Mars Hill Graduate School Library
2501 Elliott Ave
Seattle, WA 98121
www.mhgs.edu/li

D0033163

The
PRAYER

Mars Hill Graduate School

10023170

The PRAYER

DEEPENING YOUR FRIENDSHIP WITH GOD

JAMES M. HOUSTON

Victor®

The Bible Teacher's Teacher

COOK COMMUNICATIONS MINISTRIES
Colorado Springs, Colorado • Paris, Ontario
KINGSWAY COMMUNICATIONS LTD
Eastbourne, England

Victor® is an imprint of
Cook Communications Ministries, Colorado Springs, CO 80918
Cook Communications, Paris, Ontario
Kingsway Communications, Eastbourne, England

SOUL'S LONGING: THE PRAYER
© 1996, 2007 by James Houston

All rights reserved. No part of this book may be reproduced without written permission, except for brief quotations in books and critical reviews. For information, write Cook Communications Ministries, 4050 Lee Vance View, Colorado Springs, CO 80918.

This book was previously published in 1996 under the title *Prayer: The Transforming Friendship* by NavPress, PO Box 35001, Colorado Springs, CO 80935, ISBN 1-57683-118-3. Some of the anecdotal illustrations in this book are true to life and are included with the permission of the persons involved. All other illustrations are composites of real situations, and any resemblance to people living or dead is coincidental.

First Printing, 2007
Printed in the the United States of America

2 3 4 5 6 7 8 9 10

Unless otherwise noted, Scripture quotations are taken from the *Holy Bible: New International Version®*. *NIV®*. Copyright © 1973, 1978, 1984 by International Bible Society. Used by permission of Zondervan. All rights reserved. Scripture quotations marked KJV are taken from the King James Version. (Public Domain.) Italics in Scripture have been used by the author for emphasis; NASB are taken from the *New American Standard Bible*, © Copyright 1960, 1995 by The Lockman Foundation. Used by permission; and ESV are taken from *The Holy Bible, English Standard Version*. Copyright © 2000; 2001 by Crossway Bibles, a division of Good News Publishers. Used by permission. All rights reserved.

ISBN 978-0-7814-4426-2
LCCN 2007927289

Dedicated to the memory of
Erica Van Eeghen
whose example of prayerful friendship
still binds her friends together
in the Lord she loved

CONTENTS

PREFACE

For many years, prayer was probably the weakest dimension in my life as a Christian. My father was a very devout man, and I greatly respected his way of life. The problem is that moral admiration is often a cause of moral paralysis. And this was exactly my problem. I used to think that prayer was a spiritual exercise—something that needed to be worked at, like running or vaulting. But I was never any good at sports, and perhaps I would never be any good at prayer either.

After years of feeling useless and guilty, I began to realize the truth of a comment made by one of the early fathers of the church, Clement of Alexandria. He said that "prayer is keeping company with God." This began to give me a new focus on prayer. I began to see prayer more as a friendship than a rigorous discipline. It started to become more of a relationship and less of a performance.

At the same time I learned another important truth: that God calls us to use our Achilles heel, where we limp most, to lead us through our natural weakness or woundedness of personality, to grow spiritually strong. After this discovery, I made up my mind that the desire to pray and keep company with God would become my primary concern in life. Prayer would come even before my public ministry.

Like many people, I am just a beginner in prayer, speaking more from the experiences of struggle than from any skills learned. But perhaps we cannot talk about "skill" in prayer any more than we can boast of knowing how to live wisely. Even those who have given years of their life to praying say that they are just at the beginning of what prayer is all about. For ourselves, we hope that we can learn along the way, but we know we have a lot to learn about living with other people, let alone keeping company with God.

Prayer is a matter of theology and ethics, both thinking and doing. It is profoundly guided by what we believe and by how we behave. The character of our prayers will be deeply determined by the character of God as we know him and have experienced him. As we will see, the emotional education we have had since childhood will set the tone for our attitudes to God. So it is true to say: "Tell me who is your God and I will tell you how you pray."

Today, when there is so much talk about spirituality and meditation, it becomes increasingly important to know what we mean by Christian prayer, as distinct from prayer that is inspired by other religious traditions. This book takes as its structure the definition that Christian prayer is prayer to the Father, through the Son, by the Holy Spirit. The central chapters of this book deal with these themes of what we believe about prayer.

But prayer is guided by right living as well as by right thinking. True prayer means behaving in a way that is worthy of God's company. In fact, prayer expresses something of the character of God. The Bible tells us that "God is love." One medieval writer, Aelred of Rievaulx, translated this as "God is friendship." Our prayers are a response to the friendship and love of God. That is why in this book I have drawn a strong parallel between friendship and prayer.

When we pray, we allow God to live within us, so that at the deepest level it is God's Spirit who does the praying in us and through us. Archbishop Fenelon, a seventeenth-century French churchman, expressed it in this way: "Teach me to pray; pray thyself in me." If we experience prayer in this way on a regular basis, it will obviously transform our whole lives.

We are changed by prayer much more than we ever realize. Søren Kierkegaard put it like this: "Prayer does not change God, but it changes him who prays." We do not pray to inform God, as if he was ignorant of events and of what we are thinking and feeling. Instead, we pray "Your will be done" so that in our companionship with Him, as prayerful people, we really do begin to become radically different. Our whole being begins to be shaped by the life and spirit of prayer.

This ethical thrust of prayer grows out of the awareness that if we have been born again, then we must also be taught to live again. As a new person, I am in the process of changing from my old personality and temperament, to become the kind of person God always intended me to be.

In writing this book, I have benefited from many friendships, as well as from the insight of much of my work in pastoral counseling. The incidents of personal counseling included in the book are composite insights that do not portray individuals I have met with. The confidential conversations I have had remain confidential.

I deeply acknowledge the godly example of my parents, who first taught me to pray. I have also benefited from breakfast prayer groups, both in Vancouver and in Washington, D.C. These have had a formative influence in uniting prayer and friendship in my own life.

I have also been enriched by the many students at Regent College, who have responded to my classes on prayer over a number of years. My colleagues, Klaus Bockmuehl, Bill Drumbrell, Jim Packer, and Bruce Waltke have read earlier drafts of this work. While accepting some of their suggestions,

I cannot hold them responsible for any errors or weaknesses in the book!

I am also grateful to Jean Nordlund who typed so much of this text. Finally, I acknowledge the love and patience of my wife and lifelong companion in prayer, as well as our children, whose friendship in the Lord is our great blessing. They have sacrificed so many evenings of our life together to see this work completed.

INTRODUCTION

BY DALLAS WILLARD

James Houston presents discipleship to Jesus Christ as the greatest opportunity individual human beings have in life and the only hope corporate mankind has of solving its insurmountable problems.

Discipleship affirms the unity of the present-day Christian with those who walked beside Jesus during His incarnation. To be His disciple then was to be with Him, to learn to be like Him. It was to be His student or apprentice in kingdom living. His disciples heard what he said and observed what he did, then, under His direction, they simply began to say and do the same things. They did so imperfectly but progressively. As he taught: "Everyone who is fully trained will be like his teacher" (Luke 6:40).

Today it is the same, except now it is the resurrected Lord who walks throughout the world. He invites us to place our confidence in Him. Those who rely on Him believe that he knows how to live and will pour His life into us as we "take His yoke ... and learn from Him, for he is gentle and humble in heart" (Matt. 11:29). To take His yoke means joining Him in His work, making our work His work. To trust Him is to understand that total immersion in what he is doing with our life is the best thing that could ever happen to us.

To "learn from Him" in this total-life immersion is how we "seek first his kingdom and his righteousness" (Matt. 6:33). The outcome is that we increasingly are able to do all things, speaking or acting, as if Christ were doing them (Col. 3:17). As apprentices of Christ we are not learning how to do some special religious activity, but how to live every moment of our lives from the reality of God's kingdom. I am learning how to live my actual life as Jesus would if he were me.

If I am a plumber, clerk, bank manager, homemaker, elected official, senior citizen, or migrant worker, I am in "full-time" Christian service no less than someone who earns his or her living in a specifically religious role. Jesus stands beside me and teaches me in all I do to live in God's world. He shows me how, in every circumstance, to reside in His Word and thus be a genuine apprentice of His—His disciple indeed. This enables me to find the reality of God's world everywhere I may be, and thereby to escape from enslavement to sin and evil (John 8:31–32). We become able to do what we know to be good and right, even when it is humanly impossible. Our lives and words become constant testimony of the reality of God.

A plumber facing a difficult plumbing job must know how to integrate it into the kingdom of God as much as someone attempting to win another to Christ or preparing a lesson for a congregation. Until we are clear on this, we will have missed Jesus' connection between life and God and will automatically exclude most of our everyday lives from the domain of faith and discipleship. Jesus lived most of His life on earth as a blue-collar worker, someone we might describe today as an "independent contractor." In His vocation he practiced everything he later taught about life in the kingdom.

The "words" of Jesus I primarily reside in are those recorded in the New Testament Gospels. In His presence, I learn the goodness of His instructions and how to carry them out. It is not a matter of meriting life from above, but of receiving that life concretely in my circumstances. Grace, we must learn, is opposed to earning, not to effort.

For example, I move away from using derogatory language against others, calling them twits, jerks, or idiots (Matt. 5:22), and increasingly mesh with the respect and endearment for persons that naturally flows from God's way. This in turn transforms all of my dealings with others into tenderness and makes the usual coldness and brutality of human relations, which lays a natural foundation for abuse and murder, simply unthinkable.

Of course, the "learning of Him" is meant to occur in the context of His people. They are the ones he commissioned to make disciples, surround them in the reality of the triune name, and teach to do "everything I have commanded you" (Matt. 28:20). But the disciples we make are His disciples, never ours. We are His apprentices along with them. If we are a little farther along the way, we can only echo the apostle Paul: "Follow my example, as I follow the example of Christ" (1 Cor. 11:1).

It is a primary task of Christian ministry today, and of those who write for this line of books, to reestablish Christ as a living teacher in the midst of His people. He has been removed by various historical developments: assigned the role of mere sacrifice for sin or social prophet and martyr. But where there is no teacher, there can be no students or disciples.

If we cannot be His students, we have no way to learn to exist always and everywhere within the riches and power of His word. We can only flounder along as if we were on our own so far as the actual details of our lives are concerned. That is where multitudes of well-meaning believers find themselves today. But it is not the intent of Him who says, "Come to me … and you will find rest for your souls" (Matt. 11:28–29).

Each book in this line is designed to contribute to this

renewed vision of Christian spiritual formation and to illumi-
nate what apprenticeship to Jesus Christ means within all the
specific dimensions of human existence. The mission of these
books is to form the whole person so that the nature of Christ
becomes the natural expression of our souls, bodies, and spirits
throughout our daily lives.

—*Dallas Willard*

Part One

WITHOUT A PRAYER

1

WITHOUT A PRAYER IN A HOSTILE WORLD

Find the door of your heart, and you will discover
that is the door of the Kingdom of God.

—John Chrysostom

Why write another book on prayer when there are literally hundreds already in print? The answer is that a lack of prayer is such a characteristic of today's world that many different approaches to prayer are needed. On the positive side, there is a growing demand for books on prayer. This suggests that many people today are hungry for a deeper communion with God through prayer.

There is a close connection between our need for richer human relationships and our need for intimacy with God. Each dimension (our relationship with people and with God) reinforces the other. We move from the horizontal dimension to the vertical, and from the vertical to the horizontal in a constant interaction of friendship and prayer, prayer and friendship. Each dimension deeply affects the other. If we find it hard to form lasting relationships with those we see around us, then we will find it very hard to relate in any depth to the God we cannot see.

Looked at in a different way, we could obviously never claim to have a warm relationship with God in prayer if our relationships with other people were at rock-bottom.

Many people today are without friends, and without God. Perhaps this is why psychotherapists (who have been described as "paid friends") have achieved an almost godlike status in our society. Our woundedness arises almost without exception from poor or inadequate relationships. The universal experience of the human race is that we were made for relationships. We need each other, and yet we so readily wound each other.

TWO HOBOS

Samuel Becket's play *Waiting for Godot* echoes this double-edged view of relationships: we need them, and yet we destroy them. Two exotically named tramps, Vladimir and Estragon, wait beside a dead tree in the wilderness. As they wait, they become increasingly unsure if this is the right spot to wait, or the right day to do so. Like many people's prayers, they are not sure if what they are doing is right, or whether they are going to be answered.

"Godot" is the one the tramps are waiting to see, but then they are not sure if they have his proper name either. Is he God, or is Godot just another deception they face? Who knows! So they just hang around half-expectantly, half-afraid that they may be disappointed. But deep down they feel that if Godot did turn up then it would be a turning point in their lives. Perhaps all their lives this is what they were meant to seek after.

Prayer is like that. It is natural to cry out for God's help in desperate situations. It is also, at a deeper level, what we may feel we were made to have—communion with God—to emancipate us from our troubles and give guidance and inspiration. So the tramps go on waiting. The emptiness of their lives is summed up in Estragon's frustration when he protests: "Nothing happens! Nobody comes. Nobody goes. It's awful!"

Since their lives lack any substance, they begin to doubt whether they exist too. Their whole sense of uncertainty and unbelief starts to affect their relationship with each other. At one point, Vladimir wakes up Estragon because he feels so lonely. This upsets Estragon, but as he is now fully awake, he begins to tell Vladimir what he has been dreaming. But Vladimir doesn't want to hear. Pathetically, Estragon cries, "Who am I to tell my private dreams to, if I can't tell them to you?"

"Let them remain private. You know I can't bear them," Vladimir replies.

Later on, with some tenderness, Vladimir tries to make up to his companion and reaches out to embrace him.

"Don't touch me!" shouts Estragon. "Don't question me! Stay with me!"

In this way, both characters desperately need friendship, but can neither give nor receive it. And as Godot never turns up, he remains a question mark indefinitely unresolved.

Perhaps that is also the uncertainty of our prayers and of our relationships. If we have no conviction that our prayers ever ascend beyond the ceiling, and if our human relationships are superficial, we can easily start to question what reality there is to our lives. It is then that we begin to wear masks to prevent others from seeing our weakness and confusion.

"How are you doing today?"

"Oh, just fine, thanks!"

And all the time our hearts are breaking.

Two Friends

In contrast to the despair of *Waiting for Godot,* this is the story of two friends that lies behind Albrecht Dürer's famous etching, *Praying Hands.* The story is told that around the year 1490 there were two young, struggling artists who were close friends. Albrecht Dürer and Franz Knigstein were very poor and had to work to support themselves, training as artists in their spare time. However, their manual work was too demanding to allow them proper training.

In desperation, they at last decided that they should cast lots to decide which of them should carry on working to support the other in art school. Albrecht won the toss, so he went off to spend time with famous artists in training, while Franz worked extra hard to support them both.

Eventually, Albrecht returned to relieve his friend. Because he had become successful as an artist, he would now be able to send Franz off to the school. But to his horror, Albrecht discovered that the heavy manual work had ruined Franz's hands forever. Franz would never be able to become an artist. He had forfeited his own artistic future out of loyalty to his friend.

One day, Albrecht found Franz on his knees, his hands clasped in prayer, gnarled and yet offered to God in loving sacrifice. Hurriedly, Dürer sketched the moment and produced a symbol for the meaning of prayer. Ever since, the intercessory prayer symbolized by that etching reminds us that prayer and friendship belong together. The person to whom we pray had his hands pierced on our behalf.

WHY HAS PRAYER DIED?

There is a growing awareness today that modern life neglects community values, replacing them with a strong streak of selfishness and narcissism. This is not a surprising trend. Our generation has grown up on the idea that "self-fulfillment" is the panacea for all our problems. Such a faith drives us all to become Robinson Crusoes, each in our own personal desert-island paradise, living according to our own fantasies. When the family dissolves in a divorcing culture and the Me-generation takes over, then the collapse of community values is not too far behind. Prayerlessness is simply part of a larger picture of modern life, of being alone in a crowd.

One of the late-seventeenth century's best-selling books was

The Whole Duty of Man. This would not be a book to top today's lists, as our whole mind-set is now focused on "the rights of man." Taken to an extreme, this modern emphasis ends up in self-interest, whether in careerism, sexism, or even professionalism.

Many of the permanent values that keep humans human have today been declared our enemies. As we reject truth, beauty, goodness, the family, community, friendship, and the infinite significance of human life, we bring down upon ourselves catastrophic consequences. If God created us in his own image, to be like him, then every single person has an incalculable value. As C. S. Lewis thought about this awe-inspiring possibility, he stated in a famous remark:

> There are no ordinary people. You have never talked to a mere mortal.

Just as the moon reflects the light of the sun, so the dignity of our humanity is a reflection of the love and greatness of God. But if God is dead, as the philosopher Nietzsche asserted, then everything is permissible. "Nothing is true, everything is permitted." At that point, our humanity dies too.

To live without prayer is ultimately to disbelieve in God and to lose the most important human values, such as faith, hope, and love. Living without prayer is the result of going to bed with all the attitudes of a modern secular society. The New Testament would probably be blunt and call these attitudes "godlessness." It is easy to succumb to the secular spirit when we have such faith in technology, such hope in pragmatism, such love of human intellect.

All these things enable us to do what we want, how we want. In the last analysis, as C. S. Lewis put it in *The Great Divorce,* God either says to us, "Thy will be done," in damnation and loss, or else we say to God, "Thy will be done." Prayer is ultimately a battle of the will. The battle makes us choose what in the end we really want.

Prayer can die even when we proclaim that we are serving

God and not ourselves. In fact, one of the most prayerless spheres can be a seminary, or even a church. Scholarship about God, or religiosity in the name of God, can subtly become substitutes for a personal relationship with God.

A recent survey conducted by the magazine *Newsweek* revealed that theological students had become "artful dodgers of a disciplined prayer life." The survey commented:

> They use social action, spiritual guruism—in the form of psychological counseling—and a scrupulously academic approach to the study of religion as a substitute to evade the problem of a totally religious life of prayer.

Turn to the index of almost any theological textbook, and it would be a rare moment to discover an entry for "prayer," let alone to find a whole chapter in the book on the place of prayer in theological education. One theologian, John MacQuarrie, showed in a survey of 150 twentieth-century theologians that not one had related the practice of prayer to his mental, religious, or even physical wellbeing. Over a century ago, Bishop J. C. Ryle could remark: "I have come to the conclusion that the vast majority of professing Christians do not pray at all." Perhaps he would say the same thing of church life in the West today.

In all the areas of our life, prayer is the one where we can least afford to be complacent. We may spend regular times in jogging, exercising, and dieting for the sake of our bodies, but refuse to make time for prayer for the sake of our souls. We dedicate enormous effort toward developing our professional skills through expensive education, yet our time and our communion with God has become a lost art and a rejected relationship.

I'M TOO BUSY

This is probably the very first response of most people to the call to Christian prayer. It seems to be a perfectly legitimate reason—not an excuse at all! How much more can we do? One advertising page of *The New York Times* described the life of one girl, representative of today's yuppie generation:

> Can a girl be too busy? I'm taking seventeen units at Princeton, pushing on with my career during vacations and school breaks, studying singing and dancing when I can, trying to never lose sight of my five closest chums, stealing time for Michael Jackson and Thomas Hardy, working for an anti-drug program for kids, and, oh yes, I hang out with three horses, three cats, two birds and my dog Jack. My favorite magazine says "too busy" just means you don't want to miss anything....

Clearly, this attractive and vivacious girl is light years away from thinking about prayer!

The desert fathers (a protest movement against worldliness in the early church) spoke of busyness as "moral laziness." Busyness can also be an addictive drug, which is why its victims are increasingly referred to as "workaholics." Busyness acts to repress our inner fears and personal anxieties as we scramble to achieve an enviable image to display to others. We become "outward" people, obsessed with how we appear, rather than "inward" people, reflecting on the meaning of our lives.

Busyness also seems to be a determination not to "miss out on life." Behind much of the rat race of modern life is the unexamined assumption that what I do determines who I am. In this way, we define ourselves by what we do rather than by any quality of what we are inside. It is typical in a party for one stranger to approach another with the question "What do you do?" Perhaps we wouldn't have a clue how to reply to the deeper question, "Who are you?"

Since prayer belongs to the relational side of human life (to "who I am" rather than to "what I do"), it is inevitable that prayer will have a very low priority, at the very best, for people who live busy lives. None of us is too busy for the things that we regard as priorities. We are only too busy for those things that have a low order of importance in our daily schedules. We may live by the clock, but more importantly we live by our priorities. When friendship is a low priority, we have no time for our friends. And we can similarly have no time for prayer.

Our "mind-set" (the way we see and organize our lives) is therefore the key to helping us grow in Christian prayer. A botanist, geologist, or an artist will see things in a landscape that others will never see. Lovers appreciate qualities in each other that can be completely invisible to outside observers. In the same way, prayer depends on our appreciation of God.

GETTING GOD IN PERSPECTIVE

I once gave my students an exercise to find out all they could about the word "achievement" in the Bible. They searched through the book without finding a single trace of the word, until one student realized that the Bible's silence on the subject of human achievement might have a lot to say. God's achievement in his creation of all things, and our human predicament without God, puts any talk of human achievement firmly into the shade.

Our place, instead of boasting about our achievements or about human progress, is to celebrate all the things that God has made and done. Gratitude, praise, and prayer are the appropriate responses to the realities of life, rather than our crazy quest for self-significance and self-security in the things we feel we have achieved.

It is no coincidence that Sunday comes before Monday. Why is it that the Bible insists on the priority of "keeping the Sabbath day holy"? One reason for this is to show that God's achievements should have priority over anything that we might achieve under him. Our significance, security, and even our identity do not really lie in ourselves, but in the God who created us and who can save us from ourselves. The apostle Paul saw himself in this way—as a new creation "in Christ." So to celebrate the first day of the week is to celebrate that the risen Christ also lives in our hearts, giving our lives their true meaning and purpose.

So what about Monday? Monday is typically the day when we begin to squeeze all the significance, security, and personal identity that we can out of our activities. We try to assure ourselves that our identity lies in what we do and in what we achieve. This falsification of our true selves is corrected only when it is Sunday that gives proper meaning to Monday. This happens when we start to live a life of prayer and dependence upon God. Our whole lives begin to revolve around a new focus. We can then give meaning to our work rather than seeking vainly to extract meaning from our work.

This priority was recognized by the medieval monks when they lived the rhythm of *ora et labora* (prayer and work), as they prayed first and then went out to their work. When prayerfulness underlies our attitude to work, we are never too busy for the essentials of life. Our sense of perspective will have been as appropriately educated as a botanist, geologist, or artist who has been trained to see the landscape.

I'M AFRAID OF REALLY KNOWING MYSELF

Knowing ourselves is usually uncomfortable. This is why so many people live behind masks to prevent others from discovering the uncomfortable truths they have found out about themselves. Knowing yourself is not flattering. We often evade what we do not like inside by condemning other people for exactly the same weaknesses.

This is where prayer cuts across all our pretensions. Prayer is the mirror of the soul, and in it we see ourselves most clearly. Mark Twain used to say that there is at least one thing in favor of prayer, and that is that we cannot tell lies as we pray. If mother had radar-sensing to penetrate all our subterfuges when we were kids, how much more does the all-seeing God know our every thought!

Augustine, one of the great fathers of the church, was fully aware of this. He penned his Confessions, which exposed his former life of lust, while he was a bishop. For Augustine, being a bishop of the church was no cloak to cover his true identity before God. In fact, what originally attracted Augustine's attention was the voice of God which came to him while he was sitting in a garden. The voice assured him in a quote from the book of Romans: "The one who trusts in him will never be put to shame" (9:33).

The self-knowledge that we gain through prayer demands humility. Anselm, the great medieval scholar, expresses the agonizing dilemma that we all feel when approaching God with full knowledge of ourselves:

> Oh painful dilemma!
> If I look into myself, I cannot endure myself.
> If I look not into myself, I cannot face myself.
> If I consider myself, my own face appalls me.
> If I consider not myself, my damnation deceives me.
> If I see myself, the horror is intolerable.
> If I see not myself, death is unavoidable.

Humility is moral realism. Facing the realities of human sin, we stand before the righteousness and holiness of God. Physics and chemistry may be the appropriate disciplines for understanding matter, but humility is the appropriate way for anyone to understand themselves.

As we become aware that busyness is a false obstacle to a life of prayer, we also discover that humility is "constant forgetfulness of one's own achievements," as John of the Ladder expressed in the seventh century.

So what does humility mean? Humility is being aware of our own moral weaknesses, our helplessness in the presence of evil in our own lives. It also means that we are sorry for our condition and are willing to turn to God.

In contrast, pride blocks prayer, just as it did in Jesus' famous parable of the Pharisee and the taxman. We can never learn to pray if our thoughts say, "I thank you that I am not as others are," as the Pharisee prayed. Instead, prayer requires spiritual nakedness before God as we acknowledge our guilt and make a new start in our lives. It requires an honest distrust of our own sense of achievement together with a desire to learn from God—especially through the Bible.

Bernard of Clairvaux argued that comparison is the first step into pride. In prayer it can be easy to look sideways at other people, comparing ourselves proudly with them exactly as the Pharisee did in Jesus' parable. And yet this is the very opposite of what real prayer should be. Prayer is the determination to be alone before God with no gallery to play to and no distracting comparisons to make.

LEARNING TO ASK

Once we have learned humility in prayer, we will naturally begin to ask. As we recognize our own weaknesses, we turn to God for his strength. Asking is the constant heartbeat of the soul before God. God has so much to give us. The Bible says that he wants to give us "all good things richly to enjoy." Our trouble is that we are usually quite unaware of our need for God's grace and help. If only we could truly see how needy we are before God, then we would find prayer the most natural thing in the world. One seventeenth-century writer put it in this way:

> It is men's ignorance of themselves that makes prayer
> little in request: hunger best teaches men to beg. You would
> be oftener on your knees if you were oftener in your hearts.
> Prayer would not seem so needless if you knew your needs.
> Know yourselves, and be prayerless if you can.

Knowing ourselves teaches us what to ask. It helps us to identify the areas of need in our lives. It also teaches us how to approach God. In Jesus' parable, the taxman simply prayed: "God, be merciful to me, a sinner!" We can find it almost impossible to pray when we do not see ourselves from God's point of view. By knowing ourselves, we can approach God with a real desire to confess our sins and receive his forgiveness.

PRAYING FROM THE HEART OF OURSELVES

Prayer is not real unless it comes from the heart. "The heart" is a phrase that is strongly emphasized in the Bible. It is a picture of the heart of human personality, the place where all our attitudes, drive, and motivation come from. The heart is the core of our being. Prayer starts with the heart, because God longs to relate to us at every level of our being. This includes our feelings, our mind, our imagination, our love, our memory, our will. God seeks to know us intimately for all that we are. This is why prayer focuses on the very core of our being, inside the heart. John Chrysostom, the great preacher in the fourth-century church, said:

> Find the door of your heart, and you will discover that it
> is the door of the Kingdom of God.

Here is one way to picture this. Each of us was once inside our mother's womb. The heart-pulse of the mother penetrates the whole environment of the child. During pregnancy, the unborn child registers the mother's emotions of anger, fear, peace, love, desire, and excitement. All these profound influences shape us from our very earliest days. In the same way, we are profoundly influenced by God's desires for our lives. Prayer is like the heart-beat of the pregnant mother. Through God's influence, that constant heartbeat, we are shaped and grow into his image.

WHOLE, NEW PEOPLE

Prayer develops us as whole people before God. To pray to God is to be a complete person before God, a person as God has always intended us to be. It is to be open, to confess, to be forgiven, cleansed, humbled, obedient, sustained, guided, strengthened, and daily renewed and inspired. Prayer radically transforms broken people into new people—people newly created by God. We become the unique person that God originally created each of us to be.

> Let me remember,
>
> That truly to be man,
>
> Is to be man aware of Thee,
>
> And unafraid to be.
>
> So help me, God.
>
> —David Gascoyne

Prayer, in the full light of knowing about ourselves, is vitally important to sustain our life in all its different dimensions. Our life in Christ, and our genuine relationships with others, both go together as the same reality. Out of solitary dialogue with God will stream a life of enriching relationships that benefit others as well as ourselves. By contrast, we can now start to see that a life without prayer is probably the greatest impoverishment we can experience. A life without prayer and without God would be like an unborn child vibrating to the mechanical beat of an electric clock.

Prayer enables us to enter into a whole new world of relationships. To do this, we have to begin by understanding ourselves more fully. This opens our eyes to how much we really need God's help. Anselm's prayer puts this sense of need into words:

> I do desire to understand a little of your Truth which my heart already believes and loves. I do not seek to understand so that I may believe, but I do believe so that I may understand; and what is more, I believe that unless I do believe I shall not understand.

2

STRUGGLING
WITH PRAYER

Faith is simply prayer.

—Martin Luther

My prayers, my God, flow from what I am not.
I think thy answers make me what I am.

—George MacDonald

A tourist visiting the temples of Asia cannot help being impressed by the number of devotees praying to their gods, with flowers, fruits, and papers in a variety of shades. Some worship deities are identified with specific human emotions. But in a Daoist temple, it is striking that the character of each god is virtually unknown. They are addressed vaguely and asked to give luck for a bet on the horses, or for some other type of good fortune.

In contrast, people in the West assume they know precisely the nature and character of their prayers. And yet there are many fallacies in this, even among those who consider themselves "Christian" in the ways they pray. These fallacies reflect a series of misunderstandings about the nature of prayer as we see it in the Bible. And they also reflect the quality of our relationship with God.

Psychological studies in this century have focused on the crucial influence of early family life on our "grown-up" personality.

How we were treated as children influences our personality, the way we behave and relate with others, our values, and our view of life in general. Many believe that even before birth, a mother has a great influence upon her unborn child. What is not usually recognized is that our approach to prayer will also be affected by the image we have of our parents.

Take the case of one young man. His father was a distant figure to him as he grew up on a farm. His communication was limited almost entirely to instructions in the fields and when, what, and how to do things in his work. As a result, he still feels that God only gives him commands. He sees God as a taskmaster.

Another person may have been emotionally manipulated by one parent against the other, or spoiled, or even had the feeling of being somehow "different" from others. There are many ways in which our emotions can be distorted from seeing life clearly. These influences naturally affect our attitudes to prayer. Because of this, we may need to go through a long process of straightening out our damaged attitudes. We need to begin by looking at the wrong ways in which we approach prayer. There are a number of common misunderstandings.

PRAYER IS SOMETHING WE "DO"

Many people have the impression that prayer is simply another thing we do, alongside all the other activities we pack into our lives. This way of thinking, which sees prayer as an interest or a duty, may prompt us to read about prayer in exactly the same way that we learn from "how-to" books about cross-country skiing or stamp collecting.

It can be easy to become fascinated by the elaborate breathing techniques and postures for meditation that other religions have developed. We can start to pursue prayer because it makes us feel good, or to meditate because it is part of a healthier style of living. Prayer becomes an instrument of our sense of well-being. When this happens, prayer becomes an end in itself. In fact, it becomes a dead end. Absorbed in the techniques, we forget who we are praying to. We lose sight of the relationship that we wanted to have with God.

A variation on this theme is to see prayer as something that we do for God. Just as soldiers salute their superior officers, so prayer can be a way of respectfully tipping our hat to the Almighty. Prayer can become a hot-line, like the telephone link connecting the White House with the Kremlin. This is perhaps the most commonly held view of prayer—as an emergency number to dial when all else has failed. We "do" prayer after we have done everything else that was humanly possible.

However, the idea of prayer as a technique we perform breaks down when we look at prayer in the Bible. In one of Jesus' parables, two men go to the temple to pray. One man, a Pharisee, is well-versed in religious language and ritual, but his heart is far from God. The other man is a much-despised tax-man, who has no religious sophistication, but who does have a strong sense of his own guilt before God. He simply murmurs, "God, be merciful to me, a sinner." Jesus said, "I tell you that this man, rather than the other, went home justified before God." Prayer is clearly more of a posture and attitude before God than a correct way of doing or saying things.

A faith that depends on what we do has forgotten its roots. At the very heart of the Christian faith is God taking the initiative to show us mercy and to save us. Our relationship with God does not depend on the good things we do, but on God's mercy toward us. So prayer can never be made to work automatically through pressing the right buttons and following the right techniques. No human relationship works on this level, and neither does our relationship with God.

When prayer is seen as just another technique for trouble-free living, it can never compete. All the other technical solutions to the problems of everyday life will eventually kill prayer that is merely technical. Mothers in the days of high infant mortality used to pray desperately that their children would not die in infancy. Modern medical techniques have put an end to those prayers in the West. Today many people pray about the problem of cancer—but we hope that new medical advances will take care of this in the future. This swamping of prayer by modern techniques shows that true prayer is much more than praying for or about things we want to see happen.

In the Old Testament, one psalm says, "Out of the depths I cry to you, O Lord." In the modern world, our depths can seem to be less fathomless than those which the psalm-writer experienced. If we have a thousand ways of dealing with "the depths," why call upon God? It is easy to pray about problems, or to meditate using all the best techniques, without thinking about God at all.

PRAYER IS A CUSTOM

Church-going puts off many people today because of its association in the past with customs that are now clearly discredited. In eighteenth-century England, for example, the eldest son would inherit the family estate, the second son would be expected to make his career in the army or in politics, and the youngest son was left to enter the church as a gentleman parson. In the middle ages, the monastery or convent was a convenient wall behind which to hide your youngest offspring who could not be married off.

Prayer was part of the decor. True faith and true prayer had been reduced to playing the part of a detail in the social fabric of those times. An aristocratic lady of the big house in eighteenth-century England or France saw prayer as a "good thing" for the servants to do. It kept them in their place. This degeneration of the religious life was no different from the abuses that Jesus and the Old Testament prophets criticized in the Bible. Prayer that is merely a social nicety is highly vulnerable. As soon as the customs vanish, such prayer vanishes with them.

Leo Tolstoy, the Russian novelist, once told the story of two brothers who met for a weekend after a long time apart. On the first night, the older brother was fascinated to see that his younger brother knelt and prayed by his bedside. "Huh, you still do that?" he said. The younger brother did not reply, but from that time he never prayed again.

Tolstoy remarked:

> This is not because he knows his brother's convictions and has joined him in them, nor because he has decided anything in his own soul, but simply because the word spoken by his brother was like the push of a finger on a wall that was ready to fall by its own weight.

Many people keep up their habit of customary prayer because it is something they identify with their childhood. It simply "feels good" to maintain the custom. This may seem a fairly harmless habit, but the problem with it is that it can produce a self-congratulatory way of thinking that dulls the senses. Prayer that is done "because I have always prayed" inoculates us against true prayer, preventing us from ever finding a living relationship with God.

In C. S. Lewis's famous book *The Screwtape Letters,* a senior devil, Screwtape, offers words of advice on temptation to Wormwood, a junior devil. Screwtape tells Wormwood that if his patients should pray (the last thing the evil world wants to happen) then there is one well-known remedy. He should try to get them to "feel good" about their prayers. Wormwood should divert their attention from the relationship of prayer to the feelings instead:

> When they meant to ask him for charity, let them, instead, start trying to manufacture charitable feelings for themselves and not notice that this is what they are doing. When they meant to pray for courage, let them really be trying to feel brave. When they say they are praying for forgiveness, let them be trying to feel forgiven.

Habits are important for building character. But when they become unthinking and automatic, they can have a deadening effect upon our whole lives. This is especially the case when it comes to habits of prayer.

"Saying our prayers" has a long tradition, especially noticeable in the use of the Anglican prayer book, which dates back to 1549. At that time, Archbishop Thomas Cranmer introduced written prayers as a means of educating the public in Protestant (as opposed to Catholic) thinking.

The publication of the prayer book was controversial. It led to a century of argument between the champions of written prayers and those of spontaneous prayers. Both approaches to prayer have their merits, according to the spirit in which prayer is expressed to God.

On the positive side, the prayer book cultivated a spirituality with many strong emphases: confession before God, an aversion for sin, the desire to live in a new way, and submitting before God wholeheartedly. The Anglican George Herbert stands in this tradition, and he has a lot to teach us:

> Poore heart, lament.
> For since thy God refuseth still,
> There is some rub, some discontent,
> Which cools his will....
> Then once more pray:
> Down with thy knees, up with thy voice.
> Seek pardon first, and God will say,
> Glad heart rejoyce.

Following repentance, the prayer book then called for a bold approach to God in prayer. Lancelot Andrewes, another Anglican, wrote that we should pray comprehensively, almost as if commanding God. Prayer, he said, "is the key to open the day," as well as "the bar to shut in the night." Another strong element of the prayer book is that prayer made in the right spirit is acceptable and pleasing to God. And because the book provided prayers to be used by the whole church, it reinforced the church's community life.

To this day, the English prayer book (along with the Lutheran and other denominational prayer books) has been a significant safeguard for the faith of the churches—especially important when individual pastors have lacked vitality and personal conviction, because the prayer book can then play an important part in upholding and expressing the faith of the local church.

But there are dangers in the prayer book approach to God as well. Jesus spoke about the danger of "heaping up empty phrases" in an attempt to impress God in prayer. Saying prayers by rote, without serious reflection or personal intent, runs the risk of becoming the "vain repetition" that Jesus so severely criticized. This is especially the case in reciting the often-repeated "Lord's Prayer." Ironically, it was as Jesus taught his disciples this prayer that he warned them about the dangers of mindless, automatic prayer.

Real communication with God is much more than mouthing words, even when they are the beautiful words of the prayer book. This is because true communication involves giving and receiving from both parties, so that they are in tune with each other.

People who are insensitive to the need to be attuned to others are called "chatterboxes"—it does not matter who they are talking to, they simply talk. And because of their insensitivity to others, no true communication takes place. True prayer works in exactly the same way. It needs a Godward orientation of our hearts, rather than the automatic movement of our lips. One of the Old Testament prophets, speaking on behalf of God, expressed this perfectly when he said: "This people worship me with their lips, but their hearts are far off." True prayer reverses this breakdown in trust and communication between us and God.

PRAYER AS MAGIC

The use of magic in prayer is another sign of our alienation from God. Magic appears most blatantly in the prayers of religions where the gods are not known, and where spells are needed in order to coax the god into releasing power. Magic can also appear, more subtly, in the prayers of people who would be horrified to think that they were involved in magic. It is alarmingly easy for prayer to become a kind of magical device which we use to get our own way.

There are many examples of the infection of true prayer by magic. At places of pilgrimage such as Lourdes, and in many chapels, people making prayer requests leave notes pinned up on the walls together with photographs of their loved ones, and light candles, often for the purpose of invoking God to answer their needs.

Others who despise that form of faith have their own version of magic in their prayers. In an emotionally charged charismatic prayer meeting there is the attitude that if the group prays fervently, while speaking in tongues, then the prayers are more "real" and will be answered. Promote the proper rhythm, set the pulse beating wildly, raise the voice hysterically, and you have a "good prayer meeting." People who visit shrines, light candles, or pray ecstatically are obviously sincere, but the question still needs to be asked: are these the ways of knowing God more intimately?

In the West, health and wealth are the modern obsessions. Another tendency is therefore to assume that God intends us to have these goodies. We think we have every right to ask for them, and so prayer is brought in to work its magic on our behalf. In many religious groups, permanently disabled people have been condemned for not having "enough faith" to be healed from their disability. One paralytic girl was condemned by her devout mother for not getting up out of her wheelchair to walk down the church aisle as her sister's bridesmaid. Meanwhile, in the stock exchange, some dealers feel that prayer will help them to make a killing. After all, the Bible does say that their heavenly Father "owns the cattle on a thousand hills"—an expression which they take to mean that God is fabulously wealthy.

Magic also creeps in when people use prayer as a way of avoiding their responsibilities. One person asks another for real help, but the reply he gets is, "Well, I shall have to pray about it." This impressive-sounding response can actually mask a number of dangerous misuses of prayer. Am I simply avoiding something that I do not want to do? Am I trying to get divine help when it is my God-given responsibility to act straight away? Or am I asking God to intervene magically so that I can avoid my responsibilities in the situation? These tricks show how easily we can fall back on magic in prayer, hiding from real life and indulging in personal irresponsibility.

In a play by Berthold Brecht, the German dramatist, the inhabitants of a besieged town are terror-stricken to hear that the enemy is approaching. They begin to pray fearfully. In contrast, the deaf-mute girl of the community, Katarina, climbs up onto a barn roof armed with a steel drum. She pounds the drum, the enemy thinks the sound is that of a friendly platoon approaching, and they beat a hasty retreat. The plot may be unlikely, but the message is realistic. We should not expect a personal, prayer-hearing God to respond to our situations with displays of magic when we can play a responsible role ourselves.

Changing Our Perspective

In everyday life, a change of perspective can achieve great things. At the beginning of a relationship, for example, we may be set in our prejudices about the other person. Then we start to discover new facts that gradually alter our entire way of looking at that individual, and we become friends. Perhaps in the same way we can change our attitudes toward prayer.

With prayer, we also start out with prejudices. Intimate, personal prayer with God seems a formidable challenge for us to face in our world today. Even C. S. Lewis saw himself on the lower foothills of faith in comparison with the mystics who went climbing mountains. In the Middle Ages, pilgrims journeying on foot across Europe had to cross the dreaded Alps in late winter in order to reach Rome in time for Easter. This was the most treacherous season in the Alps. The pilgrims faced melting snow, the threat of avalanche, and torrential mountain streams.

No wonder they viewed the Alps with an apocalyptic apprehension, terror, and dread.

It was only much later, in the late eighteenth century, that the Romantic poets began to see beauty in mountain landscapes. A radical change of perspective was beginning. No longer seen as a barrier, the mountains began to attract invalids who had been prescribed the bracing mountain air. As mountain climbing and skiing became popular, the landscape began to change with roads, railways, ski-lifts, and hotels. The stagnant economy of the secluded alpine valleys began to flourish, taking on a new openness and international character. All this happened because of a transformed perspective on mountains.

Prayer can be rather like that change of perspective. For many people, prayer can be the most forbidding, daunting obstacle to their religious life. It often seems that we can do anything but pray. Reading the biographies of famous Christians only makes us feel more guilty because their prayer life puts ours into the shade. Even reading a book on prayer can make us feel that we will find it impossible ever to develop in prayer. When we reach this stage, it is tempting to think that the most honest thing to do is to tell God that we are giving up on the struggle. This is exactly what many people do for years on end. Other people continue with the struggle, trying desperately to break through the barriers that stand so firmly between them and a habit of regular prayer.

We are like amateur mountain climbers. We stand at the foot of Mont Blanc with an enthusiastic mountain guide who will show us the route up the vertical face of the mountain. But before he does that, we must start with the nursery slopes. Here are three beginner's lessons in prayer.

THE FOCUS OF PRAYER IS NOT PRAYER BUT GOD HIMSELF

This is absolutely basic to prayer, but it is easy to forget in today's world. We are such a technique-oriented society that we love to use tools just for the fun of using them. But all tools have a specific purpose beyond themselves. Mountain boots and ropes are used for climbing mountains. We pray not simply to enjoy the experience of praying, but to communicate with God, to submit to him, to be like him, to love and serve him. Prayer, like climbing mountains, is a challenge, but it is much more than just a challenge. We don't pray simply "because it is there." Instead, prayer is our response to God's interest in us and his love for us. To pray is to become aware of God's Spirit living within us. Through prayer, we explore a deeper and more intimate relationship with God.

One Old Testament prophet, Jeremiah, recognized that prayer can never be half-hearted. He expressed it in this way: "'You seek me and find me,' says the Lord, 'when you seek me with all your heart.'" Many people have experienced the frustration of seeking God in many different (and sometimes exotic) places, only to discover that he can be found only within our own hearts. Teresa of Avila, a sixteenth-century Catholic mystic, tried looking for God in vain for eighteen wasted years until she discovered, as the New Testament puts it, that "Christ in you is the hope of glory."

Jesus stands outside, asking us to open the door of our heart to him. This willingness to open ourselves to God is where all true prayer begins. Once we have learned to respond to God in this way, by saying "Yes, Lord, come into my life to stay," then we can begin to focus our attention on him.

Prayer Means Seeking the Mind and Spirit of Jesus

Jesus cannot simply become an occasional guest in the human heart. To allow him into our hearts means to surrender to his rule over our lives. One writer, François Fénelon, said,

> You must give all or nothing when God asks it. If you
> have not the courage to give, at least let him take.

To be robbed of our own willpower may seem a shocking indignity and deprivation. So we struggle to avoid it. However, when we place ourselves entirely in God's hands, we discover to our surprise that we have not been robbed or violated, but given a new freedom and joy in life. François Fénelon spoke about those who have not experienced this:

> They only know what religion extracts, without knowing what it offers, and they ignore the spirit of love which sweetens all the struggle.

Jesus, just before his arrest, prayed "not my will, but yours be done." When we learn to pray in this same way, we discover the amazing consequences of surrendering our self-determination to God. It leads to peace inside ourselves that strengthens and encourages us to continue along the road of surrender to God.

We quickly discover that it is impossible to live the life of Christ by our own sheer effort of willpower. It is only as we are "in Christ," receiving the power of God's Spirit, that we can live a new life. Jesus used the picture of a vine branch being joined to the trunk to illustrate this point. As the branch produces fruit only because it is in the vine, so our lives can only grow and develop as we live in Christ.

Again, we can fear the loss of self-identity in this process. But paradoxically our sense of identity only increases as we join our life to the life of Jesus. Those who try to cling to their own unique identity often end up feeling profoundly alone. If I have an overwhelming sense of my uniqueness as a person, perhaps even forcing it on others, it can become a barrier against allowing other people—or even myself—to know myself. To hand over to God the mystery of my being and identity is a great comfort. From now on, if I look for security or significance as a person, it means going to God, into whose hands they are forever committed. Since they are in the deposit box at the bank, I can never be robbed of them. This is in marked contrast to those in today's busy world who try to give their lives significance by the things they do and the salary they earn.

All this gives us a new perspective on prayer—as an opening up of ourselves before God. We can now begin to see that Jesus has more to do *in* us than *through* us. Our inner changes of heart become much more important than the things we may achieve in front of other people. Prayer makes us more flexible before God. We become open to his Spirit, begin to respond to what we read about in the Bible, and become curious about how he wants our lives to be. Prayer becomes more a matter of listening than talking. It is obvious that he has much more to say to us than we can bear at any one time. As we obey what the Bible terms God's "still, small voice," we become more concerned about knowing his mind than letting him know our thoughts.

Ignatius of Loyola, who sought to have an undivided heart before God, prayed in this way:

> Take, Lord, and receive all my liberty,
> my memory, my understanding,
> and my entire will—
> All that I have and call my own,
> You have given it to me.
> To you, Lord, I return it.
> Do with it what you will.
> Give me only your love and your grace.
> That is enough for me.

PRAYER NEEDS HELP TO WORK

Prayer is not an isolated fragment of our lives. We can live a full life without jogging or playing golf all the time. But we cannot dispense with prayer, because it expresses a new orientation of our life toward God. There are many ways in which we can encourage our growth in prayer.

The most important aid toward prayer is to begin to make our own explorations in the Bible. Jesus once said, "Man shall not live by bread alone, but by every word that comes from the mouth of God." Jesus himself was brought up to know and love the Old Testament Scriptures. Paul, the great pioneer in the early days of the Christian faith, wrote:

> All Scripture is God-breathed and is useful for teaching, rebuking, correcting and training in righteousness, so that the man of God may be thoroughly equipped for every good work. (2 Tim. 3:16–17)

Prayer goes hand in hand with discovering the riches of the Bible. As we saturate ourselves in the Bible's teachings and attitudes, we become "biblical people," focusing our lives upon the God revealed in the Bible. Like the writers of the Psalms, we discover that the Bible relates to all the moods, emotions and circumstances of our lives.

Next to the Bible, we should read some of the great classics of the Christian faith. Books become "classics" when they speak about the deeply felt, abiding principles of life before God, recognized across many generations among God's people. Such books can awaken us to fresh insights about the needs of others and about God. They have changed the lives of other people, and they can stimulate a change of heart in us as well. They may rouse us from a cultural sleep, where we are automatically following the lead of our culture in the way we behave. They can speak for us as we have never been able to do for ourselves, allowing us to know our own thoughts and feelings, perhaps for the first time. And they can also show us how other people have taken God far more seriously than we do. This is of course painful, but it can shame us into seeking a deeper relationship with God.

Another valuable support to prayer is fasting. Fasting means to deprive ourselves of any activities or habits that are deeply ingrained into our lives, but popularly it means to go without food for a set length of time. As with prayer, there is no particular value in fasting for its own sake. Fasting is practiced for greater ends than itself. It clears the mind and helps us to concentrate on a specific subject, allowing us to subordinate our bodies' needs to our spiritual need for God. Fasting can also be specifically helpful in preparing us for a special event, or in seeking guidance from God. It helps us to control our appetites before they are given the chance to control us.

One early church writer, John of Climacus, said that gluttony has many offspring: lust, hardness of heart, immorality, dirty thoughts, laziness, boastfulness, love of material things, wandering thoughts, and many other dangerous tendencies that keep prayer impure and off-target.

Stillness before God also encourages our growth in prayer. One psalm expresses it in this way: "My soul, find rest in God alone." Becoming quiet before God means to reject all intrusions that might interrupt our being with God. Such intrusions could include noisiness, anxious thoughts, or even self-consciousness. This can be a hard lesson to learn. We can achieve stillness by having a simple approach to God—the approach of a child who simply trusts its parent. A simple approach allows us to enjoy God's acceptance, and to be filled with his assurance and his confidence. Prayer at this level happens when no words are expressed, no thoughts are declared, because God's presence surpasses all that our senses might declare. The thought of Psalm 46, "Be still and know that I am God," is the climax of the life of prayer.

Community is also an important dimension of prayer. When any social group gathers together, it reinforces its shared values and provides encouragement and support for its individual members. Prayerful friendships are therefore vitally important in an age where there is so much emphasis on the individual. This is why involvement in the community of God's people is a key to growing in prayer. In the modern church, our involvement can be expressed through the church prayer meeting, through house groups or other small groups that meet together for prayer.

A final support of prayer is the increasing practice today of "spiritual direction." This means meeting with an older, more mature Christian, who is able to offer regular advice and direction in living the spiritual life. Spiritual direction is God-oriented, and its primary focus is on deepening and enriching a life of prayer. It helps us to move beyond seeing prayer as simply talking to God, presenting him with our needs, to a more meditative and contemplative way of life, with prayer at its heart.

In this way, people are able to become both more fully human and more spiritual than ever before. They come to enjoy a greater degree of inner freedom, with a greater sense of control over their handicaps, limitations, frustrations, and suffering. The life of the Trinity opens up to the worshipper as a never-ending dynamic of expanding possibilities of love, fellowship and service.

Our culture puts severe limitations on the way we carry out our relationships, and the same cultural limitations can operate in prayer, unless we resist them. Prayer sends us into an expanding universe of relationships—with God, with others and also with ourselves. The journey inward, in self-reflection, the journey upward, with God, and the journey outward, alongside others, opens up our hearts to what one of the psalms describes as "those whose hearts are set on pilgrimage." It is the longest journey of our lives, from which we cannot go back. For it is no less than walking with God.

I should like to speak to you about my prayer, O Lord. And though it often seems to me that you pay little heed to what I try to say to you in my prayers, please listen to me now very carefully.

O Lord God, I don't wonder that my prayers fall so short of you—even I myself often fail to pay the least attention to what I'm praying about. So often I consider my prayer as just a job I have to do, a duty to be performed. I "get it out of the way" and then relax, glad to have it behind me. When I pray, I'm at my duty, instead of being with you.

Yes, that's my prayer. I admit it. And yet, my God, I find it hard to be so sorry for praying so poorly. How can a man hope to speak with you? You are so distant and so mysterious. When I pray, it's as if my words have disappeared down some deep, dark well from which no echo ever comes back to reassure me that they have struck the ground of your heart.

Is my life really no more than a single short aspiration, and all my prayers just different formulations of it in human words? Is the eternal possession of you your eternal answer to it? Is your silence when I pray really a discourse filled with infinite promise, unimaginably more meaningful than any audible word you could speak to the limited understanding of my narrow heart— a word that would itself have become as small and poor as I am? I suppose that's the way it is, Lord ... If my life is supposed to be one single prayer, and my praying is to be part of this life carried on in your presence, then I must have the power to present my life, my very self to you.

—Karl Rahner

3

OVERCOMING OBSTACLES TO PRAYER

Where there is no prayer from the heart, there is no religion.
—Auguste Sabatier

Lord, I know not what I ought to ask of you.
You only know what I need. You know me better than I know myself
O Father, give to your child what he himself knows not how to ask.
Teach me to pray. Pray yourself in me.
—Archbishop François Fénelon

Most people are aware of the many potentials and possibilities in their lives. But it can be hard for us to believe that our possibilities are in fact possible at all! Perhaps this is why Jesus sometimes criticized his disciples for having such little faith. They did not trust God enough to realize what he could do with their lives.

Jesus demanded a righteousness (or a "right-relatedness") with God that dwarfed the religiosity of the religious leaders of his time. Without this "greater righteousness" of Jesus, the religious leaders had an inadequate relationship, not only with God, but also with the people around them, who saw them as hypocrites. Our relationship with God and our relationships with others are always inextricably woven together. This is reflected in the way of life which Jesus called for. At the heart of his message were two elements: the need for an inward life with God, and the call to behave in the world in a way that reflected the character of God himself.

All that Jesus did, in teaching, healing, gathering his disciples, serving the poor, dying, and being raised back to life, was to create a community of those who belonged to the King of heaven. Their whole way of life would be focused on and possessed by God. This is the whole object of prayer, to express "kingdom ways" among those who belong to God's kingdom. It is the immensity (and the radicalism) of all this that we seek to understand in this book. But first we need to look at our needs and our woundedness.

PRAYER IN OUR WOUNDEDNESS

Prayer is the way that we shape our inward life to imitate the mind of Christ. We come to God, as Augustine once observed, "by love and not by navigation." But what if we cannot pray, or cannot love? What if we are wounded as people, because of an unloved childhood, or because we are full of anger? What do we do then?

It is precisely the wounds in our relationships that keep many of us from experiencing the life of prayer. If prayer is a double search, our search for God that we later discover is really God's search for us, what happens to frustrate the encounter between us and God? If we are being invited in prayer to collaborate with God, what keeps us back from an enriching partnership with him?

Woundedness both within us and in our relationships does keep us from each other. When we are hurting, we draw back from making ourselves more vulnerable. We become distrustful when we have been deceived; unforgiving when we have been attacked; angry when we have been cornered into impossible, loveless situations. All this makes us feel unwanted, let down, unloved, and perhaps even destroyed.

Such feelings have a deep effect throughout our personalities. God has created us as relational beings. We were made for others, destined to love, to receive love and to share love. But when pain or anger is smoldering deep within us, this balance of giving and receiving is broken. This hidden pain and brokenness may explain why we face a blank wall when we try to pray. Anger has blocked us more than we realized was possible.

One person had an overwhelming sense of guilt and frustration with God which rose out of her relationship with her father. Unfathered himself, he was unable to show her affection and kept her at a distance from him. The result was that she had a poor sense of her own sexuality and lacked confidence with men. She was angry with God for her broken relationships, fearing that marriage would always elude her. Meanwhile, God stood far off, possibly indifferent to her efforts to pray and relate to him.

Another person was a perfectionist who could only gain attention in childhood by coming home with good grades from school. His relationship with God was played in the same attention-seeking way, but God seemed strangely unimpressed by all that this person tried to achieve. Still another person had experienced so much rejection in her relationships that rejection had become a way of life. She set herself up deliberately to be further rejected, and this too was reflected in her relationship with God.

How is prayer affected by all these types of personal woundedness? When we look at life through emotional dark glasses, then our view of God and prayer becomes distorted. If I have been manipulated as a person when young, the odds are that I will go on manipulating other people throughout my life, and I will try to manipulate God as well. Then I will have a frustrating prayer life indeed.

Yet this cycle of woundedness and rejection can start to be broken in very simple ways. We can be surprised to discover that despite our wounds some people do accept us, love us and even trust us. A healing friendship opens us up to the possibility that we can also accept ourselves in all our woundedness. As we open ourselves up to such friends, we can be encouraged to begin opening ourselves up to God too. We begin to learn at an emotional level how profoundly God has accepted us in Christ, because his love for us is infinite. Then with a deeper acceptance still, we learn that in his acceptance of us, we can accept ourselves. This happens not because we work to receive acceptance, but simply because he has already forgiven and accepted us.

We go back to the roots of our being, to the little wounded child within us. Jesus speaks directly to us as the children we are:

> Except you become as a little child, you cannot enter the kingdom of heaven. (See Matt. 18:3.)

The sad, confused child within me needs to experience the healing love of Jesus, who invited little children to come to him. In this way, the protective barriers of our lives can be removed, allowing us to become vulnerable to God's love, intimacy, and acceptance. When this happens, prayer takes on a new reality, bringing with it a deep healing. As we accept our woundedness, we learn that our wounds now become positive assets, showing us exactly where we need God's help in our lives.

PRAYER IN OUR ACTIVISM

Those who have been hurt by life often have a powerful drive to achieve, as they look for compensations, recognition, and significance. If we have been ignored, then we can buy acceptance. In our culture, we are defined by our function in life—by what we do and by our position on the tribal totem pole. We try to manipulate things to suit ourselves, so that we come out on top.

These conscious and unconscious drives work against a spirit of prayer, where we seek God's will rather than our own, and where we need to be still and listen to God rather than pump ourselves full of the narcotic of busyness. The words of one of the psalms, "My soul, find rest in God alone," are death to a spirit of self-importance and restless ambition. Sometimes we cannot stand to listen to such a radically different message when the world is seducing us to listen to its own claims.

Of course, we can always deceive ourselves by arguing that we are simply the achieving, activist type. The church is full of people who do argue in this way and who secularize the Christian message by infecting it with a spirit of busyness. They end up defining themselves and their faith by their activities, like the "cosmopolitan girl" of chapter 1. If we are such workaholics, addicted to activity, what hope can there be for us to have a meaningful prayer life? Research has shown that such people may even step up their adrenalin flow when they are praying, as if prayer is also a part of the competition, no less strenuous than running a race.

Unfortunately, despite all the effort, the achiever will always fail in prayer. His competitive spirit makes true prayer impossible. He will probably also fail in personal relationships, because the temptation to manipulate others will be so great. Prayer is not the controlling hyperactivity that the activist is familiar with. Instead, it will be an alien world to him, where he will need to become passive and receptive.

Activists can take their first steps in prayer by listening to their dreams, or by becoming aware that their dreams are never allowed to surface. We can ask God to allow us to wake up remembering what we have dreamed. Dreams are not in our control, so they can open up to us areas of our lives that are cloaked in mystery.

Our ordinary lives can also provide us with pointers to how our life in prayer could be. In the give and take of personal relationships, among friends or in the family, we can begin to see the possibilities of an even more radical give and take with God. Belonging to a small group or receiving spiritual guidance from a trusted friend may also help us to work toward nonachieving ways of handling our relationships. Behind our struggles to change and be changed, we may just begin to see that we have never learned to be gentle with ourselves, let alone with other people. We have never given others much patience, or allowed them "space" simply to be themselves. Allowing others and ourselves more space and time also allows God to work in our hearts, to change our ways and give us hope. It is clearly absurd to expect God to do great things for us if we are unwilling to allow him to interfere in the way we run our lives and relate to other people. That is how prayer can remain static and unreal for us. We have stopped listening—we have stopped living too.

DISTRUST OF GOD

Our culture dictates that we are most comfortable when we are dealing with personalities rather than persons. The difference is that personalities are the masks we wear before others, while the real person hidden beneath the mask fears the rejection that might come if the mask of personality was removed. Our mask is accepted, because everyone else is also wearing masks at the ball. A great deal of our life is spent in dancing and playing around each other's subterfuges. Of course, a small amount of openness is allowed. We call this "letting your hair down." But the real fear is what we would do if we took off our masks and discovered that we had no faces.

Here again we can see the evidence of our woundedness. We do not like the little that we know about ourselves, and we certainly do not want others to catch even a glimpse of the reality beneath the mask. If it is more natural for us to wear a mask than to show our faces, then how and when do we expose ourselves to God?

Perhaps we begin by realizing that we cannot handle our own uniqueness, and that we need to trust God with who we really are. Perhaps I really do need to consider that I need God to help me run my own life after all. When we come to this realization, then we will start to take prayer more seriously, starting the day with God and reflecting on all that lies ahead of us during the day.

When we have started to make daily morning prayer a necessity, perhaps we will then begin to see that life is much more full of mystery than we had dared to imagine. We begin to see what before was hidden. Seeing life mysteriously prompts us to see more and more of our helplessness and need. We start to recognize the many areas of life where we simply do not have the answers or the wisdom to cope.

The philosopher Pascal said, "The heart has its reasons, which are quite unknown to the head." In other words, we simply cannot understand, by mere thinking, why we behave as we do. And if it is true that the heart has its own secret ways of working, then how much does the whole mysterious struggle between good and evil also have its own secrets? Rational thinking can only cope with "things" rather than people, and it certainly cannot cope with the irrationality of evil. We could go mad trying to find reasons for the irrationality we see inside us and all around us, erupting like lava from a volcano, or like a flood that sweeps away the human landscape beneath it.

What else can we do but become vulnerable? We can only be awed by the great mysterious forces of evil all around us and within our own hearts, too. In the face of it all, prayer begins to become decidedly more attractive and relevant. Prayer allows us to throw ourselves onto God, who alone understands and brings light to our darkness.

However, this raises the whole problem of how we can trust God in the first place. How can I trust him if I dare not or simply don't want to share my inner longings with him? If we face this sort of inner obstacle, we need to ask whether we are still worshipping our father and mother in place of God. The image of our parents can easily usurp the place God rightfully has in our lives. When this happens, we turn Jesus' prayer upside down by saying, "Thy will be done in heaven as it is on earth." Earth, and not heaven, then becomes our way of mapping our reality—but it is a false reality. If we decided to navigate by the nearest telegraph pole rather than by the Pole Star, we would soon be completely lost.

Once we have realized this, we may need a friend to help us break the outer shell of our false self. An admirer may see my outward personality, but a true friend knows something about me as a person, and may be able to help me to be real before God. After all, God is the one who knows me completely. One of the psalms expresses it in this way:

> O Lord, you have searched me
> and you know me.
> You know when I sit and when I rise;
> you perceive my thoughts from afar.
> You discern my going out and my lying down;
> you are familiar with all my ways....
> You know it completely, O Lord. (Ps. 139:1–4)

God is the only one I can trust in the absolute sense. I can give him my whole heart, entrusting him with my identity. I can begin to experience what one monk, Brother Lawrence, called "practicing the presence of God." God becomes fully entrusted with my thoughts and aspirations.

When I was a child, I lived with a recurring fantasy. My birthday and Christmas are very close together, and so at that time of year I would think about the two series of gifts about to come my way. I used to avoid hoping for specific presents, as I told myself that I would only be disappointed. Instead, if I kept my desire for presents vague, then I might just get what I really, secretly wanted. As the years went by, my sense of desire was stifled by my defense against being disappointed.

Many of us grow up in this way toward God. If we feel we can never expect much from God, then prayer and desire shrivel up within us, paralyzing our inner life. We need to develop our ability to desire, to counteract the doses of cynicism that have inoculated us from ever expecting very much out of life.

The absence of desire can kill prayer, because how can God give to us if we do not expect or want him to do so? A Zulu proverb says that "hope is the pillar of the world." James, in his

New Testament book, speaks about the amazing generosity of God toward everyone. And twice in the Gospels the disciples are assured of Jesus' promise (Matt. 7:7; Luke 11:9).

> Ask and it will be given to you; seek and you will find; knock and the door will be opened to you.

We are called to believe what the Bible tells us about God. Against the evidence of our own wounded lives, we have to disbelieve the mean picture we may have of God's character. Jesus spoke in extravagant terms to show how our lives and our prayers can be transformed when we believe in the generosity of God's giving. He spoke about our prayers casting mountains into the sea and said, "Therefore I tell you, whatever you ask for in prayer, believe that you have received it, and it will be yours" (Matt. 11:24).

God's character is not restricted to our prudent, short-sighted ways of tackling everyday life. God takes us out of the mean and narrow ways in which we relate, to open before us the great open spaces of potential for our lives. But this can only happen if we expose our true selves to his love.

FEAR OF OUR INNER DARKNESS

Beyond the defects in our character that we know about, lurk deeper fears and anxieties that are a secret even to ourselves. This subconscious darkness may be more terrifying and crippling for some people than for others. One person spent his early childhood on a hospital cot. He had no experience of his mother's warmth and affection, and had to guard the territory of his cot from older children. This has made him a highly disciplined, successful military officer. However, his rigid emotions left him with a broken marriage and an inflexible system of rules for living. It was only after many years that the love of God helped him to laugh at himself and to become vulnerable. He discovered that God is a relating God who was able to receive all his fears and uncertainties.

Some people have experienced so little love and so much violence in childhood that their prayer life is full of violent images. Their prayers are spelled out in terms of struggles against principalities and powers, exorcisms, and a strong fascination with demonic forces. Everything they pray for comes from a powerful sense of endless struggle, of violence in heaven as well as on earth.

Others may see life only in terms of addiction, compulsive habits, guilt, or a weak self-image. The dark shadow that haunts them is an overpowering sense of failure and the hopelessness of living. Some people fear to look inside themselves at all. It is as if looking into one's soul is to look through a window of the heart into a bottomless pit.

Then there are those people who appear to have inherited psychic powers of intuition and foresight, which make them afraid of themselves, or cause them to reject themselves because of their "abnormalities." Whatever the darkness inside, our natural instinct is usually to hide and repress it. Prayer can be extremely threatening, because it calls for us to face our darkness and to uncover it. Our encouragement to do this is that God has already dealt with the forces of chaos—with cosmic chaos far greater than we can ever imagine. Because of this, we can go to him in prayer with a confidence spoken about in Psalm 139:

> If I say, "Surely the darkness will hide me and the light become night around me," even the darkness will not be dark to you; the night will shine like the day, for darkness is as light to you. (vv. 11–12)

Paul the apostle also echoes this thought in the New Testament. Paul says that the same Creator who commanded starlight to shine in the darkness of space, also shines his light into our hearts, "to give us the light of the knowledge of God in the face of Jesus Christ." The same creative, redeeming force which has dealt with the vastly mysterious reality of chaos also expels the darkness and violence within us. Experiencing this feels as if we have been raised from the dead, which in a sense we have. God is able to raise us to new life morally, spiritually, and psychologically. Receiving the creative power of God to drive out our darkness enables our prayer life to grow in confidence. It removes our deeply repressed anger, our desperate fears and compulsive habits. And it destroys our sense of helplessness and despair, our consciousness of failure, the guilt of living a lie and our feelings of emptiness and futility—to name just a few of our besetting shadows!

We can learn that God lies beyond the shadows, that he transcends all our enemies and that he is still the King of Kings, however powerful the forces that rule our lives may seem to be. This gives us hope to reach out to him, simply praying: "Lord, I believe. Help my unbelief." Our trust in God is a realization that he is already working for, in and through us, calling us to a new, whole life beyond our broken lives. The darkness will not win through, because light will overcome the night and love will destroy evil and hatred.

Encountering darkness in our lives should not drive us from prayer, but drive us to prayer. Darkness only becomes an obstacle when we fail to see God as the powerful ruler of our lives, able to overcome the evil we face in spite of our own fears and feelings. It is worth taking time to meditate on this prayer given by an early Cistercian monk, Aelred of Rievaulx. He had lived in the king's court in Scotland, but turned away from it all to live the life of prayer.

> Lord, look at my soul's wounds.
> Your living and effective eye sees everything.
> It pierces like a sword, even to part asunder soul and
>   spirit.
> Assuredly, my Lord, you see in my soul the traces of my
>   former sin;
> my present perils, and also motives and occasions for
>   others you see also.
> You see these things, Lord, and I would have you see
>   them.

You know well, O searcher of my heart,

that there is nothing in my soul that I would hide from
     you,

even had I the power to escape your eyes …

Lord, may your good, sweet Spirit descend into my
     heart,

and fashion there a dwelling for himself,

cleansing it from all defilement both of flesh and spirit,

pouring into it the increment of faith, hope and love,

disposing it to penitence and love and gentleness.

—PASTORAL PRAYER

4

ENTERING INTO
PRAYER

The power of knowledge of the thinking man is hardly enough, without the help
of grace, to know himself, even this is of no value unless from the knowledge of
what he is he rises to Him from Whom he is, to Him who is above him.

—William of St. Thierry

Religion," says the philosopher A. N. Whitehead, "is what
a man does with his solitariness." This quotation contains ideas with which we will want to both agree and disagree.

In the sense that each of us has to "keep accounts" with
God, it is certainly true. The seventeenth-century puritans used
to say that just as a doctor keeps his case-studies of patients, or
as a sea captain keeps his logbook, so a Christian has to keep
accounts with God, especially in his prayer life.

The negative side to A. N. Whitehead's quotation is its strong
emphasis on individualism. The Reformers, such as Luther and
Calvin, were the first to teach that each of us has a call from God
that transcends our particular job or profession. But in the modern world, this idea of an individual "calling" has become
secularized. Our jobs have become our calling, giving us our
sense of identity and our place in society. Western culture, partic-
ularly in North America, has become highly individualistic. This

concentration on "me" is in the end incompatible with true religion, just as it is incompatible with personal life, which grows and develops with our human relationships.

Prayer is the mirror-image of individualism, even though it may appear to be a highly individual activity. Withdrawal into solitariness is necessary for us to listen to God, but true prayer must also relate to the needs of others, and send us back with new life into our relationships. A relationship with God that does not relate to other people is unreal. Our withdrawal into solitude, prayer, and meditation is also an affirmation of personal dependence on God to live in the world, rather than to escape from it.

It has been wisely observed that no one is safe in the marketplace of human affairs if they have not also spent time in the desert of solitude with God. But the reverse is also true. We pray to a God who loves the world, and so our prayers will be false if we do not respond by loving other people as well as loving God. Whether our prayers are made in the stark simplicity of a Quaker meeting, in the structured use of the Anglican prayer book, in the ornate ritual of the Orthodox liturgy or in a lively, fervent house church, prayer should always have the same social consequences: that we love others and God more sincerely.

PRAYER EXPRESSES RELATIONSHIPS

A Russian book, *The Way of the Pilgrim,* illustrates the close link between prayer and relationships. It describes how a young Russian, living in the nineteenth century, sells all that he has after both his parents have died. He travels the length and breadth of Russia to find out the meaning of the words of Paul: "Pray without ceasing." On his journeys, he meets many people who tell him their own diverse experiences of prayer, some more helpful than others. The pilgrim discovers that prayer is a great matter, vaster than the land he journeys through, deeper than all the experiences of individuals. And yet, despite this mystery of prayer, it draws him into warm relationships with many, many people. On the surface, the pilgrim's life seems solitary, but in reality he is enriched by the different experiences and perspectives shared by his fellow pilgrims.

Significantly, the pilgrim discovers three sources of companionship: his own incessant practice of daily prayer; the daily reading of the *Philokalia,* a collection of the meditations of the saints; and the conversations he has with the people he so frequently meets.

The book is saturated with the sense of God's presence. It shows how joy, love, and strength enter the inner being of a man because he keeps in close touch with God, and how in turn he is able to reach out and be a presence for so many other people.

We, too, need a climate of prayer that enables us to travel with a free (or even a transcendent) spirit. Others will then be able to see that not only is God's presence of supreme importance in our lives, but also that everything we are and do is dependent on living prayerfully.

A WORLD IN FRAGMENTS

There is a widespread feeling that our modern age, with all its glittering technical prospects, is slipping away from us into disillusionment. We live in an in-between age, where the old and new grate against each other painfully. The poet John Donne, writing in the seventeenth century, witnessed the beginning of the modern age, and described those changing times:

> Tis all in peeces, all cohaerence gone;
>
> All just supply, and all Relation:
>
> Prince, Subject, Father, Sonne, are things forgot,
>
> For every man alone thinkes he hath got
>
> To be a Phoenix, and that then can bee
>
> None of that kinde, of which he is, but hee.

Donne lived in a passing world where feudalism, with all its ties to family, property, and village life, was dissolving. Few people could see what the radical consequences would be. In our age, we also see "all coherence gone," as the fragmentation of life takes place at every level. In science, there is increasing specialization. In everyday life, there are more and more professionals, expert in their fields. In religion, there is frantic activity geared toward selling faith as a marketable commodity. All this specialization shows how our society has broken up into separate fragments.

Prayer alone can give us a sense of coherence in the broken-up world. Prayer at the beginning and end of each day and each meal, prayer at the beginning of each week and with each cycle of the year, reminds us that our practical, everyday pursuits are not the whole of life.

Prayer shows us that life makes little sense if this is all it is: making money, making love, making a name for ourselves, making idols. The poverty of affluence, the failure of success, the emptiness of material plenty, the moral laziness of being busy—all these only make us hungry for something deeper. They drive us to a new concern for our inner needs, for friendships that last, and for spiritual resources that strengthen us inside. They make us long for a personal relationship with God to replace the emptiness of modern life.

Prayer, too, can overcome our own fragmentation inside. Many people have an internal division between what they think and what they do, between belief and action. In fact, many religious people see their faith as a set of beliefs, rather than as a living relationship with God. Only a life of prayer can bring healing to our divided selves, and to our divided relationships with other people.

FIVE VISITORS

While prayer can bring healing to broken relationships, it is also deeply affected by them. During the writing of this chapter, five visitors called on me, one after another, whose stories illustrate the way in which prayer can collapse under the weight of bad relationships.

The first visitor was a young woman who said that she was afraid to pray. She lacked the emotional assurance of being herself. Since her childhood, she had been sexually abused, and she was afraid that God, too, might abuse her if she was too vulnerable before him. The result was that her prayers were dutiful, but distant and unreal. She felt dissatisfied and guilty.

The second visitor was a young medical doctor whose strong, domineering mother had had a permanent effect upon his adult life. He constantly felt manipulated by other people, and yet put himself into situations where others found it easy to manipulate him. Rebellion had become a way of life, so it was more natural to rebel against God than to be vulnerable before God in prayer and obedience. The children of alcoholic parents often have the same dilemma of being emotionally manipulated by other people, becoming skillful actors in hiding their true feelings. They find it almost impossible to take prayer seriously into their hearts.

The third visitor was an older woman whose relationship with her father had always been distant. She had a deep sense of rejection from him until he died. Her mother had married "beneath herself" socially and the result had been an unhappy marriage. To compensate for this, the mother had drawn her children around herself, which only generated in the daughter an intense dislike for her mother. Rebellion was the daughter's only response—against home, faith, and her own two marriages. Coming back to God was a long, painful journey. Her central struggle was to see God as someone who truly cared for and accepted her.

The fourth visitor was a middle-aged man who had recently resigned as the pastor of a very difficult church. The church's worldly members were not prepared to tolerate his biblical views. He was prepared to stick with the situation indefinitely, as he had the spirit of martyrdom in his blood. But he found the experience devastating. He had always been the "good" child of his family, in contrast to his brother who played the black sheep. Looking back, he could see that he had tried to buy his parents' acceptance in being good, and had done the same to gain God's acceptance too. When this strategy failed in his church, he was emotionally shattered. He came to realize that his prayers had always been affected by his upbringing. They were an unreal, necessary obligation. He spoke to God like someone speaking through misted glass. He could only see God's shadow, but not his face.

The fifth and final visitor was a young church worker who grew up in an actively Christian home. She grew up watching her mother counseling others, but having no time for the home, and her father working late into each evening on committees, growing apart from his two daughters. Religious life focused around what other people approved of rather than what you yourself believed and felt. She grew up as a valued church worker with a secret life of rebellion and sexual adventure. She had never discovered prayer, because she had never discovered her own heart. She knew that prayer is a matter of the heart. But did she have a heart?

Reflecting on these stories, we can see that prayer, like all our relationships, is not done in isolation. John Donne tells us that "No man is an island, entire of itself...." All of our relationships are affected by the relationships we have had in the past and which continue into the present. There are times when we need to uncouple ourselves from an unhealthy relationship, such as a wounding parental influence in the past, so that our relationship with God is allowed to grow toward maturity. Jesus spoke about our life in him as the branch on a vine. As it is pruned back, it goes on to grow and bear more fruit than it would have produced unpruned. Growth in prayer may mean that we will have to go through a process of emotional pruning.

It is clear that prayer and the rest of our lives are closely linked and deeply affect each other. In the 1960s and '70s it was recognized that events on one side of the earth could have a massive impact thousands of miles away. When penguins in the Antarctic were affected by pesticides, the cause was found to be crop spraying by farmers in the midwestern United States. We now know that the earth is a series of interlocking life-systems, each system producing responses in all the others. The same is true in the world of relationships. Human sin is like a pollutant which crosses all known boundaries. Its effects are passed down from parents to children in an unending sequence of generations. This pollution would be relentless and lethal if it was not for the redeeming action of God who intervenes when we request his help. Prayer is that request, said and lived out unceasingly.

The relationships of parents and children, friends and work colleagues, and the whole family of mankind are interconnected in ways beyond our imagination. All the time we are influenced and affected by their invisible waves. Yet if each person is a unique individual, how can this sinful, self-directed, self-preoccupied world survive with its five billion people, each looking after number one?

Prayer is the means that God has given us to survive. Through prayer we can sustain our human dignity and the freedom of our uniqueness but still love other people as well. Through prayer we can be freed from the suffocating influences of bad relationships, past and present. The rich communication between us and God in prayer enables us to relate to other people as he relates to us. Prayer makes it possible to contribute positively to our relationships, making the world less of a jungle teeming with wild animals, more of a realm of friendships.

PRAYER EXPRESSES GOD'S CLAIMS

Encountering God in prayer is not always comfortable. Prayer exposes us to the character of God, who comes up against our own sinfulness. God's character also collides with the sinful character of the culture in which we live and which deeply infects us as people. We see this collision between God and modern culture at a number of different levels.

The Old Testament shows us that God related to a community of people, the Israelites, and not simply to the individual. God's agreement with his people was summed up in the words, "I shall be your God, and you shall be my people." It was God himself who sustained the solidarity of the community and gave them their unity. This view of people relating to God in community is in marked contrast to today's individualistic, dog-eat-dog mentality. Prayer is an antidote to the spirit of modern culture, a daily reminder that our duties toward God come before any talk of human rights in society. This is because human rights cannot be sustained without first establishing the priority of God's rule. Prayer expresses our awareness of the prior rights of God.

Our culture is also engaged in a new series of mental adventures in trying to define what is personhood, or when human life in the womb begins. Such attempts to bring personality into the laboratory are consistent with the way we see human beings today. Our society increasingly treats people as commodities in the marketplace, as sex objects in lust, as untold millions of babies to be incinerated, as the old who can be disposed of by euthanasia. All this occurs when we alienate ourselves by denying the value of human personality. For it is the nature of human beings that they should be known in the acceptance of love rather than by clinical analysis.

Prayer helps us to recognize that we are imprinted with the image or likeness of God. We have the God-given ability to relate to and communicate with others and with God in prayer. Recognizing this can renew all our relationships. It is this that enables me to get into the habit of silently praying every time I meet someone in the street, in the office or if I am calling on them. I can say to myself before God:

> Lord, help me to see this person as unique in your sight, as someone for whom you died, and who you love so much that you want to spend eternity with them in friendship. I have no resources to make our encounter meaningful without your Spirit. But in your presence, help me to be kind, giving territory to the uniqueness of the other person, awed by the mystery of being human together!

If prayer like this was offered to God as the breath of our relationships, just as oxygen is the breath of our bodies, there would pulsate through the world of other people a mighty renewal for the human race. For as we reflect upon it, sin brings alienation against God, and evil is what depersonalizes the human person. In the New Testament, the apostle Paul gives a number of formidable lists which detail the forms in which sin appears. All the sins he mentions dehumanize us, causing man's inhumanity to man in rebellion against God. Pride is the supreme source of egocentric isolation, and from this stems anger, arrogance, covetousness, drunkenness, faithlessness, foolishness, hatred, homosexuality, idolatry, immorality, jealousy, malignity, murder, sexual evil, sorcery, stealing, swindling, and viciousness. Human inauthenticity is made up of all these things and they keep us isolated from ourselves, from other people and from God.

Prayer works to destroy these evils, because prayer unites the human soul with the life and vitality of God. Prayer allows us a direct relationship with the one person who can save us from the evil that invades our hearts. So we can pray for ourselves throughout each day, "Create in me a clean heart, O God, and renew a right spirit within me."

However, there is a cost to being human. It is the cost of being claimed by God. John Calvin put it like this:

> The first rule of right prayer is to have our heart and mind framed as becomes those who are entering into converse with God.

Everything that is unworthy of God—selfish desires, sinful thoughts, mean ways—must be discarded in a spirit of humility. We cannot pray if we are arrogant or distracted by the world, nor if we remain self-confident. And it is here that we reach the point of struggle.

Every well-meaning person who tries to live a life of prayer quickly discovers that the strategies and masks that they use to shield them from a painful world also insulate them from truly reaching out to God. These strategies might include working hard to gain recognition, being "good" to buy affection, or manipulating others to establish position. They may help us to win success in the world, but, as we have seen, they really signal our failure to redeem our childhood. Brought into the world of prayer, they suddenly appear for what they are: death-giving rather than life-giving. The painful cost of prayer is to confront these signs of our brokenness, allowing God to heal our humanity.

So in order to become prayerful people, there are costs that we must accept. True prayer involves agreeing to conditions that reflect the character of the God to whom we are relating. The rest of this chapter examines four of the most significant costs of prayer.

ENCOUNTERED AND SHATTERED BY GOD

Prayer will always remain a vague, safe exercise until we are impacted by God. This happens when we stop looking at ourselves through the mask that we like to wear for other people, and start to see ourselves as God actually sees us.

Imagine a wealthy, powerful businessman who has ruthlessly built up his empire by trampling all over the feelings of others. He has an arrogant image of himself. But if his cruelty is suddenly exposed through a takeover of his company or through bankruptcy, then his world and his image of himself are shattered. The shattering of leadership can be a revelation indeed.

Many ordinary people, who take fewer risks than high-flying businessmen, escape being shattered in this way. But exactly the same process can happen for them if their marriage partner walks out, their parents die, or their children run away from home. The rapid rate of change in our culture makes us all vulnerable to what has been called "future shock."

To be a Christian means to be "shocked" by Christ. He has encountered us. Our defenses have been shattered. We have heard the shocking call to abandon our much-loved securities and to follow him. The cult of self-fulfillment, which makes us so selfish and self-directed, creates a brittleness in us that simply shatters when we meet God personally.

We can see this moment of impact at many points in the Bible. When Jesus called a rich young man to leave all his possessions to follow him, we read, "At these words, the man's face fell. He went away sad, for he had many possessions." At another point, a man who saw heaven opened recorded his immediate, instinctive response: "When I saw him, I fell at his feet as though dead."

The paradox is that this shattering of our personality is essential before we can follow God and become intimate with him in prayer. We cannot behave before God as we behave before other people, even when the ploys we use are amusing or winningly attractive. Our mask may be beautifully made, drawing admiration from everyone who sees it—but it is still a mask. And it must go.

ABANDONED TO GOD'S GOODNESS

Homesickness for God is a mark of the life of prayer. Once we recognize that we are in love with God, then we will want to experience his presence as a daily reality. This is why some people decide to devote themselves completely to prayer by living behind monastic walls. The radical nature of encountering God can shatter any other alternative resource for living.

Peter, Jesus' disciple, recognized this when he once cried out: "Lord, to whom can we go?! You alone have the words of eternal life!" This means moving out of the human city to live in the desert alone with God. For some people, this is a literal renunciation. If we understand what it is that has motivated people to seek the monastic life, we can learn a great deal for our own prayer life, even though we still live in the world.

The desert fathers in the fourth century left the fantasies of power and status, which had infected the church of that time, to be authentic before God. This protest movement at a worldly church marked the very beginning of monasticism. The aim of the monastics is to surrender our self-will to the will of God, and to control the body through prayer and fasting. Solitude is an important part of all this, as it allows space for us to listen to God. Through listening, we are able to identify the addictive, compulsive habits that tyrannize us, and from which we must be freed to practice the presence of God.

The early monastic vows set themselves against the addictions of possessiveness, sex, and power, in the threefold vows of poverty, chastity, and obedience. Monastic life was a counter-culture, just as Jesus' Sermon on the Mount is an alternative to the spirit of the world. Prayer belongs to this counter-culture and our prayers are frustrated whenever we compromise between our praying and our living. Prayer should determine the spirit in which we live our lives. Too often we turn this upside down, turning the agenda of our everyday needs into shopping lists for prayer.

Our life in the body deeply affects our prayer-life in the soul. So we pray that God will help us to control our physical addictions, not simply by placing restrictions on our bodies, but also by enlarging our souls. We do this by improving the quality of our relationships with God and with other people. When we restrict our souls through poor relationships, we become lonely and self-concerned, which in turn makes the body uncontrollable in its lusts. Our lust then becomes a measure of how far we are alienated from those around us and from God. So the whole point of denying ourselves is to free the soul and allow us to grow in our vitality for God.

True self-denial is the way in which we make room in our lives for the presence of God. We can do this in a number of ways: we can learn to become silent, listening to God; we can find solitude and become uncluttered in our desire for God; we can give him our attention, to be more deeply aware of how we need him; we can become obedient to his will, surrendering ourselves to his rule.

Self-denial sounds negative, but its aim is to give us a fuller, richer life. Augustine said that fasting gave greater space to the soul, allowing it freedom to discover God. One of the desert fathers prayed, "We beg of you, make us truly alive." As we deny the excesses of our bodies and release our inner lives, we discover a new quality of living. This determination to exchange something of lesser value for one of greater is exactly the discipline an athlete goes through. Doughnuts take second place to winning the prize, and the aches and pains of the body are less important than running in the Olympics.

In the same way, the life of prayer is a call to exchange the less important for the more important. We deny not only our bodies but ourselves, replacing a selfish way of life with the joyful acceptance of the rule and presence of God. It is only by emptying ourselves that we create room to receive the gifts God brings to us. Through emptying we are filled with his love, his Spirit, and his friendship. This is the goal of self-denial. We receive more of God, becoming more fully human, renewed and healed in ourselves and in all our relationships.

TRUSTING GOD

We can only fully deny ourselves when we deepen our trust in God. Like a child that takes a leap into Daddy's strong arms, we need to have that same fearlessness that characterizes trust. Prayer lives on this fearless trust in God.

But what if we cannot trust? What if we were brought up in a home where love was in short supply and where we felt without worth? We would probably feel that faith and trust were the very realities we most lacked. And if these qualities are absolutely necessary to prayer then we would be defeated right from the start.

We need to recognize that God takes the initiative with us. His love for us comes before our love for him. The apostle John tells us:

> This is love: not that we loved God, but that he loved us and sent his Son as an atoning sacrifice for our sins. Dear friends, since God so loved us, we also ought to love one another. (1 John 4:10–11)

A much-loved child will also love much. We imitate the love we receive because being loved gives to us the sense of self-worth we need to love, trust and relate to other people. It is when we feel we belong that we can start to relate. This is also true of prayer. When we begin to realize that we belong to God, because he first loved us, then we will be able to love and trust him in a growing relationship. By being accepted and loved by God we receive a new self-regard and self-respect. One New Testament writer put it in this way: "We have been accepted in the Beloved (that is, in Jesus Christ)." In other words, God loves us with the same love that he has for his Son. This is the rock upon which our prayer life is established firmly and forever.

If we are loved by God, then we are also known by him. A true friend will know everything about me and will accept it all because he loves me. In the same way, God reaches into the depths of our beings, into our alienation and sin, where we are most helpless and lost. While much of our inner life may be hidden from friends (and from ourselves), God knows us completely. In the Gospels, there are many incidents where Jesus clearly knew exactly what people were thinking or deciding in their inmost hearts. Jesus' disciples also realized that their lives were transparent to him. But they also discovered that Jesus understood and identified with their sorrow and bereavement, their suffering, weakness and temptation.

Jesus, who knows me completely, understands me in the same way. And since his knowledge of me is high above my own understanding of myself, he is qualified to be the supreme judge of my whole life. In one of the visions of the book of Revelation, John, the author, describes Jesus as having "eyes like blazing fire." As John fell at Jesus' feet in fear, Jesus told him, "Do not be afraid."

Behind the eyes which see everything is a love that accepts and heals.

Psalm 139 also expresses the all-seeing knowledge of God:

> When I was woven together in the depths of the earth,
> your eyes saw my unformed body. (vv. 15–16)

For some, this may seem a gross invasion of our privacy, but to those who put their trust in God it is an encouragement to give their whole persons to him. This faith in God gives us great freedom, as we commit ourselves to his protection. We have faith in God not just for our future beyond death, but that he will preserve our identity in Christ in the present also.

The child of God is able to live an entrusted life, safe in God's keeping and direction. Prayer becomes a joyful experience of belonging, trusting, and sharing with God in all of our life and relationships. Such a relationship with God gives unity to the whole person, and union with God himself. We achieve what has been called "holy simplicity"—a life that has become simple in its wholeness and integrity, its devotion and inner freedom; a life that simply belongs to God alone. Our thoughts and actions, our words and deeds are no longer divided but are fused together in a way of life that is for God and in God. We become one with ourselves in God.

Remaining an Attacked Human Being

The picture we have just painted would be too idealistic if we left it there. For in life we remain in conflict. When Antony withdrew into the desert in the fourth century to live for God, two-thirds of his time was spent in battling the temptations he faced as an athlete for God. We all experience the reality that prayer is a persistent struggle. We are attacked and confronted by evil thoughts. Our devotion to God is tested as we struggle against invisible influences and subtle forces that try to undermine our relationship with God.

We also discover that a change of scene does not automatically bring with it a change of heart. Just as the monks, alone in the desert night, could still imagine the dancing girls of the city brothels, so we should not be too surprised to find our prayer interrupted by dark thoughts and passions.

In fact, a life more dedicated to God enlarges our consciousness of ourselves. The thoughts that we used to repress now come to the surface, revealing the inner world of our heart which needs to be brought under the rule of Christ. This is a disturbing process, as the filth from the cellar of our inner lives bubbles up, exposing the things that threaten and damage us deep inside. But it is also a life-giving process, allowing us to be forgiven and healed by God.

So when we think we are making progress spiritually and are deluged without warning by evil thoughts, we should not think that our spiritual journey has suddenly gone into reverse gear. Instead, we should rejoice that God will be able to deal with us on a new level as we bring our evil before him in confession and repentance.

The philosopher Socrates once said that "an unexamined life is not worth living." Suffering can make us pay attention to ourselves before God, forcing us into narrow straits to be tested, and to come through them proved. We cannot avoid struggle if we are determined to live by our convictions. So when we pray,

"Lead us not into temptation," we are not asking for a way of escape, but for the strength not to be overcome by temptation.

At a deeper level, we discover that there are demonic forces which we will have to fight. Origen, one of the early church fathers, asked a question:

> If it is true that the devil and his legions have been destroyed, how is it that we still believe him to be so powerful against the servants of God?

His answer was that the demons' evil activity was directed most against those who were far from God, because the Devil no longer has any power over those who belong to God. The evidence of the truth of this is in the way that prayer works.

Prayer can cast demons out from the lives of people who have been invaded by evil. Prayer can and does protect us from demonic activity. Reading the Bible prayerfully provides us with great power against evil forces. Paul spoke about putting on "the whole armor of God" to guard us against evil. He ended his description of the protective armor by calling us to "pray in the Spirit on all occasions with all kinds of prayers and requests."

However, there can be a tendency for us to blame demonic powers when we need simply to examine our own hearts. We live in a society that is becoming more and more neurotic, so perhaps we too are becoming too self-indulgent, too much an easy prey for temptation. A life of prayer meets trial and temptation head on, never avoiding the issues. The struggle really begins when we start to resist the evil that comes from within our own hearts.

One of the desert fathers helpfully drew up a catalog of the different types of temptation that attack us. His list later became the basis for the famous "seven deadly sins." The description of these various temptations is valuable in helping us to know our enemy, and in learning how to battle with them in prayer.

The first temptation in the list is gluttony, which the writer also calls "stomach-madness." This rivets our attention on our bodily appetites.

The second temptation is fornication, "lusting after other bodies," which is closely connected with gluttony. Then there is greed, which often grows out of insecurity. We long to have more money, more pleasure, a greater reputation. Greed is the itch for more and more that can never be satisfied.

Discontent is the fourth temptation. Discontentment in life leads to depression and discouragement. This is why it is so vital that we should receive the encouragement God longs to give us through prayer.

The fifth temptation is anger, an emotion which should never be used against other people, but only against evil. Anger in human relationships tends to escalate into more and more anger, like a nuclear reactor set on self-destruction.

Then there is despondency, or what the monks called "the noonday devil." Despondency is usually a form of spiritual cowardice, where we escape from the painful duties of life into a fantasy of how nice life would be if only....

The seventh temptation used to be called "vainglory," but we might now call it self-congratulation. Ironically, this is a temptation that becomes stronger as we make progress spiritually and think we are really getting somewhere. As evil retreats, its traps become ever more subtle.

The final temptation is pride, which is closely related to self-congratulation. This is the temptation to feel that we have finally arrived. In a sense, it underlies all the temptations in that it tells us that we can look after ourselves and make our own decisions about how to run our lives. Pride is essentially self-enclosure, which is the greatest of all the sins. It denies the fundamental character of our being, that we were created for God and for relationships with others. To deny this is sin of the first magnitude. Pride is a blasphemy against God's creation of us as human beings.

Behind all these temptations is our basic addiction to loving ourselves to the exclusion of anyone else. The philosopher Plato tells us, "Man is by nature his own friend: it is legitimate." But then he goes on to admit: "This great friendship for oneself is then for each the cause of all missteps."

Allied to this exclusive self-love is our inclination to indulge in temptation, and our astonishing ability to justify our own evil actions to ourselves. One of the great passages of the New Testament tells us, "If we say we have no sin, we deceive ourselves, and the truth is not in us." Our obstinacy can often lead us to deceive ourselves that we are on the right road.

Prayer, then, is a spiritual warfare against all these temptations and evil tendencies. We should expect attacks against our prayer life, and we need to know exactly how we will be attacked. At the heart of each attack is the temptation to achieve self-fulfillment If we are deeply convinced that God made us for himself, that he made us to give and receive in relationships, then any temptation toward self-fulfillment will be seen as destructive of the way God made us. Believing in God, entrusting ourselves to his keeping, and receiving from him the source of our life are the only antidotes to the poison of our fallen world and its demonic realities. As Jesus said, "Watch and pray, so that you will not fall into temptation" (Mark 14:38).

Father in heaven! Well do we know that thou art everywhere present; and that should anyone at this moment call upon thee from his bed of sickness, or one in greater need upon the ocean cry out to thee—or one in still greater need in sin—that thou art near to hear him. But thou art also in thy house where thy community is gathered together, some perhaps flying from heavy thoughts, or followed by heavy thoughts, but some too coming from a quiet daily life of contentment, and some perhaps with a satisfied longing hidden in a thankful heart enveloped in joyous thoughts—yet all drawn by the desire to seek God, the Friend of the thankful in the blessed trust; consolation of the weak in strengthening communion; refuge of the afflicted as thou dost count their tears; last comfort for the dying as thou dost receive their souls. So let thyself be found with a good gift to everyone who needs it, that the happy may find courage to accept thy good gifts, that the sorrowful may find courage to accept thy perfect gifts. For to men there is a difference of joy and of sorrow, but for thee, O Lord, there is no difference in these things; everything that comes from thee is a good and perfect gift.

—Søren Kierkegaard

Part Two

EXPLORING BIBLICAL TERRITORY

5

EXPLORING PRAYER IN THE OLD TESTAMENT

The man who knows God hears his step in the tramp of daily events, discerns
him near at hand to help, and hears his answer to the appeal of prayer in a hun-
dred happenings outwardly small and insignificant, where another man can talk
only of remarkable coincidence, amazing accident, or peculiar turns of events.
That is why periods when the life of faith is strong, and men have enthusiasti-
cally surrendered themselves to God, have also been times rich in miracles.

—Walter Eichrodt

Prayer is wider than the world, deeper than the heart, and older than the origin of humanity, because prayer originates from the very character of God. Its possibilities are infinite and so our explorations in prayer can be vast. The easy way in which some people claim to have "found it" in their spiritual experience only shows up more clearly the mystery of prayer and the mystery of God longing for friendship with us.

We now live at a time when humankind has become a technological giant but a moral pigmy. We have become fearful of our knowledge and cleverness. We are even becoming aware that we need more than clinical therapy to sort out our confused emotions. Our lust for knowledge needs to be placed in the deeper setting of once more "knowing God." He is the only person who can show us the place where knowledge fits into human life.

This is where the Old Testament can help us. Our culture and view of life are of course far removed from the ancient Near East of the Old Testament. But at heart we are still the same in our unchanging need for God's companionship and friendship. Exploring the world of prayer in the Old Testament is simply an effective way of getting back to our roots. It allows us to gain a sense of perspective on the fullness of relationship that we can enjoy with God.

A New World of Prayer

To pray is to declare loyalty to a spiritual reality above and beyond the human realm of self-effort and control. Prayer can be idolatrous, the worship of false gods. This can come about when our emotional needs are distorted and we attempt to manipulate and control others. So when we talk about "prayer," we need to qualify what we mean by linking it with the character of God himself.

If we refuse to approach prayer in terms of God's character, then our own thinking becomes the deciding factor in our lives. This is exactly what has happened to us culturally. The philosopher René Descartes assumed that human reason could call all reality into question, and his approach led us into the darkness of modern rationalism.

This is what also happened in the story of the fall in Genesis chapter 3. Adam and Eve sought to rival God's powers of knowledge. The symbol of this comes when they snatch the forbidden fruit of the knowledge of good and evil, seeking knowledge outside their relationship with God. So to pray to false gods, or not to pray to the only true God, are both expressions of sin and our fallenness.

A modern novelist who gives hints of what this may mean is William Golding. His perceptive novel, *The Inheritors,* is a satirical rejection of evolutionary optimism—the idea that the human race is steadily progressing to a higher and higher form of life.

Golding turns this idea on its head by taking us back to the world of Neanderthal Man (said to have lived one hundred thousand years ago). The Neanderthals are depicted as much nearer to the garden of Eden than we are. They are gentle, kindly, and innocent, living close to the mysteries of life. They have a poor reckoning of cause and effect, but this only frees them to a more childlike imagination, with a great sense of wonder and reverence for life. In the book, the Neanderthals are not wholly innocent. They have evil thoughts and practices. But the species *homo sapiens* is much worse, as they live "without pictures." They are not conscious of and do not respond to the mysteries all around them. Instead, they are boastful creatures, conscious of their own intellectual powers. Their creation of language reinforces their sense of guilt, anxiety, and fear of each other, and eventually they turn in anger on the Neanderthals and destroy them.

The Old Testament does not speculate in this way on how the human race fell by "eating from the tree of knowledge of good and evil." But it does repeatedly emphasize that the kingship of God lies at the heart of all true worship. Unless prayer recognizes and celebrates Yahweh as King (Yahweh is the Hebrew name for God), then worship degenerates into idolatry. This is because Yahweh is the creator of all things. Everything else that exists, including the gods devised by human idolatry, are under his irresistible rule. When the Israelites called upon God as Yahweh, they acknowledged his kingship over creation, history and the destiny of the nations. His character gave meaning to their worship, as well as giving them a sense of personal identity as the community of God's people.

So "Yahweh" says everything about God's revelation to us, and of our response to God. Psalm 100:3 celebrates this exuberantly:

> Know that the Lord is God.
>
> It is he who made us, and we are his;
>
> we are his people, the sheep of his pasture.

Psalm 95 echoes this by inviting the worshipper:

> Come, let us bow down in worship,
>
> let us kneel before the Lord our Maker; ...
>
> and we are the people of his pasture,
>
> the flock under his care. (vv. 6–7)

Over fifty times in the book of Psalms Israel is called God's people. Israel is "the people he has chosen," "his flock," "his servants," and "his possession." We too need to enter into this deeply personal sense of loyal allegiance to God as our King and Lord. Our own instincts of superiority and of belonging to an advanced, technique-oriented culture will block us from giving loyalty to God. Unless we overcome these false instincts, then prayer will become a futile exercise. We will either feel that it would be "more honest" to give up, or we will feel a nagging sense of guilt that we can never achieve anything in prayer.

Our first prayer needs simply to tell God, "Oh, God, help me to pray, because I cannot pray by myself." Such a prayer helps us to recognize how prayer expresses our deepest need before the kingship of God.

One person expressed her feelings about prayer to me in this way:

> I used to feel that all the praying I was doing amounted to nothing more than a pile of words. I was fed up with the hollow echo of organized religion, and hearing endlessly the same old sermons. I had poured out all my energies on what I now realize was a form of self-satisfaction that had very little to do with God. It was only when I came to myself, aware of my great limitations that took on a frightening shape of fearful, painful, personal inadequacy, that prayer became for the first time a real and intimate way of living for me. I still have a lot of the same kind of responsibility for other people as I did before, but my whole approach is completely reversed,

> turned upside down and inside out from what it once
> was. Even though the structures of my life still look the
> same on the outside, the inside is radically different.

My friend's attitude toward God and prayer has arisen from a whole new experience of how she can trust God. She is able to relax in his goodness and mercy and surrender to him her instinct to manipulate life. Like Israel in the Old Testament, each of us needs to experience our own exodus, our own deliverance from the technological society of Egypt in which we live and are enslaved.

LIVING AS FREED SLAVES

Israel's experience of God in the Old Testament was dominated by the exodus, when God released his people from slavery in Egypt. The Hebrew word for "Egypt" literally means "bondage" or "affliction." The Israelites were enslaved in Egypt under an idolatrous ruler, because the pharaohs saw themselves as gods. The deliverance of the Israelites only happened when Moses fled into the desert of Midian and met with the true God at the burning bush. In that encounter, God spoke these words to Moses (Ex. 3:7–8):

> I have indeed seen the misery of my people in Egypt. I
> have heard them crying out because of their slave drivers,
> and I am concerned about their suffering. So I have come
> down to rescue them from the hand of the Egyptians and
> to bring them up out of that land into a good and spa-
> cious land, a land flowing with milk and honey.

This experience of Israel is true for us too. We are enslaved by an idolatrous way of life, and it is only as we meet God in the silence and struggle of our own hearts that we can be freed to know God for ourselves. When we are completely self-preoccupied it may appear that God is indifferent to us. But as we begin to take him seriously, to desire God, then we discover that God takes us seriously and specifically in response. As the slaves in Egypt cried out to God, he saw their misery, heard their cries, and came down to rescue them. In the same way, God knows our condition and meets our personal needs.

After their deliverance, the Israelites were filled with joy and gratitude toward God. They praised God by singing:

> I will sing to the Lord, for he is highly exalted.
> The horse and its rider he has hurled into the sea.
> The Lord is my strength and my song;
> he has become my salvation.
> He is my God, and I will praise him,
> my father's God, and I will exalt him. (Ex. 15:1–2)

This is the experience of everyone who finds their salvation in God. But the Israelites quickly discovered (and the same is true for us too) that the journey through the desert is not a shortcut in living. We are not suddenly freed from all our problems. Instead, we have a long journey through many other temptations and challenges.

The poet T. S. Eliot, in one of his *Four Quartets,* expressed it in this way:

> In order to arrive at what you are not
> You must go through the way in which you are not.

We now begin to realize that our Achilles heel provides the direction for our spiritual journey. We are led and redeemed to become the opposite of what we were when we started out on our pilgrimage. So if I start out timidly, then I will end up courageously. If I begin as a grumbler, finding it hard to trust others, then I will complete my journey praising God and full of faith.

This can only happen if the life of prayerful companionship is really what we want from our relationship with God. But we need to be warned. There will be many temptations and tests in the desert. We will often find ourselves estranged from God and attacked by our enemy before we reach the end of the wilderness.

LIVING PRECARIOUSLY

The world of the Old Testament was precarious. Compared with the assured systems of irrigation in the great civilizations of the Nile, the winter rains in Palestine were uncertain for the Israelites. Politically, Israel lived between the two great powers of Egypt and Babylon. These powers, each with an aggressive approach to diplomacy and culture, encircled Israel like two giant claws. It is small wonder that Israel turned to prayer in the pursuit of its own national identity:

> Blessed is the nation whose God is the Lord,
> the people he chose for his inheritance.
> From heaven the Lord looks down and sees all mankind;
> from his dwelling place he watches
> all who live on earth—
> he who forms the heart of all,
> who considers everything they do.
>
> No king is saved by the size of his army;
> no warrior escapes by his great strength.
> A horse is a vain hope for deliverance;
> despite all its great strength it cannot save.
> But the eyes of the Lord are on those who fear him,
> on those whose hope is in his unfailing love,
> to deliver them from death and keep them alive in
>   famine. (Ps. 33:12–19)

Set between what is called the bronze age and the iron age, the exodus and the making of Israel as a nation took place during a period of intense activity. International treaties were being made, the horse was becoming domesticated, and iron weapons and chariots were appearing on battlefields. All this led to struggles for power and influence in the Middle East. Small powers such as Israel lived under the shadow of the great superpowers of the time.

In this setting, Israel's agreement with God, made on Mount

Sinai, was seen as central to the Old Testament faith. This agreement had to be put before any other agreements or treaties with the nations around them. The agreement opened with the words: "I am the Lord your God who brought you out of the land of Egypt." This reminder of what God had done in releasing his people from Egypt showed how God's power dealt with military threats. Under the leadership of Moses, God's people learned how God would never forget his agreement with them, and how those who sought God with all their heart would find him.

These promises were put to the test when the Israelites stormed the land of Canaan, which they had been promised by God. They discovered that when they were faithful to God, and when they cried out to him for help, he would deliver them from their enemies. These discoveries were often made the hard way, as the people rebelled against God's rule. The smaller nations began to fear Israel, because, as one prophet put it, "the shout of a king is with the Israelites." That shout was enough to demolish the walls of Jericho.

All these experiences of God's people in the Old Testament show how God cannot be opposed. When we pray, we understand the character of the God who makes and sticks by his agreement with us. As he is faithful, he calls on us in turn to be faithful to him.

LIVING INTIMATELY WITH GOD

In the ancient Middle East, there was a great confusion among the pagan religions as to which god you should speak to in your prayers. You never really knew if some gods might be roused to jealousy because they were not being addressed, or if the god you were praying to was bothering to listen at all. This prayer from the Hittite Empire (in present-day eastern Turkey) records the pathos of such uncertainty:

> The lord in his anger of heart looked at me;
> the god in the rage of his heart confronted me;

> when the goddess was angry with me she made me
>   become ill.
>
> The god whom I know or do not know has oppressed me;
>
> the goddess whom I know or do not know has placed
>   suffering upon me.
>
> Although I am looking constantly for help, no one takes
>   me by the hand.
>
> When I weep they do not come to my side.
>
> I utter laments, but no one hears me.

This sad prayer is in stark contrast to the experience of the people of Israel. In the first book of Samuel, Hannah prays to God that she might have the child for which she has longed over many years. God hears her prayer and answers her. Hannah's response, after the birth of her son Samuel, was a hymn that reveals how different God is from the gods of other nations:

> My heart rejoices in the Lord;
>
> in the Lord my horn is lifted high.
>
> My mouth boasts over my enemies,
>
> for I delight in your deliverance.
>
> There is no one holy like the Lord;
>
> there is no one besides you;
>
> there is no Rock like our God. (1 Sam. 2:1–2)

The two books of Samuel continue by recording the personal prayers of Samuel and David. The lives of these two leaders of Israel reveal the faithfulness of the God who does care personally for his people, and who hears their prayers. In fact Samuel, whose life started with the prayer of Hannah, becomes a man of prayer himself. He sees his work in terms of prayer. On one occasion he told King Saul, "God forbid that I should sin against the Lord in ceasing to pray for you." When Saul was later rejected as king because of his disobedience to God, we are told that "all night long, Samuel cried out to the Lord."

In the same way, David constantly consulted God in prayer. Even when he sinned by committing adultery with Bathsheba, the wife of one of his soldiers, he turned back to God, confessing before him in prayer. This moving prayer of David is recorded for us in Psalm 51. At the end of his life, David combined thanksgiving with a victory song.

King Solomon, who ruled after David, showed what could happen when this close relationship with God in prayer was lost. He started his reign, after the death of his father David, by asking God for wisdom to rule Israel. And after he had built the magnificent temple in Jerusalem, Solomon dedicated the building with a long, formal prayer. After this point, Solomon and prayer seem to have parted, because there is no more mention of Solomon praying to God. Instead, Solomon turned away from God to other gods. After Solomon's time, the different kings of Israel and Judah are judged as "good" or "bad" according to the strength of their relationship with God.

LIVING TRANSPARENTLY BEFORE GOD

The Old Testament prophets saw prayer as a matter of life and death for the nation. For the earlier prophets such as Elijah and Elisha, prayer was used literally to make the difference between life and death for two young children.

Elijah also used personal prayer to face 450 prophets of the pagan god Baal. The worship of Baal had been gaining ground among the Israelites, so Elijah challenged the false prophets to call down fire from heaven to demonstrate publicly who was the true God. While the prayers to Baal failed, Elijah's prayer brought down fire, providing a turning point in Israel's history.

As the prophets clarified the character of God, they insisted that God rejected worship by people whose hearts were far from him. To be a part of the people of God was not like a free insurance policy. Instead it demanded that people should treat others and approach God in a way that reflected how God treated them.

The prophets Isaiah, Hosea, and Amos lived at a time when prayer had become a dutiful exercise of empty ceremony and meaningless words. The people's prayers bore no relation to the cruel and oppressive ways in which they treated their fellow Israelites. The response of the prophets to this empty worship was that God refused to listen to their unreal prayers. The prophet Micah linked worship with the rest of life:

> What does the Lord require of you?
> To act justly and to love mercy
> and to walk humbly with your God. (6:8)

In the life and confessions of Jeremiah we can see one of the finest examples of a heart wholly surrendered to God. Jeremiah had a profound awareness that he was destined to be a prophet for God. He heard God say to him, "Before I formed you in the womb I knew you, before you were born I set you apart." For Jeremiah this was sometimes too much to bear, because his task as a prophet was extremely difficult. He was called to bring God's message of anger against his own people, because of their disobedience to God. He so closely identified with the message of God's anger that he was rejected along with the words he spoke.

This led Jeremiah to throw himself upon God. He prayed,

> O Lord Almighty, you who examine the righteous and
> probe the heart and mind, to you I have committed my
> cause. (Jer. 20:12)

Yet at the same time, Jeremiah has hard questions to ask God. Why do evil people prosper? How can God allow people to curse him? Why should good people suffer? The answer he received was that he should dig himself in even more deeply by committing himself to God, regardless of the painful consequences.

After the time of Jeremiah, God's people were taken off into exile in the Babylonian Empire. The prophets of those times saw human helplessness stretch even further. Because of their extreme circumstances, the people were forced to recognize their own helpless situation and to realize that profound changes were needed in their lives. Ezekiel looked forward to the coming of Jesus in seeing the need for a new agreement with God that would radically change people's hearts.

The Old Testament men and women of prayer are models for us to imitate in our own praying. They call us to live a life oriented on God, hearing his words to us, discovering his will and living entirely for God. This means that we live transparently, with a consistent love for God and for those around us. In this way we will be able to pour out our whole being before God in spontaneous prayer from the heart.

THE PRESENCE OF GOD AND CONTINUAL PRAYER

In the Bible, whether God was seen as "Yahweh" (in the Old Testament), or as "Father" (in the New), he was always seen in the light of his agreement with his people. Prayer always evoked the experience of a God who cared and acted for those who trusted him. To pray "in his name" was to share in all the benefits of his character and promises.

God's people were therefore a prayerful people. When all your significance, security, identity, and future are in the hands of God, then prayer is bound to follow. As a result, the godly Israelite was much less inhibited about prayer than we are today. The questions that we often raise (such as where, when, how, and what we pray about) were unthinkable to the Old Testament people because of their experience of God.

On the question of where we can pray, the Old Testament tells us that prayer can be made anywhere. Prayer was not restricted to holy places or to using special formulae.

On the "when" of prayer, the Israelites prayed at the morning and evening sacrifice. They recited their confession of faith, known as the *shema* (see Deut. 6:4–9), every morning and evening. The prophet Daniel prayed three times a day. This practice is also mentioned in the Psalms.

How an Israelite prayed was by not being inhibited. Abraham prostrated himself on the ground before God. Solomon "knelt upon his knees with his arms spread toward the heavens." Daniel simply knelt in his window in Babylon, looking toward Jerusalem. The most common practice seems to have been to stand, and to sing praise to God. Others crouched. The posture taken by the person praying reflected his or her emotions before God.

What was prayed for is indicated by the rich variety of terms used for prayer throughout the Old Testament. The Hebrew language does not have a single word for "prayer" as modern languages tend to. Instead, there is a wide range of words and ideas. The range is as wide as the terms used to describe human emotions: to entreat, to ask God for deliverance, to seek guidance, to beg for mercy, to intercede, to invoke God, to cry in distress, to sigh, praise, magnify, exalt, rejoice, and adore. All these words or phrases summarize a vast realm of emotional life lived out before God, the Lord of Israel. All express the character of God's saving help, his redeeming grace and loving-kindness. They also express the character of prayer as a transforming friendship with God.

The poet George Herbert captured the way the people of Israel approached God in prayer:

> Teach me, my God and King
> In all things thee to see,
> And what I do in any thing,
> To do it as for thee.

THE NARRATIVE OF PRAYERFULNESS

For an Israelite who took prayer seriously, it was an activity related to the whole of life. Because of this, the Old Testament is saturated with accounts of prayer. The book of Psalms provides the focus for prayer in the Old Testament, but the historical books also contain what can be called prayer narratives. These narratives contain over ninety references to worship in the temple, and an additional 140 references to acts of individual prayer. In about 100 of these, the words of the prayers themselves are reported.

The most common form of these prayers is a simple request to God, as when Moses prays for the healing of his sister Miriam: "Oh God, heal her!" The Egyptian pharaoh, unable to bear the plagues which God sent in the time of Moses, says to him, "Pray to the Lord." When the people of Israel saw the Egyptians pursuing them after they had escaped from slavery in Egypt, "They cried out to the Lord."

These prayers were offered in times of crisis, emergency, and distress. So we read about the people praying during a battle with their enemies, or how the King of Judah begged to be allowed home from exile, or how the frightened sailors threw the prophet Jonah overboard after praying to their god during a storm. These are all very natural human responses to dire need.

However, more elaborate expressions of prayer are also to be found in the Old Testament. Probably the most striking example was the experience of Jacob one night when he was preparing to meet his estranged brother, Esau. Jacob then discovered that prayer can be like a wrestling match with God. In utter helplessness in God's grip, just as Jacob was, we can be made permanently aware that such an encounter with God will make a dramatic change in our life. It certainly left Jacob with a perpetual limp, and he was also given a change of name. From this time onwards, Jacob was called "Israel," meaning "a prince with God."

There are other Old Testament prayers where the person who prays comes to God because he or she knows something of God's character. When prayer is motivated by the character of God, then we have a deeper sense of what we really need from him. This type of praying is distinctly different from the more common kind where we bluster before God without knowing our true needs in the light of who he is.

In the Old Testament, the sequence of such true prayers follows this order: addressing God, declaring our humility before him, describing our distress and concluding with the motive for our prayer.

There are also prayers in the Old Testament which are set in the middle of a story. In his old age, Abraham commissioned his servant to go to the land of his relatives to find a suitable wife for his son Isaac. From the beginning to the end of the story, the characters show an attitude of prayerful trust that God will guide the whole affair.

The servant begins by praying: "O Lord, give me success today, and show kindness to my master Abraham." Then he prays that God will help him to identify the right girl for Isaac. (This was important because Abraham was concerned that Isaac should not marry a pagan girl who would seduce him to go back to her people.) Before the servant's prayer is finished, he sees Rebekah drawing water from the local well. All that follows then fits neatly into place. Rebekah is willing to go, her parents are happy with the arrangement, the journey home goes smoothly and Isaac is ready to marry her. It is a story of prayer and romance, all in one!

In the same way, Hannah's prayer for a child to be given her in her old age was only the beginning of a whole background of prayerfulness in the life and work of the child she eventually produced—the prophet Samuel. Hannah declared about Samuel:

> I prayed for this child, and the Lord granted me what I asked of him. (1 Sam. 1:27)

Then she added:

> So now I give him to the Lord. For his whole life he will be given over to the Lord. (v. 28)

Samuel lived in the "temple" at Shiloh, growing up in the presence of God. At a time when Israel lacked strong faith, he heard God's personal call and became one of the great leaders of the Old Testament. The whole prayerful life of Samuel was clearly recorded to inspire Israel to live as Samuel did before God, submitting to his authority.

Samuel was later forced to rebuke Israel's first king, Saul, for failing to obey God:

> Does the Lord delight in burnt offerings and sacrifices as much as in obeying the voice of the Lord? To obey is better

> than sacrifice, and to heed is better than the fat of rams.
> (15:22)

The prayer narratives of Samuel's life and ministry follow each other in turn, warning as well as inspiring us. They reveal how a lack of prayer can mean rejecting the kingship of God in our lives.

BLESSING GOD FOR HIS GOODNESS

The Old Testament is also full of instances where people who have been blessed by God publicly acknowledge what he has done for them. A fairy tale wraps up a happy ending with the words: "And they all lived happily ever after." But the Old Testament stories end with words to the effect of: "Blessed be the name of the Lord!"

When Abraham's servant found a wife for Isaac, he concluded his search: "Praise be to the Lord, the God of my master Abraham, who has not abandoned his kindness and faithfulness to my master." This ending makes the point for all those who hear the story that God hears and answers prayer.

The life of David was full of escapades, reverses in fortune, and death-threats. On one occasion he was grateful to a woman that she had prevented him from killing her husband's family. He tells her: "Blessed be the Lord God of Israel, who sent you this day to intercept me." And on his deathbed, sure that his crown will pass to his son Solomon, he declared,

> Blessed be the Lord God of Israel, who appointed a successor to my throne, whom I can see with my own eyes.

These declarations of God's goodness express the natural attitude of those who trust in God. One of the psalms says:

> I will bless the Lord at all times.
> His praise shall be continually on my lips. (34:1)

In the book of Ruth, where the quality of life with God is so beautifully expressed, the phrase "Blessed be God" appears frequently. It expresses the joy given to those who recognize how God works on their behalf.

These are a few of the many Old Testament instances of how people respond to the love and faithfulness of God in their daily lives.

GOD'S PRESENCE IN THE PSALMS

The Psalms vastly exceed in number and variety all other expressions of prayer in the Old Testament, and indeed in the whole Bible. Only five of the psalms bear the title tephillot, meaning "prayer." Despite this, the five books of psalms are the epitome of Israel's prayer life, in praises, laments, confessions, supplications, prayers of thanksgiving and confidence, cursings and intercessions. We are invited to praise God, to know him better, to love him loyally, and find all our delight and happiness in him.

By submitting to God's will and trusting in his kingship, we will find true happiness:

> Taste and see that the Lord is good!
> Happy is the man who finds refuge in him! (Ps. 34:8)

The psalms written out of David's personal experiences are full of this elemental experience of God's nearness. David knew God as the one who sticks through thick and thin, through a thousand deaths. As a young shepherd boy, he had experienced this as he fought off lions, wolves, and later the giant Goliath.

This confidence in God is expressed in the most famous of all the Psalms, Psalm 23, the shepherd psalm. When David sins and openly confesses his need of cleansing, in Psalm 51, we are with him too. In this way, the Psalms contain the language of experience, expressing life before God, the friend above all friends. The richness and variety of the Psalms are impossible to exhaust. They contain a great density of theological thought, coupled with the emotional depth of human experience.

These two aspects of the Psalms are complementary. These songs are concerned with the character both of God and of human need, personal and communal. Because of this balance, they are neither aloof and theological, nor emotionally subjective.

The Psalms celebrate our encounter with God, but they also encourage us toward further encounter by deepening our appreciation of him in worship. They help us to become more realistic and intimate with God. The result is the praise of God in the Psalms. Praise allows us to admire, celebrate and focus on God himself as the result of our experience and because of what we know of his character.

Joachim Neander's beautiful hymn summarizes the central character of the Psalms in praising God:

> Praise ye the Lord!
> O let all that is in me adore him!
> All that hath life and breath
> Come now with praises before him!
> Let the Amen
> Sound from his people again:
> Gladly for aye we adore him.

Just as the temple was at the heart of Israel's national life, so the Psalms are at the heart of the Bible, and the Christian's prayer. In the 1,500 years of monastic life, these songs were the daily focus of life and worship. Of all the books in the Bible they reflect the daily pulse of the ordinary Christian. But why is this?

One answer is that we can best appreciate God's kingship when he is enthroned in our own hearts, touching every emotion that wells up from the depths of our beings. The Psalms express our emotions and God's response to them perfectly, speaking for us before God.

John Calvin, the sixteenth-century reformer, remarked at the beginning of his commentary on the Psalms that they could be called "an anatomy of all parts of the soul":

There is no emotion anyone will experience whose image is not reflected in this mirror. Indeed, here the Holy Spirit has drawn to the life all pains, sorrows, fears, doubts, hopes, cares, anxieties—in short all the turbulent emotions with which men's minds are commonly stirred. Here the prophets themselves speaking with God uncover all their inner feelings and call, or rather drag, each one of us to examine himself. Thus is left hidden not one of the very many infirmities to which we are subject, not one of the very many vices with which we are stuffed. True prayer is born first from our own sense of need, then from faith in God's promises. Here will the readers be best awakened to sense their ills, and, as well, to seek remedies for them. Whatever can stimulate us when we are about to pray to God, this book teaches.

Because of the many different emotions expressed in the Psalms, it is no surprise to find that the book contains a variety of different styles, each with its own mood and atmosphere. There are hymns that call the listener to praise God, inviting us to "sing to the Lord." These begin with a call to worship. They explain why God should be praised: perhaps for the wonder of his creation, or the mighty deeds which he has performed in history, or because of his goodness to the individual worshipper. These psalms usually end in a final burst of acclamation. Their mood is unrestrained joy in the presence of God.

Then there are the psalms of thanksgiving. These also begin with praise, and then express a lament that is now over, with its release of hurt emotions now either healed or in the process of healing. These psalms may be either personal or communal. They end by declaring that "the Lord has heard me," or "he drew me out of a horrible pit," or some similar expression of redemption. The joy at the end of the psalm is shaped by the pain or sorrow that has been overcome.

There are also a large number of psalms of lament: distress calls sent in God's direction. In these, the psalmist begins by crying to God and pouring out the problem in all its terrifying intensity. He then calls on God for specific help, listing reasons why he should intervene. This is followed by the certainty that God will hear and answer, and a vow which closes the prayer. The vow is usually a promise to praise and thank God with a renewed awareness of what it means to live before him. Some of the laments in the Psalms are personal (covering sickness and false accusations), while others express the grief of the community (calling for protection against national enemies and reflecting defeat in battle). Communal laments often end by affirming that God will protect his people again, as he has always done in the past. Over one-third of all the Psalms contain an element of lament or request to God.

Psalms of confidence celebrate the trust of the worshipper in God, even though enemies and assorted perils seem to deny that he cares. Here the worshipper is at peace with God, submitting to him in complete trust. Such psalms also contain words of mourning, but it is clear that an inner peace enables the speaker to rise above his or her immediate circumstances.

Psalms of remembrance recall the great acts of God in the past, especially in the events surrounding the exodus from slavery in Egypt. It was only natural that the nation should look back to its beginnings and praise God for what he did then. These psalms are full of the mighty acts of God and invite the hearer:

> Sing to him, sing praise to him; tell of his wonderful acts!

To recite God's acts is to praise him, because they specify how God has dealt with his people. Psalm 136 is one psalm with a repeated chorus at the end of each verse. It throbs with the pulse: "His love endures forever."

The psalms of pilgrimage celebrate specific points in Israel's religious year. Moses had been commanded by God that all the men of Israel were to appear before God at the temple three times a year. These three festivals were Passover, Pentecost, and the Feast of Tents—joyful celebrations of God's goodness and blessing in the past. One of the high points of the journey was catching a first glimpse of Jerusalem: "How lovely is your dwelling place, O Lord of hosts!" During the journey, and while the pilgrims were in Jerusalem, they would sing psalms of praise and thanksgiving.

There are also psalms of wisdom, reminding the hearer of the great divide between the way of folly and evil and the way of wisdom and godliness. Psalm 1 stands guard at the beginning of the whole book, teaching us the vital need to live wisely before God:

> Blessed is the man
> who does not walk in the counsel of the wicked
> or stand in the way of sinners
> or sit in the seat of mockers.

Wise people avoid all these postures of evil. Instead, they are dependent on God and on the words he has spoken. Psalm 119 is the most outstanding example of these psalms. All 176 verses are devoted to the way in which a godly person can focus his or her life on the words of God in the Old Testament Scriptures. Those who saturate themselves with the Scriptures through meditation, day and night, become people of the word.

Finally, there are the royal psalms. The whole book of Psalms is stunningly rich in imagery. But perhaps the most striking and persistent image is the enthronement of God as King of the universe, the Lord over all lords, and uniquely Yahweh. God's kingship underlies all the psalms and provides the foundational motive for praise.

For God's kingdom stands forever, despite all the immediate causes for lament, all the threats of danger, all human sinfulness. The king's loyalty to his people, his righteousness, and his understanding as wisdom personified, generates praise and confidence in prayer. The royal psalms celebrate the enthronement and rule of the King of kings. We can only echo the words of these psalms to the extent that we have opened our own hearts to his rule, bringing our deepest thoughts and feelings under his kingship. Only then can we proclaim him as King.

The many different types of psalms enable each of us to open our inmost being to the entrance of the King. All our emotions, all our most concealed fears and needs do not have to remain behind closed doors in the darkness. We can throw open the doors to allow God in:

> Lift up your heads, O you gates;
>
> be lifted up, you ancient doors,
>
> that the King of glory may come in! (Ps. 24)

We do this for ourselves personally. We also do it as the community of God's people, past and present. And we also throw open the doors in anticipation of the final victory of God over all spiritual powers and rulers.

A prayer of John Calvin gives the flavor:

> Grant, Almighty God, that as we must carry on a warfare in this world, and as it is your will to try us with many contests—O grant that we may never faint, however great may be the trials which we have to endure. As you have favored us with such an honour as to make us the framers and builders of your temple, may all of us present and consecrate ourselves wholly to you. As each of us has received some spiritual gift, may we strive to use it in building this spiritual temple, so that you may be worshipped among us perpetually. Especially may each one of us offer himself wholly as a spiritual sacrifice to you, until we shall at last be renewed in your image, and be received into a full participation of that glory which has been attained for us by the blood of your only begotten Son.

6

APPLYING
BIBLICAL PRAYER
TO OURSELVES

Unless we are ready to surrender ourselves to the divine fire and to become
that burning bush of the desert which burned and was never consumed, we
shall be scorched, because the experience of prayer can only be known from
the inside and it is not to be dallied with.

—Archbishop Anthony of Sourozh

Prayer must be a personal experience of God if it is to be personally convincing. This may seem an obvious statement, yet many people hope that God will hear them without much conviction that he will do so.

There are many parts of the Bible that encourage us to seek immediate communion with God. The writer of Psalm 13 puts it directly:

> How long, O Lord?
> Will you forget me forever?
> How long will you hide your face from me?

Another writer (of Psalm 27) says:

> Hear my voice when I call, O Lord;
> be merciful to me and answer me.
> My heart says of you, "Seek his face!"

> Your face, Lord, will I seek.
>
> Do not hide your face from me....

In true, biblical prayer, the person praying is confident not only that God hears his or her prayer, but that God can be met in a personal, intimate way. This personal encounter with God has a profound effect. As one psalm says: "You who seek God, may your heart live!" Jeremiah the prophet spoke on behalf of God:

> You will call upon me and come and pray to me, and I
> will listen to you. You will seek me and find me when
> you seek me with all your heart. (29:12–13)

This warm, personal language is very different from the cold, impersonal language used by philosophers in talking about God. To talk about God in the abstract is like talking about people behind their backs only to make the horrified discovery that they are within earshot. When we are confronted by the person we have talked about, our language and ideas about them change. This is exactly what a personal encounter with God in prayer achieves. But is this what we expect from prayer?

In a recent book, twenty-one Christians talked about their most memorable encounters with God. They were able to list only one or two such encounters in their whole lives. Surely we can expect prayer to be more of a continual relationship than this.

THE ABSENCE AND THE PRESENCE OF GOD

A young man decided that it was about time he took prayer more seriously. He was a good sportsman and decided that, as he found it difficult to get up early to pray, he would also take up rowing for his college. Rowing involved two solid hours of pre-breakfast exercise on the river. This meant that he had to get up at 4:00 a.m. in order to pray and row before breakfast. This worked well until he left the boat crew. He was amazed to discover how much of a struggle it was to get up at even 7:00 a.m. for a time of prayer!

Why can prayer be so difficult? And what is it that prevents prayer from becoming the personal relationship it was intended to be?

Simone Weil, the French writer, once remarked that friendship consists of meeting to identify with each other, and then learning to say goodbye to trust each other. This is a wise insight. We cannot tolerate other people suffocating us by always being around. This is why "gushy" relationships never last long; we need space to mature the bonds between us. Perhaps this is how prayer works, too, with a conscious sense of both the presence and the absence of God. We learn different insights about our friends' character and relationship to us when they are absent and when they are present.

This is exactly what happens in infant life. At first the mother gives her baby almost unlimited time and attention. The newborn baby has an eye focus of about twelve to eighteen inches, so as he feeds at her breast he can easily see the approving signals of his mother's face. However, this stage cannot go on forever. Step by step, the mother withdraws her presence from the child, teaching him to learn from his frustration when she is absent.

This withdrawal is an important stage in the child's development. It helps to clarify the difference between the fantasy that lies behind the child's demanding crying, and the reality that the mother is not there simply to serve the child's self-interest.

A similar mixture of God's absence as well as his presence helps us to make prayer a personal, real experience. If we always experienced the presence of God whenever we prayed, we would never learn to distinguish between prayer and our own fantasies. The reality is that God, like the mother, has his own existence apart from us.

We learn of the reality of God through the experience of guilt. In the Psalms, the absence of God is usually associated with confessions of guilt. "Hide your face from my sins," is a necessary cry of guilt, and yet the writer couples this with an opposite emotion: "Do not cast me away from your presence." The first reaction of Adam and Eve when they sinned in the garden of Eden was to hide themselves from God. In the same way, we usually have a shrewd suspicion that if we meet a blank wall in prayer, it is more than likely that unconfessed sin or hidden anger is blocking us from an encounter with God.

By contrast, the psalms' imagery of meeting God face to face is linked with the idea of a righteous life—a right relationship with God. As one psalm puts it, "In righteousness I will see your face." However, it may not be wrongdoing that keeps us from meeting God for ourselves. Take the case of a man who was angry with God for apparently not answering his prayers. His younger brother had been turned down for the job that he had wanted so badly. So the older brother prayed, fasted, and did everything he could about the issue. Nothing happened. He ended up more frustrated than his younger brother, and then his anger really boiled over at God. It took a third person to gently point out to him how all his life he had tended to absorb suffering and hold it to himself. He began to see that his sense of God's absence had allowed his bitter feelings to rise to the surface, where they could be healed.

This is like our own babyhood. How would we ever have learned to trust the deeper realities of love if our mother had not withdrawn her breast and face from us, leaving us to ourselves? As we realize that God is separate from us, and that he is not there simply to give us what we want, we learn to see ourselves more realistically.

Being able to laugh at ourselves is a great gift. It helps us not to take ourselves too seriously. When we think about it, it is highly incongruous that we should be made in the image of God in this fallen world. It seems unlikely that we will one day be conformed to the likeness of Christ, we are so far from that glory now. Of course it is true that we are made in God's image, and that we will one day be like Christ. But these truths can generate great illusions about our own importance. We can begin to see the world purely from our own point of view. To correct this, we need to exercise prayer in the absence of God. Not that God is truly absent, but he withdraws from us so that we can learn to know God as God. God is not our patron, our wish-fulfiller, or the generator of more illusions about ourselves. He is himself.

A mother's absence pushes her child's relationships on to greater maturity than mere wish-fulfillment. An absent lover teaches new insights in letters sent home. An absent friend teaches us by his absence how much we have learned about true friendship. And so the absence of God teaches us about his holiness, his otherness from our narrow view of his character and thoughts. Familiarity does breed contempt, unless it is tempered by the distancing of reverence, awe and worship. We need God's absence in order better to appreciate his presence. We tend to think that we fully understand and enjoy God's presence, when in fact it is far beyond our understanding. The absence of God, with its pain and loneliness, takes us beyond our feelings and illusions to see more clearly what his presence really means.

This was the experience of one of the psalm-writers, who sensed both the absence and the presence of God at the same time:

> My God, my God, why have you forsaken me?
> Why are you so far from saving me,
> so far from the words of my groaning?
> O my God, I cry out by day, but you do not answer,
> by night, and am not silent.
> Yet you are enthroned as the Holy One;
> you are the praise of Israel.
> In you our fathers put their trust;
> they trusted and you delivered them.
> They cried to you and were saved;
> in you they trusted and were not disappointed. (22:1–5)

In these verses, the writer compares his futility in getting God's attention with the experience of Israel in trusting God and receiving his goodness. Does this mean that the personal experience of absence can lead through to a deeper, renewed appreciation of God's presence after all?

One small child was once enraged that his mother was not around when he wanted her. He looked out of the window and saw her playing a game of tennis on the lawn with a group of guests. She was obviously enjoying herself in a way that the child had never seen before. God's absence from us teaches us that God is greater, wiser, and more loving. He is above and beyond all our fantasies about him.

However, it would be wrong to think that God is playing celestial tennis when he is absent from us. George Bernard Shaw grew up as the only son of a hardworking mother in Dublin. While she worked to make ends meet, Shaw's father spent his time in playing cricket. Shaw decided that if God was like his father, a celestial cricketer, then he would forget him, as he had obviously forgotten about a fatherless boy. As a result, he became an atheist, with a great sense of relief that the problem of God had been dealt with.

But this solution is too easy. The prayer written by the psalm writer was spoken by Jesus on the cross. "My God, my God," he cried, "why have you forsaken me?" Our experience of alienation, our sense of being deserted by God because of our sin, all our darkness and ignorance were carried by God himself. In our humanity, God entered into this most painful of all human experiences, to be separated from God, so that we could know the joy of his presence. This is one of the astonishing paradoxes of the cross: that there, where Jesus experienced God's absence, we can experience God's presence. In other words, we most deeply know God's presence in prayer when we experience a sense of sin, forgiven by the cross.

The poverty and the suffering of God on the cross make his presence most real. And in the same way, it is in humility of heart and poverty of spirit that we can reach out to where his presence and absence are one.

MOODS OF TRANSFORMING PRAYER

This fundamental reality of experiencing God as both present and absent removes our illusions and reinforces our faith in God. The light and shadow of God help to deepen our relationship with him, guiding us as we push out beyond the shallows. Some of our deepest experiences of love with a marriage partner or a friend arise when we are vulnerable, or even broken —when nothing is sensible, logical or reasonable. One hymn writer expressed this vulnerability in prayer:

> Thou art oft most present, Lord,
> In weak, distracted prayer;
> A sinner out of heart with self
> Most often finds thee there.
>
> For prayer that humbles, sets the soul
> From all delusions free,
> And teaches it how utterly
> Dear Lord, it hangs on thee.
>
> Thrice happy be the darkness, then,
> This deep in which I lie;
> And blessed be all things that teach
> God's dear supremacy.

Instead of feeling discouraged or depressed by our dark feelings, we can emerge from them, liberated from our self-illusions to become more flexible for God, and with a greater sense of realism about what freedom from self entails. Bishop Westcott, writing in the last century, wisely observed:

> A saint is not a man without faults, but a man who has
> given himself without reserve to God.

We only give ourselves to God wholeheartedly when we have seen the profound depths of sin and contradiction in our own souls. Only God can save us from these depths.

We are all familiar with the idea of having a "lifestyle." This is a collection of attitudes and habits that we display before other people. A lifestyle can include our pace of life, our activities, clothes, interests, and all the expressions of our gifts and our temperament before others. But at a deeper level we also have what can be called a "life-mood." This relates to our inwardness before ourselves and God. The Danish philosopher Søren Kierkegaard tells us about his life-mood.

He had a pious, God-fearing father, who lived with a deep-down disquiet, as though his fear of God and his piety were powerless to give him peace. This inner disturbance was passed on to young Søren, who came to the conclusion that God was not, after all, infinitely loving. This tragic life-mood caused him great suffering, especially in his relationships.

We all inherit our own life-mood, which to a different extent needs to be exposed, corrected and transformed by our prayer life as we relate to God. Prayer can take many forms as we experience this change in mood. James Montgomery expressed the different moods of prayer:

> Prayer is the soul's sincere desire,
> Uttered or unexpressed,
> The motion of a hidden fire
> That trembles in the breast.
>
> Prayer is the burden of a sigh,
> The falling of a tear,
> The upward glancing of an eye
> Where none but God is near.

Prayer is the simplest form of speech
That infant lips can try;
Prayer the sublimest strains that reach
The majesty on high.

Prayer is the contrite sinner's voice
Returning from his ways,
While angels in their songs rejoice,
And cry, "Behold, he prays!"

Prayer is the Christian's vital breath,
The Christian's native air,
His watchword at the gates of death;
He enters heaven with prayer.

MOVEMENTS OF THE SOUL

Prayer is needed at every stage of the Christian's journey through life, and every aspect of his or her life-mood. This is why the Psalms can be divided into a variety of prayers, some full of praise, others despairing, and still others reflecting the changes made by God in the heart of the worshipper. The Psalms are like a textbook of prayer, guiding us in our praying, so it is worth stopping at this point to reflect on them.

There are first songs of praise and worship that help to assure us of God's goodness and to focus our lives upon him. These prayers consolidate our experience of God. They strengthen our good attitudes, deepen our convictions, strengthen our faith and provide us with the language we need to express our praise to God. They teach us what Martin Luther called "the naked realities of life before God," helping us to give God priority over everything else in our lives. Praise and worship belong to those elemental certainties that God alone is to be adored, served and surrendered to as the King of kings. No one can ever usurp his place in our lives.

Psalm 119 is one of these psalms, celebrating the rock-like dependability of God's word. It provides a sacred canopy over our lives where we can live in safety, in a well-ordered world of God's revelation.

Psalm 119 was written by a skillful writer. This long psalm is divided into twenty-two stanzas, each containing eight verses. The eight verses in each set all start with the same letter, the stanzas working through all twenty-two letters of the Hebrew alphabet in turn. Each group of eight verses uses at least six different words to describe God's Law, and the whole psalm is a celebration of the wonders of the Scriptures. In reading the psalm, the impression is that God's word, which embraces the whole of life, can be examined from every conceivable angle.

Psalm 119 is an excellent meditation to use over twenty-two weeks, taking a verse each day, a stanza each week, and reciting the whole stanza daily with a renewed focus on a verse each day. This helps us to meditate on God's word, exactly as the writer of the psalm intended.

Using a daily discipline in this way will help us to learn that there is nothing more important than meeting with God over his word. This will enable us to take on our daily lives with a new strength and confidence, seeking God's will in all that we are, say and do. We discover what it means to "walk in the law of the Lord." Hearing the voice of God in this way means freedom from other voices in my life, allowing us to receive God's wisdom for authentic Christian living.

There are many other psalms that offer God our praise and thanksgiving. As an introduction to the book of Psalms, Psalm 1 describes life with God as living in an oasis. The living water of God's presence keeps us alive spiritually while others are in the desert. Psalm 14 confronts those who live without God. Psalm 37 reassures those who put their trust in God, even though they see evil people succeed in what they do. Those who trust God will see the "success" of evil vanish in a puff of wind. As family psalms, Psalms 127 and 128 point out the need for families to pray together, so that we can see the faith being handed down from generation to generation. Other psalms, such as 103 and 104, celebrate God's care for us. And Psalms 131 and 133 show how God is trustworthy in all our social relationships.

These psalms present a sure faith, which frees us from all distracting emotions, confusions of thought, doubt, cynicism, and anger. We are freed from our confusions to worship God for his reliability, which gives stability to our lives. At times of such wellbeing, we can enjoy the beauty of God's creation, the richness of the relationships in which he has placed us, and his faithfulness which underlies our very existence.

However, the Psalms also express a second movement of the soul which is the polar opposite of praise and thanksgiving. These are the psalms of disorientation—expressed in confession, lament, petition and supplication. When life is going well for us, we can become soulless and complacent before God, putting ourselves out of touch with his mercy. God may put us through periods of intense emotional and moral disorientation, during which we can do nothing except lament before him.

The book of Psalms is full of such prayers. These songs of lament and confession are characterized by certain recurring features.

The writer begins with a plea that God will correct his desperate situation. He addresses God personally, declaring that he trusts God despite great distress, or even intense anger.

A long complaint at the desperate situation then follows. This could be a case of prolonged illness, an agonized conscience, isolation, imprisonment, or the destruction of life. God is accused of allowing these things to happen.

The writer now asks God to act quickly and decisively. He uses strong language to plead for justice, or mercy, suggesting that if God had been more attentive, then these things might never have happened!

Having vented his feelings so strongly, the writer can now recognize some of God's true motives, which he was unable to see before. He begins to achieve a better perspective on his troubles. A few self-doubts creep in. Perhaps he was wrong in the way he accused God. Anger and cursing may still linger as an echo of the bitterness and resentment within. The writer's old way of life has not yet been completely changed.

Once he has received healing and forgiveness, the writer can praise God with the assurance that his prayer has been heard. He promises to serve God in a renewed life, full of praise and worship.

This type of prayer is an act of cleansing. It purges sin, dissolves misunderstanding about God, removes doubt about God's actions, and washes out all the deceitfulness that sin has created within us. Confession is therefore a great antidote to the poison of mistrust in our lives. Such honest exposure of our condition before God shows up any secret, lurking distrust within us. It helps to weaken addictive, sinful habits. It is the nature of sin to deceive us, living in the shadows of our darkened lives.

There is a vast realm of stress-related illness in our society and within ourselves, caused when we repress our anxiety and guilt. If prayer helps us to counteract selfish living, it also provides us with the release of suppressed emotions. We bring untold suffering on ourselves by allowing bitterness, hidden anger, and so many other negative emotions to live inside us.

The letter of James sees a direct connection between confession and health:

> Confess your sins to one another, and pray for one
> another, so that you may be healed. (5:16)

As we open the depths of our lives to God, we will grow in the use of prayer that cries out to God for help. Many Christians have discovered from their own experience that short prayers for help are more effective than long, exhaustive prayers. A simple prayer from the Psalms, such as "Create in me a clean heart, O God, and renew a right spirit within me," repeated throughout the day, can help us to find the attitude we need to take before God. The Psalms are full of these short prayers, and we

THE PRAYER

can ransack the book to find the ones which best meet our needs.

The Cloud of Unknowing, a fourteenth-century Christian classic, called these short prayers "arrows flashed to heaven." It also revealed why these arrows are so effective:

> Their naked intent is like a shield and spear in peace and war alike. With this sword you will hammer the clouds and the darkness above you .... Why does it penetrate heaven, this short little prayer, even of one syllable? Surely because it is prayed with a full heart, in height, depth, length and breadth of spirit of him who prays it. In the height, for it is prayed in all the might of his spirit; in the depth, for in this little syllable is contained all that the spirit knows; in the length, for should it always feel as it does now, it would always cry to God as it now cries; in the breadth, for it would extend to all men what it wills for itself.

This reorientation of ourselves in prayer is a world away from our more instinctive cries of "Give me, Lord!" Learning to pray in this way transforms us before God. Karl Barth, a twentieth-century theologian, once said,

> The Christian asks, and by this asking the doors of heaven are opened wide and the gates are lifted high, so that the King of glory may come in!

Our growth in prayer is a journey. This journey begins, as we have seen, with the assurance of an oriented faith, through a deep sense of disorientation, and finally to the reorientation of our whole lives.

So the third stage of the psalm-writer's experience of God is the reorientation of life in thanksgiving, intercession and contemplation. The spiral of prayer rises and expands upwards into a greater, fuller appreciation of God, and of all that he has been and done for us in the past. Lament gives way to thanksgiving; petition for our own needs gives way to intercession for the needs of others; and in place of self-interest there is now a contemplation of the glory of God.

Some of the psalms that show this reorientation toward God are Psalms 30, 40, 65, 66, 124, and 138. The wounded writer of the lamenting psalms now becomes the skilled musician, the full range of his abilities now tested and tuned to the glory of God. The book of Psalms ends with one of these songs, closing the whole book with the joyful words,

> Let everything that has breath, praise the Lord!

In the margin of my Bible, I have written the name of my friend Myrtle opposite Psalm 30. As she fought hard against cancer, she had underlined these words from this psalm:

> I will exalt you, O Lord,
> for you lifted me out of the depths
> and did not let my enemies gloat over me.
> O Lord my God, I called to you for help
> and you healed me.
> O Lord, you brought me up from the grave;
> you spared me from going down into the pit.

Is Myrtle then a success story of signs and wonders? No. She died soon after she underlined these words; she died much younger than her friends ever wanted. But at her funeral service, instead of banks of flowers there were groups of people who had witnessed her love of God.

One group was there because they had all discovered faith in Jesus through the way she lived. Another group was thankful for her teaching in a Bible class. Another group remembered how she had shown hospitality. Still others were there because they had seen her transcendent spirit as she fought her long, painful illness.

THE PRAYER

The reorientation of our lives does not mean becoming a "success story" as the world counts success. Instead, our lives are turned to God as we experience him in sickness, doubt, despair, or any one of a number of broken human situations. It is then that God mysteriously intervenes in our lives to overcome and change our attitudes, to give us a new spirit and a changed heart. When this happens, we will be able to say with Psalm 30: "you lifted me up," "you healed me," "you spared me." These are the specific expressions of personally knowing God.

PERSONAL ENCOUNTER

Early on in the Bible, we read how Abraham "walked with God," and about the appearances that God made to him and the other early Old Testament figures. In these events when God appeared personally to individuals, we are significantly told more about what was said rather than what was seen. These people were told: "I am the Lord," or "do not be afraid," or "I will be with you." We can learn a great deal from reflecting on the Old Testament's encounters with God. So in this section we will look at a number of them.

A number of common features characterize these tangible meetings with God. First, they are overwhelmingly real. Second, God initiates them himself. The experience is never premeditated or expected; it comes from God's own initiative. Third, God's appearance always strikes fear into the hearts of those who see him. Fourth, the encounter is always very brief, but its effects are both lifelong and life-changing. And finally, the experience of God always makes ethical demands, calling for major changes in the way the person lives. Rather than being simply a seen or heard experience, the encounter imprints itself on the very soul. It is as if the whole person is saturated with the truth of what God has said and done.

One of these encounters took place when Abraham was tested by God. God had given Abraham a son, Isaac, in his old age. Abraham loved Isaac more than anything else. So God tested Abraham's loyalty to himself by asking him to offer up Isaac as a sacrifice. Abraham took Isaac to Mount Moriah. They left their donkey at the foot of the mountain and prepared an altar at the top. Just as Abraham was about to kill his son in obedience to God, God called out to him to stop. One medieval writer, William of St. Thierry, reflected on how this event speaks beyond its own time:

> Come, let us ascend unto the mount of the Lord, to the house of the God of Jacob. There he will teach us his ways. Intentions, thoughts, longings, affections, all that are within me, let us go up to the place where God sees or is seen. Cares, worries, anxieties, toils, concerns, and all effort involved in the conditions of my bondage, all must be left behind with the ass (that is my body) while I and the lad (I mean my intellectual faculties) will hasten and go up the mountain. When we have worshipped, we will return again. Yes, we shall return, and that unfortunately all too quickly.

Just as Abraham had to be ready to give his only son, so William of St. Thierry was willing to offer up to God his own intellect, his own great source of self-control, and to sacrifice it for God. God does not rob us of our gifts and abilities, but he does want them simply to be instruments for loving God, rather than ends in themselves.

In another encounter, Jacob wrestled with God all night in his tent before a difficult meeting with his brother Esau. This account in the Old Testament touches us because of our own self-ambitions. We are told elsewhere in the Bible that even in the womb Jacob had struggled with his twin brother Esau. It was Jacob's fear in meeting Esau, whom he had cheated of his birthright years earlier, that set the scene for his encounter with God. The stranger wrestled with Jacob until daybreak, and permanently wounded him in the hip. Jacob learned that God being with him implied human brokenness, which would enable God to transform his character. He would no longer be called Jacob (a name which meant "the cheat"), but would have the name Israel (which means "God fights"). This change of name symbolized Jacob's change of character. In the words of Charles Wesley, we too can invite God to change us:

> Come, O thou traveller unknown,
> Whom still I hold but cannot see!
> My company before is gone,
> And I am left alone with thee.
>
> With thee all night I mean to stay
> And wrestle till the break of day....
>
> My prayer hath power with God.
> His grace unspeakable I now receive:
> Through faith I see thee face to face—
> I see thee face to face, and live!

In another Old Testament encounter, Moses experienced God at the burning bush in the desert of Midian. Moses saw a bush that burned but was not consumed. As he went near out of curiosity, a voice from the bush told him to take off his shoes because the ground where he stood was holy. God then called Moses to lead the Israelites out of slavery in Egypt, and assured him that he would be with him in all that was to happen. This picture of a bush that burns but is not burned up was perfect for Moses, who was reluctant to take on this impossible calling. It tells us that God chooses the weak and the unwise to overcome those who seem to be strong and wise.

There are many other startling meetings with God through-out the Old Testament. God appears on Mount Sinai to give the Law to Moses. He calls out to a young boy, Samuel, as he sleeps in the darkness of the Shiloh "temple." He speaks in a "still, small voice" to the prophet Elijah. He appears to the prophet Ezekiel, exiled in Babylon, in a strange and fearful vision.

The response of those who met with God in these ways is summed up in the vision seen by Isaiah the prophet. He saw the glory of the Lord filling the temple and watched as the seraphim (angelic beings) covered their faces and feet in reverence before the majesty of God. Isaiah responded by becoming overwhelmingly aware of his own naked sinfulness before God. And then he responded to God's call by saying, "Here am I, send me!"

These personal encounters with God can inspire us in our faith and lead us into new levels of praying. But it is fair to ask whether God still appears today. One person whom I know well suddenly woke up one night with the intense awareness that the presence of God was in his bedroom. It was not so much a "sight" as the deepest possible conviction to surrender his career, his personal ambitions, and his future into the hands of God. It took ten years or more for him to fully understand and put into practice what God told him that night.

Another incident happened to a tax-lawyer who was not a Christian. He came home from work one evening, took his usual drink by the fire before supper, and fell into a reverie about his life. Suddenly, quite unexpectedly, he felt a tap on his shoulder. He knew that he did not need to turn around to see who had touched him, because he was completely sure that it was God who wanted his attention. In this strangely mystical way, he knew that God was calling him to hand over his life and his future. Since then, tough-minded lawyer that he is, he is thankful that he needs no further proof of God's existence, because he has met with God in a life-changing way.

MYSTICAL PRAYER

Many people find any talk about the mystical rather threatening. In English, the word has associations with the occult, and with religious feelings that have no connection with rational thought. This is perhaps where other languages serve us better. In German, *mystizismus* refers to what is psychic or occult, while *mystik* refers simply to what is mysterious.

The different world religions have their own definition of what mystical experience is. In Christian mysticism, experiences of God are determined by biblical guidelines. This means that the experience of Christian mysticism will be different from the mysticism of another faith in just the same way that their doctrines differ. As a result, the experiences of Christian mystics down the ages can be tested for their reliability by referring them back to the Bible. The true Christian mystic always lives within the reality of certain Christian truths.

First, God is our creator, and is distinct and separate from us. Any talk of union with him will never be a union of substance, but of will and love.

Second, God reveals himself to us as a Trinity of three persons in one God. Christian mysticism does not experience God as a nameless absolute, but as the Father, the Son, and the Holy Spirit.

Third, God became a man in Jesus Christ and suffered on the cross to mediate between us and God. The mystic can therefore never make any spiritual progress without referring to the life and death of Jesus.

Fourth, our relationship with God depends entirely on God's initiative with us.

And lastly, the true mystic recognizes that he or she belongs to the church, the community of God's people. The mystic has things to say to the church, but knows that the truth of God is held communally as well as personally.

The mystics' experience of God is different from our own in terms of quality. They enjoy a greater unity between their faith and their experience. Their love of God is more intense and consistent than the love which we have experienced. They are also more "extreme" in the way they deny themselves and devote their lives to prayer and contemplation. Above all else, they are seen as great lovers of God and friends of Jesus Christ.

> Give us, O Lord, a steadfast heart, which no unworthy affection may drag downwards; give us an unconquered heart, which no tribulation can wear out; give us an upright heart, which no unworthy purpose may tempt aside. Bestow upon us also, O Lord, our God, understanding to know you, diligence to seek you, and a faithfulness that may finally embrace you; through Jesus Christ our Lord. Amen.
>
> —PRAYER OF THOMAS AQUINAS

7

THE HOLY SPIRIT AS THE TRANSFORMING FRIEND

He who would pray acceptably, must pray in his heart and spirit.
He who would pray in his own spirit, must pray in the spirit of God. For to
pray in the Spirit is the inward principle of prayer ...
it comprehends both the spirit of the person praying, and the Spirit
of God by which our spirits are fitted for and acted in.

—William Gurnall

The landscape of northern France is sharply divided into two major types of country, called *bocage* and *plaine*. *Bocage* is characteristic of most of Normandy and Brittany, where the Allied invasion at the end of World War II found its sheltering coppices, high hedgerows, dense woodland, and small villages with curving roads and narrow lanes. These features were ideal for an invasion. In contrast, *plaine* is a grandly open landscape of rolling plains, wide views of the sky, straight roads, large fields, and fat villages. While the people of the *bocage* are individualistic and poor, the *plaine* dwellers tend to be marked by a communal atmosphere and by wealth.

Our inner life also contains these two types of landscape. Left to ourselves, we are like the *bocage*. In our spiritual poverty, we struggle to become independent of God. We are hedged in by hidden emotions and by our own unconscious drives and inner attitudes. We are full of concealment which limits any spiritual panoramas we might otherwise have. As a result, our actions tend to be restricted by self-interest and willfulness, and we remain unconscious of any issues bigger than our miserable self. This environment of soul is highly vulnerable to invasion by other powers that tyrannize and enslave us.

The spiritual man or woman who lives with the resources of God's Spirit is very different. His or her inner landscape is the *plaine,* which is spacious and open to God's direction. This way of life is enriching and communal, as the person shares with others all that they have received from God. Compared with the spiritual life, the self-interested life is claustrophobic and restricted.

The apostle Paul drew this same contrast when he distinguished between what he called the "natural" and the "spiritual" person. He said that it was impossible for the natural person to understand about God simply by using his or her natural faculties, because God can only be understood when we are alive spiritually. We are only brought to life spiritually when we surrender ourselves to God and his Spirit comes to make his home in us. When this happens we begin to experience spiritual realities in the way that God intended. When we are forgiven by God, then we experience the sense of being forgiven. When we are adopted into God's family, then we also know this reality with a profound sense of being accepted. If we are in God's presence, then we are given the deepest conviction of sensing his presence with us.

The Spirit of God speaks to us in our inmost being, revealing the plans that God has for us. The prophet Jeremiah expressed this:

> "For I know the plans I have for you," declares the Lord,
> "plans to prosper you and not to harm you, plans to give
> you hope and a future. Then you will call upon me and
> come and pray to me, and I will listen to you."
> (29:11–12)

All this gives us the confidence to pray to God, knowing that he hears us.

THE INADEQUACY OF OUR OWN PRAYERS

In the last two or three decades, the charismatic movement has swept through the church worldwide. This movement has been characterized by a joyful, lively approach to worship, stressing the immediate presence of God, and his power to heal his people and speak directly to them. The movement has ranged across many of the church's traditional divides, from the Pentecostal churches through to the Roman Catholic Church, with much evidence of spiritual renewal. As a result, people have been praying with more of a sense of God's closeness. However, the danger is that people have often interpreted God's presence in cultural rather than biblical terms.

Many people tend to emphasize the Holy Spirit as a power that is given to us. It is true that the first Christians experienced power from the Holy Spirit, but an emphasis on power can easily be misused. Some people seek power for its own sake, to work magic. Magic is a sign of alienation from God, because the magician always seeks to use supernatural power without knowing where that power comes from. Those who want power but do not want a personal relationship with God end up having false relationships with other people too. We can believe that people have amazing psychic powers, but to use them outside of the friendship and love of God is extremely dangerous.

Unlike those who claim to have special powers today, Paul the apostle spoke about the power of God's Spirit in a very different way. He said that the Spirit gave him power to bear trials with humility, to live contentedly through times of hardship as well as times of success. He also spoke about the power to bear "a thorn in the flesh"—rather than the power to live as a superstar or a salesman of his own ego!

Others see the work of the Holy Spirit as a performance.

They stress the outward "gifts" of the Holy Spirit, which are exercised in the community of the church. Some of these gifts include "speaking in tongues" (where the speaker praises God in a language unknown to him), "giving prophecies" (where someone speaks the words of God in the first person), and healing. Since we live in a function-oriented culture, where our identity is associated with what we do, it is not surprising that so much emphasis is given to these activities. The spiritual gifts are valid, but their true purpose is not to boost our own egos or establish our own credibility, but to build up others in the Christian faith.

Jesus warned his followers about miracle-workers who would cast out demons and perform many miracles, claiming that the power to do this came from him. But he added, "I will tell them plainly, 'I never knew you." The lesson of this is clear: spiritual powers can be exercised by sorcerers, but the only way of knowing God is by doing his will. Performances of power are no substitute for a personal and prayerful knowledge of God.

On another occasion, Jesus said,

> Do not rejoice that the spirits submit to you, but rejoice
> that your names are written in heaven. (Luke 10:20)

Immediately after this, Jesus is described as being "full of joy through the Holy Spirit," because of his unique relationship with God the Father. For us too, entering into this rich friendship through prayer is profoundly more significant than using magical powers. As we enjoy the presence of God the Holy Spirit, we learn to see him more for the relationship we have with him than for any particular phenomena he brings. If emotionalism was a sign of truly having the Holy Spirit, then the dour Scots or the taciturn Scandinavians would never have the same opportunities as the dramatic Welsh or the passionate Italians. Neither the exuberance of one type of temperament, nor the gravity of another can ever be proof that God's Spirit is in us. Instead, the evidence lies in our relationship with God and our willingness to submit ourselves to the rule of Christ. Only the Holy Spirit can help us truly to give ourselves to God.

The Old Testament prophets, as we saw in the previous chapter, constantly emphasized that God's presence depends on our willingness to seek him. Jeremiah said, "When you seek me with all your heart, I will be found of you." This is also why King David, in Psalm 51, wrote:

> Create in me a pure heart, O God,
> and renew a steadfast spirit within me.
> Do not cast me away from your presence
> or take your Holy Spirit from me.

Clearly, for David the enjoyment of God's Spirit and God's presence are one and the same. He had experienced mercy from God's Spirit, showing him tender compassion just as a mother shows toward her child. And he had also experienced God's "loving-kindness," his imperishable loyalty in keeping his promises toward David. It is no wonder that David desperately wanted God not to remove his Spirit from him.

Later in this same psalm, David speaks about having a "broken spirit" and a "contrite heart" for the things he has done wrong. We too discover that our own frustrations and sufferings can drive us to rely on God's Spirit rather than to rely on our own resources for strength. Paul writes of this in the New Testament:

> The Spirit helps us in our weakness. We do not know
> what we ought to pray, but the Spirit himself intercedes
> for us with groans that words cannot express. And he
> who searches our hearts knows the mind of the Spirit,
> because the Spirit intercedes for the saints in accordance
> with God's will. (Rom. 8:26–27)

When we are so personally inadequate that we do not know how to express our inner emotions in any rational way, we can only cry out to God, or groan in our frustration. The next four sections look at this frustration in our prayers.

OUR PRAYERS ARE INEXPRESSIBLE

We groan, as I have known on two important occasions in my own life, when we are wholly frustrated in being able to tell God what our problem or need is. I did not know how I needed help and comfort, or even what to ask from God.

When this happens, we may speak in tongues to express out of our subconscious selves our need for the presence of the Holy Spirit. This can be communicated in speaking or singing, and helps us to articulate our needs and limitations before God. This is best done as a private exercise, as speaking in tongues can easily be used as a form of emotional manipulation in a group, as a power-play, or even as a form of self-indulgence.

The gift of tongues was misused even in the earliest days of the church, by Christians who did not have a balanced prayer life to help them understand what was happening. But despite this, the apostle Paul was grateful that he could speak in tongues more than anyone else. At the same time, he clearly said that we should not expect all Christians to speak in tongues. It is wrong to grade Christians, as some people do, according to whether or not they have spoken in tongues.

There are other ways in which we can express our inexpressible yearnings to God. We can use the language of the Psalms, allowing them to speak for us when we cannot speak for ourselves:

> As the deer pants for streams of water,
> so my soul pants for you, O God.
> My soul thirsts for God, for the living God.
> When can I go and meet with God?
> My tears have been my food day and night,
> while men say to me all day long,
> "Where is your God?" (42:1–3)

Because prayer is a two-way relationship, we are caught in a deep dilemma. We need to pray to God, but since we are so unlike him, how can we know for certain that he hears us? In fact, the more spiritually aware we become, the deeper this dilemma seems. We start to realize exactly how different our actions and thoughts are from the way God acts and thinks. How can our broken humanity ever express true thoughts and right worship to God? We clearly need the help of the Holy Spirit to grow in true prayer. Paul can help us here:

> He who searches our hearts knows the mind of the
> Spirit, because the Spirit intercedes for the saints in
> accordance with God's will.

Not only does God's Spirit teach us how to pray, but he prays for us himself.

OUR PRAYERS LACK INSIGHT

Many times, our greatest difficulty is to find out precisely what is the will of God, so that we will know how to shape our prayers. The problem is that in our short-sightedness, when we can see only our own needs, we may pray for things that God simply does not want to give us.

Encouragingly, this sort of thing happens to the most godly people. The apostle Paul was afflicted with an illness, which he called his "thorn in the flesh." He prayed three times that God would release him from his suffering, until God told him that the illness was there for a specific purpose.

Monica, the mother of Augustine, prayed many times that her wayward son would not leave his home in North Africa. However, he did leave home and became a Christian while he was living in Milan.

We have to admit that unless we submit to the will of God then we will never know how to pray. To present God with a shopping list of our requests is more likely to indicate our willfulness than our submissiveness to his rule over us. Our relationship with God would be greatly improved if we saw prayer as listening to God rather than talking to him. Think of those boring people who talk endlessly to others (or rather, at others). All their words show that they are distanced from others rather than close to them. Could this also be the reason why our prayers lack insight into the character of God? Openness to God, submissiveness to God, listening to his "still, small voice," may give us far more insight than the constant chatter which we are used to calling prayer.

The New Testament writer Jude says in his letter:

> Dear friends, build yourselves up in your most holy faith
> and pray in the Holy Spirit.

These two realities—being built up in the faith and praying in the Spirit—go together. As we learn more about our faith and grow in our relationship with God, then we will be able to pray more sensitively and wisely, understanding more about the will of God. This spiritual discernment comes only when we surrender ourselves wholly to the will and Spirit of God.

We will discover that prayer in the Holy Spirit will probably be the exact opposite of our natural temperament. If we are extroverted, given to great dramatic displays, we will become quiet, modest and inwardly directed by God's Spirit. If we are shy, timid and withdrawn, we will become much more committed to our relationships, bold, and even confrontational when necessary. We will learn to engage deeply with other people in a life of prayer. These new insights about ourselves before God lead to insights about other people too, so that we learn to pray with greater insight.

OUR PRAYERS ARE SELF-FOCUSED

Another reason why we "groan" in our prayers is that they are so biased toward ourselves and our own view of our needs. This obsession with the self is strong evidence that sin has invaded us as persons.

Self-pity is one of the most subtle ways in which our selfishness expresses itself, for have we not the "right" to be sorry for ourselves when others hurt us? Selfish ambition is another expression of this tendency. Self-display is another, much loved by the Pharisees of Jesus' time. They indulged in attention-seeking even when they thought they were worshipping in the temple. If prayer is "the very soul and essence of religion," as William James put it, then it is only natural that we should groan when our prayers remain so self-preoccupied.

In the garden of Gethsemane, hours before his death, Jesus prayed:

> "Not my will but yours be done."

When we can make this prayer our own, then we will have discovered true prayer. This prayer does not mean the destruction of the self, as a Buddhist monk might interpret it, but the true realization of the self as created by God. The self achieves personal communion with God the Father, through the Son, and by the Holy Spirit.

Within the Holy Trinity, each person is for the others. The work and identity of the Holy Spirit is to make the Father and the Son more of a reality in our lives. Because we are made in God's image and likeness, our true identity shines out most strongly when we are relating fully to God and to other people. Selfishness is not just a bit of harmless naughtiness, it is rebellion against the way we were created. It distorts God's intention in creating us as he did, and also his intention of restoring his image in us. The presence of the Holy Spirit in us is therefore vitally important, because he teaches us to pray and relate to God as we were always meant to. As long as we remain in slavery to our self, then we will continue to groan in our chains. We will only be able to say with Paul,

> What a wretched man I am! Who will rescue me from
> this body of death? (Rom. 7:24)

OUR PRAYERS ARE HUMAN

True prayer, as the writer C. H. Dodd once expressed it, is "the divine in us appealing to the divine above us." But there can be nothing divine in us unless the Holy Spirit moves into our lives to live with us. Very often our prayers are cold and formal, an automatic ritual where the movements of our lips have nothing to do with what we truly feel inside. Only the Holy Spirit can make the vital connections in us that bring unity to our lives, linking what we are inside to the way we relate to God.

We have many human weaknesses in our prayers. They tend to be irregular. We lack self-discipline or the motivation to pray. Sometimes we are simply lazy, or we get discouraged easily. Paul painted a powerful image in one of his letters to encourage his readers that they could strengthen their humanity in their spiritual struggles; we find this in Ephesians 6. He talked about putting on combat gear to defend ourselves against attack by evil. The result will be that we are able to pray:

> Pray in the Spirit on all occasions, with all kinds of
> prayers and requests. With this in mind, be alert, and
> always keep on praying for all the saints.

Our prayers also lack faith. This is why many of our requests to God are so empty and half-hearted, lacking energy and trust in God.

This is where the words of James can challenge us:

> If any of you lack wisdom, he should ask God, who gives
> generously to all without finding fault, and it will be
> given to him. But when he asks, he must believe and not
> doubt, because he who doubts is like a wave of the sea,

> blown and tossed by the wind. That man should not
> think he will receive anything from the Lord; he is a
> double-minded man, unstable in all he does. (1:5–8)

This is where we need the Spirit to give us faith. We will then be able to pray with the full confidence that Paul once expressed when he prayed that God would "do immeasurably more than all we ask or imagine, according to his power that is at work within us...." Human prayers are not enough. We need the Holy Spirit to transform our humanity and enable us to pray as God intended.

THE SPIRIT AND HUMAN TEMPERAMENT

Paul used a multitude of different words in describing our humanity. Two of them were implacably opposed to one another. He spoke of sarx, a Greek word that literally means "the flesh." He used this in a variety of ways, to describe us as physical beings, or in the sense of being addicted to lust, gluttony, and other physical pleasures. But mainly he means people who live in a purely worldly way, without any reference to God at all. "The flesh" is therefore the deadly enemy of *pneuma,* or "spirit." The person who is "spiritual" lives his or her life related to God, through the power of the Holy Spirit.

It is this quality of life, rather than a purely earthbound existence, that we need to discover in our prayers. Those who are spiritual are sensitive and obedient to the influences of the Holy Spirit. They live with a vivid awareness of another realm, with its own way of living.

A problem arises because even those who are spiritually aware have to struggle against their purely natural instincts and temperaments. Writing to a worldly, aristocratic lady, Archbishop Fénelon spoke words of deep wisdom:

> One thing is certain, namely, that I daily ask with all my
> heart that you have all the recollection and faithfulness

to God's Holy Spirit which you need to conquer the difficulties of your position. For you have much to fear
both from within and without. From without, the world
smiles on you, and that side of the world which is most
adapted to you flatters your pride, fosters it by all the
considerations that you hold at court. Then within you,
you have to conquer your taste for a refined life, your
haughty, disdainful temperament, and long-formed habit
of dissipation. The real remedy for so many difficulties is
to match, in spite of everything that hinders you, some
fixed hour for prayer and reading.

Our development as spiritual persons is often handicapped by the powerful combination of our natural temperament and the environment to which we naturally gravitate. This double enemy—the enemy inside and outside—blocks our prayer life and with it our spiritual progress. Because of this, we need to become critical both of the culture in which we live, which so often promotes self-fulfillment as the ideal, and our own inner temperament.

We have already taken a critical look at modern culture, so we now turn to look inside at our temperament. In the past decade, a great deal of study has been made of human temperament. Temperament is the vitality that we inherit in our central nervous system, our hormonal balance, and all the other ways in which our body influences our moods, thoughts, and feelings.

While we are free to make choices in life, it has been found that we have certain preferences, according to our temperament. These preferences have been described as extraversion or introversion, sensing or intuition, thinking or feeling, and judging or perceiving. People who are outwardly oriented, or extraverted, can be seen to fall into the four classical distinctions of the sanguine, the phlegmatic, the choleric, and the melancholy.

The first step we should take is to recognize how our prayers reflect our natural temperament. A sanguine person becomes restless if he or she spends more than ten minutes alone in prayer. This is because sanguine types are very active. They generate enthusiasm, act spontaneously, and find discipline very trying. They therefore find prayer in the company of other people much more easy than long hours spent on their own. Phlegmatic people, by contrast, are much more dependable, stable, and conservative. They find security in routine, and so find it easy to develop a daily discipline of prayer. Phlegmatics are faithful, but they are not usually creative or spontaneous in their worship.

The choleric person tends to be logical and rational, lacking in feelings and in the quality of relating well to others. One choleric who struggled with prayer said, "My prayer life is all exegesis, like preparing a series of sermons!" Cholerics need plenty of space for their times with God, but they do not experience the ecstasy of others who pray.

The melancholic are creative, persuasive, and imaginative people who think reflectively and deeply. But they can also be touchy, or set themselves impossible standards. Their prayers are often creative and spontaneous, but they happen more intermittently.

Having spotted the connections between our style of prayer and our natural temperament, the second step is to make the most of our natural temperament, strengthening our habits of heart before God. We do not need to feel guilty that we do not pray in exactly the same ways and for the same lengths of time that we admire in great Christians from the past. Instead, we can draw encouragement from and thank God for the different ways in which we see growth and enrichment in our times with God. We need to be careful that we do not simply let ourselves off the hook because of our temperament, giving up on prayer entirely. We have to plan for the changes we hope to see happening in our prayer life. The spiritual life is always forward-looking, always calling us to move on to further exploration and journeying. The journey never ends, because we are exploring the mysteries of God.

The third step is to anticipate change in our temperaments, because this is exactly what God longs to achieve in us. As long as we refuse to believe that God could ever change us to become a different person, we will remain blind to our own weaknesses and deficiencies. But if we believe that our spiritual growth lies in the opposite direction to our natural temperament, then we can begin to anticipate how the Holy Spirit will change us. It becomes exciting to anticipate that I will become the exact opposite of what I once was. This is where we can take the opportunity to use weekend retreats, leisure time and Sundays to alter the approach we normally take toward God in prayer. Our prayers can become times when we reach forward in faith to take hold of what we will one day become.

We can discover our weaknesses as we probe our inner selves with significant questions. Which of the four functions (intuition, sensing, feeling, and thinking) most exhausts me when I try to focus on them? When am I most easily upset, disturbed, or distracted? What do I find most difficult to sustain? When do I feel least confident? When am I most negative and unassured? When do I most need powers of concentration and peace of mind?

As we begin to answer these questions in the presence of God, we will begin to realize that they cluster around one of the four functions, enabling us to identify our inferior function. As God begins to change our lives, we will see this weaker function become a new source of strength and change in our temperament. While the terms used for these psychological functions are modern, behind them are several biblical phrases which describe the person who is being changed by God's Spirit.

Intuition: "The Fear of the Lord"

Of all the functional changes we may seek to make, the area of intuition is perhaps the first. Our materialistic and rationalistic society is afraid of intuition, because it awakens us out of the sleep of a false world with shallow values. The Devil is afraid of it, because it activates an awareness of the spiritual, inward life.

We begin to exercise intuition when we see how truth is not a flat view of things, but is much closer to paradox. Intuition allows us to discover how much of our life is surrounded and enveloped by mysteries. In the light of this discovery, it is absurd to flatten life out into questions and answers.

As the realm of the mysterious grows, the relevance of the spiritual dimension of our lives increases in importance, giving prayer a higher profile for us. This may mean that we begin to pay more attention to our dreams, so that we can deepen our inward awareness. For years I assumed that I never dreamed at night, as I never woke up with any memory of dreams. But it occurred to me that I might be robbing myself of insights about my inner life that I could share with God. So I began to pray last thing at night that during sleep God would guard my unconscious state and awake me with dreams to ponder over. As soon as I did this, I discovered that I had been dreaming for years, but had simply been unaware of what was taking place inside me.

Many people in the Bible had significant dreams which guided them at key points in their lives. Jacob dreamed that a ladder connected heaven and earth. Joseph dreamed that his brothers would all one day bow down to him, which they eventually did. In a dream, King Solomon asked God to give him wisdom. The Old Testament prophets Jeremiah and Zechariah attacked the false prophets of their time for neglecting their dreams, considering hem to be passing memories with no significance. Reflecting on our dreams can make a deep impression on us as we open up the world within.

Deep though intuition and dreams are, "the fear of the Lord" is the deepest intuition we can ever have. In the wisdom books of the Bible it is recognized as the beginning of all wisdom. When we begin to exercise greater spiritual intuition in our lives, in the fear of the Lord, we can expect to see real inner changes of heart before God.

Sensing: "Waiting upon the Lord"

The faculty of sensing means to use all five of our bodily senses. Ignatius of Loyola, the founder of the Jesuits, wrote one of the great classics of prayer, *The Spiritual Exercises*. In this book, he encourages everyone who meditates on Jesus' life to use all five senses as they travel through the Gospels. This is not to everyone's taste, but even the temperamentally unimaginative will surprise themselves as they do this exercise in the presence of God.

As we wait upon God, we can begin to discover the inner beauty of many of the things around us that we normally take completely for granted. A blade of grass, a flower, the song of a bird, the texture of wood, the sense of the inner harmony of life, and even "the rumour of angels." We start to see things for the symbols that they are. One poet expressed this discovery:

> Earth's crammed with heaven
>
> And every common bush afire with God;
>
> But only he who sees takes off his shoes;
>
> The rest sit around it and pluck blackberries.

The poet William Blake also comments on this transcendent use of our senses:

> If the doors of perception were fully cleansed, we would
>
> see everything as it really is, infinite.

The Old Testament describes this new sense of perception as "waiting on the Lord." When natural abilities are exhausted and strength has become weakness; when what seemed permanent has disappeared, then waiting on the Lord becomes a new dimension of reality.

There are eight or more meanings in the Old Testament's use of this phrase. They range across waiting in tension, in humility, in persistent asking, in eager expectation, and in shared companionship. Despite these many meanings, the outcome is always the same. Waiting on the Lord gives us a new sense of God, his purposes, and his world. It is an exciting experience to be awakened to the realm of music when I have not a single harmonious bone within me! Or to open my eyes to the world of art when I cannot draw a simple figure. But there is even more than this. There is the delight of being awakened to the sheer beauty of God's Spirit within me, after the long, dark sleep of indifference to his presence.

FEELING: "LIFTING UP OUR HEARTS TO THE LORD"

We often complain that today's world is so impersonal. People seem to have little feeling toward others and can be indifferent to their needs and loneliness. The impersonal facts of science, technology, politics, and bureaucracy seem to play an ever-increasing role in our society. Even the Christian faith can be packaged and sold at a profit, or at the opposite extreme, organized and institutionalized to death. If feeling people are those who are most likely to get hurt, why cultivate more sensitivity in an unfeeling world?

Greater sensitivity of feeling is exactly what the Christian gospel does produce. The good news is felt. It is sensed. It is expressed in joy and in strong feelings toward God. If love does not produce love, then it was never love in the first place. The purpose of the Christian life is not to fill our heads with doctrine, but to awaken us to a spiritual quality of life that excites, energizes, and enriches us with a more genuine human life. So when we open ourselves to the influences of the Holy Spirit, it is like a black-and-white film that suddenly bursts into full color.

This is what it means to "lift up our eyes to the Lord." We actually lift up the whole core of our beings to the Lord. This means to live a God-inspired, God-directed, God-focused life. In the Old Testament, the expression of "lifting up" or "casting down" the eyes was used frequently to show how a person stood before God. So right at the beginning of the story of human worship, when

Cain's sacrifice was rejected by God, he became "very angry and his face was downcast." Later, we read that King Nebuchadnezzar of Babylon was condemned to live like an animal, with "downcast face." When his "sentence" was finished, he exclaimed:

> I, Nebuchadnezzar, raised up my eyes toward heaven, and my sanity was restored. (Dan. 4:34)

"Looking up to heaven" is another way of saying that we have been given transformed feelings for God, and that he has forgiven and accepted us.

Eliphaz, one of Job's comforters, reassures us:

> Surely then you will find delight in the Almighty and will lift up your face to God. You will pray and he will hear you, and you will fulfill your vows. What you decide on will be done, and light will shine on your ways. (22:26–28)

THINKING: "WALKING BEFORE THE LORD"

It is thought that most distinguishes the human race from the rest of the creation. Our culture is spellbound by its massive advances in science and technology. And yet there are relatively few people who have thinking as their dominant function. Many more of us are dominated by the sensing or feeling functions. Perhaps this is a good thing. The great thirst for knowledge can be ruthless, proud and defiant of God. The power of the mind is often arrogant and self-sufficient, thinking that relationships can be replaced by mental concepts. This cold, intellectual spirit is incompatible with Adam's delight in walking with God. And yet true knowledge is exactly that: using our minds in the companionship and friendship of God.

Thinking can become a powerful and effective instrument of God's grace in our prayer life, and in transforming our temperament. Yoked together with intuition, thinking in prayer can provide us with a rich succession of insights which will enrich our lives before God. As we exercise our minds before God, we reach a fuller agreement with him and receive a common direction and goal. Thinking before God shows us the need of a greater degree of balance in our lives. Our natural temperament begins to fade into the background in comparison with the transforming change of heart, mind and spirit that the life of prayer is beginning to become for us.

As the deepening of our prayer life becomes more related to the shadow side of our character, we become more open to our weaknesses and repressed hurts. The task of knowing the full truth about ourselves is never finished. However, we are assured by the words of Jesus:

> You shall know the truth, and the truth shall set you free.

THE FRIENDSHIP OF THE HOLY SPIRIT

The challenge to see prayer as the agent of change in us is daunting. We clearly need help from within. This is precisely what we are offered in the person of the Holy Spirit, who works inside us to change us from the inside out.

When the twelve disciples of Jesus met with him for the last time over the last supper, they were shocked by the possibility that he would be taken from them. They were about to lose their companion, guide, friend, and counselor. In this context of fear and loss, Jesus promised the disciples that the Holy Spirit would be given to them. He would be "another counselor," which implies that he would be to them all that Jesus had been during his time on earth. He would be personal as their friend, authoritative as their leader, and reliable as their guide.

The Greek word used to describe this person, *parakletos,* is someone who is "called to one's side." This word is used to describe a friend who comes alongside to help, or a professional, such as a defense lawyer in a trial or a doctor in sickness. However, the word is almost untranslatable from Greek to English because of the vast range of meanings it contains. The Holy Spirit completely embraces all our social and personal needs. He is personal, rather than an impersonal force or energy. There are four outstanding features in his role with the disciples and with us.

First, he is the friend who reminds us.

Paul wrote that the Holy Spirit "takes of the things of Christ and declares them to us." He reminds us of everything that Jesus said to his disciples. This is why the teaching of Jesus has never been lost to the church. Where there has been an outbreak of heresy in the history of the Christian faith, then the truth has been recovered again and again. This truth about the church is also a truth for us personally. The Holy Spirit sustains the truth of the gospel within our hearts, making it more relevant to us and deepening its impact on our lives. If we allow the Holy Spirit to be active in us, then our faith will be dynamic and prayer will be a true relationship between us and God. As John Calvin expressed it:

> The principal exercise which the children of God have is to pray; for in this way they give a true proof of their faith. And prayer is the inevitable outcome of the presence of faith in the human heart, for wherever faith exists, prayer cannot be sluggish.

The Spirit is also the friend who warns us in advance.

As the person who comes alongside us, the Holy Spirit quite literally befriends us. Like a true friend, he is honest with us even when it hurts. He exposes wrong relationships and false situations in our lives, saving us from the confusion and worry that always result when we trust these things. We can all think of friends or acquaintances who have gone bankrupt or have been divorced partly because they did not have good friends who could give them sound, tough advice. The Holy Spirit is not like a fair-weather friend. He is a true friend. He shows us things as they really are.

Jesus said that the Holy Spirit would "convict the world of guilt in regard to sin, righteousness, and judgment." He reveals to us how the world is affected by sin. He also convicts the world of righteousness in showing us how far short of God's standards secular society has fallen. And he convicts the world of judgment by showing us how the world has and will be judged. By the death and resurrection of Jesus, the power of evil has been overthrown and the Devil, "the prince of this world," has already been defeated.

The counselor who befriends us also forewarns us of what is yet to take place as his righteous judgments unfold. He gives us insight into the future. It is as if, just when Hitler was about to seize power in Germany, we were given a film preview of the judicial proceedings at the Nuremberg Trials fifteen years later. Warned in advance, we would be given courage, insight, and the strength to resist all the cultural pressures and natural weaknesses of our own temperaments. In the same way the Holy Spirit gives us an eternal perspective, allowing us to see events from God's point of view. This keeps our prayer life courageous and pure before him.

Third, the Holy Spirit is the friend who makes heaven real to us.

When Jesus told his disciples that he would have to leave them, they were deeply troubled. But he promised them that rather than ending his relationship with them, there would be a deepening of it. The Holy Spirit makes it possible for everyone (not just the group of twelve disciples) to know Jesus in a personal relationship. Through the Spirit, Jesus is closer to us than our hands or feet, more intimately close to us than breathing. Paul the apostle gives us two metaphors to bring this home.

From the world of commerce, he enlists the word *arrabon,* "a down payment," to describe the work of the Spirit. A down payment represents an advance that guarantees that the full amount will eventually be paid. The gift of the Holy Spirit is an anticipation of what our relationship with God will be like in heaven. All our prayers are expressed in the light of this promise, which has still to be fulfilled. In our prayers now we experience a small taste of the communion we will enjoy throughout eternity.

From the world of craftsmanship Paul describes the work of the Holy Spirit as *sphragizein,* to "seal" or "imprint a trademark." These marks were used in the time of Paul to indicate ownership or the quality of a product. Just as a jar of wine or oil was sealed with the mark of the vineyard or olive grove, so we too bear the mark of our possession by God. Paul says that we are "sealed with the Holy Spirit."

Both these symbols remind us of our heavenly destiny. It is the role of the Holy Spirit in our life of prayer to prepare us for our life beyond death. But such change does not take place overnight. Just as it can take many years for an analyst to help his patient to overcome depression, or for an activist to become a quiet contemplative, so our natural temperament is stubbornly resistant to change.

Archbishop Fénelon once gave some advice to a worldly courtier who could not understand why he found prayer difficult. Fenelon told him that his whole life was overburdened by his many distractions. He recommended that he should pray in advance about all his day's business. This would enable him to go into the day's pressures in a heavenly frame of mind, with peace and assurance.

It has often been claimed that some people are "so heavenly minded that they are no earthly use." But the opposite is true. Our lives become most useful on earth when they are controlled by the Spirit who makes heaven real to us.

Last but not least, the Holy Spirit is the friend who is always with us. When we meet someone whom we like intensely, and begin to make friends with them, there is often a tinge of fear that he or she might not want to continue the relationship once they know us better. The Holy Spirit is the friend who will never leave us.

Jesus told the disciples at the last supper:

> I will ask the Father, and he will give you another
> Counselor to be with you forever. (John 14:16)

Without the presence of the Spirit in our lives, we would never have any hope of a change of temperament, and all our efforts to pray and to follow Jesus would be in vain.

Just as the Spirit caused Jesus to be conceived in Mary, so he lives in us so that our bodies can become what the New Testament describes as "the temple of the Holy Spirit." Then our spiritual life becomes real, meaningful and transforming. He takes away the meanness, the alienation and the meaningless-ness of our life, drawing us closer to God. And because he stays with us forever, this process goes on.

The Holy Spirit is the person who makes the presence of God a living experience. He comforts us when we feel forsaken or when we are in mourning. He enters into our most personal temptations, strengthening us to resist them. There are many times when we are not sure if God has really heard our prayers, or whether he really understands our circumstances. At such times we can experience the consoling role of the Holy Spirit in our lives. In all these ways we discover that the Spirit living in us is an active Spirit, making real to us the presence of God.

Consider this paraphrase of Paul in Romans 8:26–28:

> We do not even know how we ought to pray, but in our
> inarticulate groans the Spirit himself is pleading for us,
> and God who searches our inmost being knows what the
> Spirit means, because he pleads for God's people in God's
> own way; and in everything, as we know, he co-operates
> for good with those who love God and are called accord-
> ing to his purpose.

Abandoned by words, we wait on the Holy Spirit to articu-late for us. In our struggle against our own temperament we often find out that we simply do not have the strength to become what we want to become. This is where we benefit from the faithful presence of the Holy Spirit. He both prays on our behalf and makes it possible for us to become fully human, as God longs us to be.

Spirit divine, attend our prayers,
And make this house thy home;
Descend with all thy gracious powers:
O come, great Spirit, come!

Come as the light; to us reveal
Our emptiness and woe;
And lead us in the paths of life
Where all the righteous go.

Come as the wind: sweep clean away
What dead within us lies,
And search and freshen all our souls
With living energies.

Come as the fire: and purge our hearts
Like sacrificial flame;
Let our whole soul an offering be
To our redeemer's name.

Spirit divine, attend our prayers,
Make a lost world thy home;
Descend with all thy gracious powers:
O come, great Spirit, come!
　　　—Johann Cruge

Part Three

Entering the Heart of God

8

FRIENDSHIP WITH JESUS CHRIST

Day by day, day by day,
O, dear Lord, three things I pray:
To see thee more clearly;
Love thee more dearly;
Follow thee more nearly,
Day by day.

—Richard of Chichester

The Holy Spirit becomes our friend primarily to give us a deeper quality of relationship with God the Father and Son. We saw in the previous chapter how the Holy Spirit is the person who comes alongside us, sent to us by the Father, and promised to us by the Son. This is why Jesus left his disciples, so that they (and we) could know him in a far deeper sense through the Spirit. Because the Spirit is the Holy Spirit, and the Spirit of consolation, to receive him is to have a holy life as well as a consoled life. As the Spirit works in our prayers, we can expect to see significant changes in our attitudes and in our spiritual growth.

For in the reality of the Holy Spirit we have both the transcendence and the immanence of God. In his holiness, he is transcendently "the other," unlike us in his deity. But in his immanence, his Spirit is intimately personal, "closer than breathing." As both, he is the Spirit of Jesus Christ, who remains with us always, "the same yesterday, today and forever." So, like the disciples who walked and companioned with Jesus, we have the same privileged friendship, to be always with him. As the Spirit works in our prayers, we can expect to see significant changes in our attitudes and in our spiritual growth.

Our faith will be increased, our hope will be extended, our love for God will grow, and joy, peace, and inner assurance will enrich our inner being. In turn, the way in which we pray will be radically changed. We will experience a greater freedom of communication with God as we become more and more sure that he accepts us as we are. We will become stronger in our determination to follow Jesus and to be his friend. As we escape from the slavery of self-importance, we will be able to see ourselves in a new light. We become more critical and discerning about our weaknesses, and at the same time less threatened by seeing ourselves in this way. This is because our identity is now "in Christ" rather than in ourselves.

The New Testament tells us that "No one can say 'Jesus is Lord,' except by the Holy Spirit." The Spirit is the person who gives us the inner strength we need to give ourselves to the rule of Jesus. So in our prayers we will continue to call on his Spirit to make Jesus an ever-greater reality in us.

JESUS AND OUR PERSONALITY

When we read the four Gospels, which tell the story of Jesus' life, we are overwhelmed by the sheer mass of incidents that took place: Jesus' healings, parables, miracles, and his meetings with so many different people. As we listen to the teaching of Jesus, we become like the first disciples. We simply cannot absorb all the implications of his teaching, because it has so many repercussions for our lives. It means renouncing all self-will, abandoning ourselves to the Father, and living for God in ways that we can barely imagine.

When we look at the prayer life of Jesus, we have to admit that we have scarcely begun to pray. Like the disciples, who watched how Jesus prayed, we too ask him, "Lord, teach us to pray." I cannot begin to imagine how vastly different I would be as a husband, father, son, brother, or friend, if I truly followed Jesus in the way I prayed and related to others. I cannot imagine what impact it would have on my wife and family, on my colleagues at work, on my career, and on all those I come into contact with each day. And what would be the effect of truly following Jesus on my church?

Following Jesus is so radically different from what the world of today allows that we can begin to see why the New Testament calls us "strangers and pilgrims" in the world. Because we still have one foot in the world, we see Jesus half as a friend and half as a stranger. So for much of our lives we look at Jesus, as we see him in the Gospels, with a mixture of love and revulsion, attraction and fear, desire and disobedience. The stranger has hopelessly outclassed me and overwhelms me whenever I am in his presence for too long.

Despite our mixed feelings about Jesus, we still want to pray and to relate with God. And just as our temperaments need to be changed, so too do our personalities. In the Greek-Roman world around the time of Christ, people's personae were seen as no more than the theatrical masks worn by actors performing a drama on stage. They had no real substance as persons. In the same way, we wear our personality masks, which we display to the outer world. This is especially true of professional people, who project a particular image of themselves in the attempt to impress other people.

Our personality is shaped by the way in which we were brought up as children. The way in which we were parented will also have a deep effect on the way we pray and relate to God. If a person grew up to be a "good girl," always trying to win the approval of her parents, then the odds are that she will carry on doing this with God when she is grown up. One person even went overseas as a missionary in her attempts to be a good girl. She thought that by doing something she considered unpleasant she would win God's approval.

On the other hand, the "bad boy" who rebels against his mother's emotional manipulation of him will probably suspect that God is trying to do the same thing. The judgmental person may have been deeply influenced by her mother's criticism of her father, so that negativism becomes a way of relating to others and to God.

Prayer, as a relationship, is affected by our upbringing in exactly the same way as all our other relationships. Just as our personality is disordered, so too are our passions. Western culture places a distorted emphasis on the needs of our sexuality, which affects all of us.

In his book *The Great Divorce*, C. S. Lewis tells the story of a man in purgatory who carries a mean little red lizard of sensuality on his shoulder. The lizard keeps whispering into the man's ear about all the fun they will be able to have together. A great angel pleads with the man to allow him to destroy the lizard, which the man is too terrified to allow. But eventually he gives in. The angel grabs hold of the lizard with his burning hand and flings it broken onto the ground:

> Something seemed to be happening to the lizard. At first I thought the operation had failed. So far from dying, the creature was still struggling and even growing bigger as it struggled. And as it grew it changed. Its hinder parts grew rounder. The tail, still flickering, became a tail of hair that flickered between huge and glossy buttocks. Suddenly, I started back, rubbing my eyes. What stood before me was the greatest stallion I have ever seen, silvery white, but with a mane and tail of gold. It was smooth and shining, rippled with swells of flesh and muscle, whinneying and stamping with its hoofs.

The man climbs onto the horse and gallops away.

This striking picture represents how the death of our old nature leads to a newness and greatness of life with unimaginable consequences. We discover how useful it is to have passions, real passions for God that enable us to hate sin and evil with new energy. The Psalms are full of passion for God which is channeled by the worshipper into acclaiming God as the King of kings. Our emotions are so often misdirected toward ourselves instead of being directed to God. This is why we must express all our emotions prayerfully before him. Our job is not to suppress and hide our true feelings, as we have done since childhood, but to expose them to him so that he can heal us and make us whole people. When this happens, we enter prayer more deeply than ever as the reparenting of our old personality, discovering the Father of Jesus as our own father. I no longer worship and serve the god of my fallen parents, but Jesus' God and Father. This is what it means to be born again.

These words will be completely useless if they are read simply as words, without becoming a part of our own living experience. So this may be a good point to pause and pray that God will enter our hearts. We need the "heart transplant" that the prophet Ezekiel predicted we would one day have:

> I will give you a new heart and put a new spirit in you; I will remove from you your heart of stone and give you a heart of flesh. And I will put my Spirit in you and move you to follow my decrees and be careful to keep my laws. You will live in the land I gave your forefathers; you will be my people, and I will be your God. (36:26–28)

In prayer, imagine what a spiritual heart transplant would mean to your whole person. Imagine if your heart, which beat almost 24 million times in your mother's womb and which has beaten many more times since—in fear, anxiety, desire, anger, despair, envy, insecurity, and lust—now beats only in the presence of God's love. Imagine spending time with Jesus, so that you bless the little children as he did, you help to feed the hungry crowd of five thousand as he did, and you touch the lepers or AIDS victims as he would do. This change of heart, at the very roots of our being, helps us to long for the deepening friendship of Jesus Christ.

These changes in the way we relate to others are important for our prayers. The apostle Peter wrote:

> Husbands, be considerate as you live with your wives ...
> so that nothing may hinder your prayers. (1 Peter 3:7)

Or as another writer has put it,

> The sighs of the injured wife come between the
> husband's prayers and God's hearing.

Our relationship with God can never be right when our relationships with other people are wrong.

Wrong relationships take place at many different levels. There is alienation between parents and children, employers and employees, the rich and the poor, and between people of different races. Because men have seen women as "the weaker sex," they have sinfully abused womanhood right down the ages. At a deeper level, marriage is often a cockpit for unresolved conflict, as two fallen personalities struggle with their own inner conflicts, frequently blaming them on each other.

In an age that demands its rights, the New Testament makes revolutionary reading. In his New Testament letter, Peter calls for submission in a whole range of relationships: a slave to his master, a wife to her husband, a husband to his wife. The grounds for this is that Jesus set us an example by submitting to the humiliation and death of the cross.

Far from demanding our rights in our relationships, we need to take on board the humility of Jesus. Our old attitudes have to be put to death so that we can become new people in Christ. We need to pray, as the poet Crawshaw prayed, "Leave nothing of myself in me." If we draw back from this, then our prayers will be blocked. We need to die to ourselves, just as Jesus allowed himself to be killed. The poet William Blake expressed it in this way:

> Jesus said, Wouldst thou love one who never died
> For thee, or ever died for one who had not died for thee?
> And if God dieth not for Man and giveth not himself
> Eternally for Man, Man could not exist, for Man is Love,
> As God is Love; every kindness to another is a little death
> In the Divine Image; nor can Man exist but by
> Brotherhood.

As Jesus died, so his followers believe that the death of self is the only way to true life. We say goodbye to our old personality—clever, successful, and adaptable as it has been in the world of fallen relationships—and enter into communion with Christ. It is only by doing this that we can be truly ourselves before God in prayer.

JESUS AS THE WAY, TRUTH, AND LIFE OF PRAYER

Although prayer is a universal experience, found in all the world's religions, there are two elements of prayer which are unique to the Christian faith.

The first is that prayer can be offered to Jesus himself by those who follow him. This happened in many of the gospel stories about Jesus. In Matthew's gospel, for example, a man with leprosy knelt before Jesus and said to him, "Lord, if you are willing, you can make me clean." On some of these occasions, we are told that people worshipped him, in the same way that they worshipped God.

The second new element is that prayer is offered in the name of Jesus. It is John's gospel which teaches this whole new dimension. John is fascinated by the inner life of prayer. He emphasizes that Jesus longs for his followers to enter into the same relationship that the Father and the Son share with each other. He teaches us that to enter a life of prayer is nothing less than entering into the heart and being of God himself.

We can view John's gospel as a new school of prayer. It is new because it is about prayer directed to Jesus, as well as prayer that links us to the Father and the Son, through the Holy Spirit. The incidents we read about in John all point in this direction. The noises in the crowd, the requests for personal help, the cries of distress and anguish, the declarations of faith and love are all directed to Jesus. They are all prayers to him. Yet they are all set against a dark background of whispered plots, carping criticism and the swelling prejudice and hatred of the crowd and its leaders who will eventually crucify him.

This environment, in which Jesus embodies the reality of prayer, echoes the words of one of the psalms:

> With words of hatred they surround me;
> > they attack me without cause.
> In return for my friendship they accuse me,
> > but I am a man of prayer.

In the Hebrew in which this psalm was originally written, the last line literally means, "But I am a prayer." This is precisely what John portrays about Jesus. The friendship of Jesus Christ is prayer on our behalf. Jesus is therefore the way, the truth and the life of prayer. In the rest of this chapter, we will look at what this means.

The way of prayer is defined by Jesus' own character and life. To be like Jesus, who was God living as a man among us, becomes the destination of our journey in prayer.

THE WAY OF SUBMISSION

Submitting to others and to God is the key to prayer.

How many people have destroyed their marriages because they have demanded control of the relationship and have defended their rights to the death? Behind this spirit of selfish control lurk other, more sinister spirits. One man who is afraid of his own inner life might tyrannize and even physically abuse his wife, attempting to control her, break her own spirit, and eliminate her personality. Or a woman who finds she cannot physically dominate her husband might manipulate him by constantly criticizing him and teaching him to fear and avoid confronting her.

We retain control over ourselves, others, and God in many different ways—some of them extremely subtle. The scholar is always ready with a cleverly argued reason for everything he does. The young girl smiles sweetly at the people she is determined to win over. The disciplinarian jogs every day and manages his faith in exactly the same way. At the heart of our lives is the fear of losing this control and renouncing our self-will. This is what sin does to us; we cannot bear the thought of self-surrender.

In one of his Narnia books, *The Voyage of the Dawn Treader,* C. S. Lewis pictures this process of losing self-will as stripping off a heavy dragon's skin to uncover and free the true person inside. This is the way and the mystery of prayer. We begin to pray in Jesus' name and to live his life of submission.

Prayer is something that we do "in the name of Jesus." But what does this actually mean? To pray in his name is to reproduce the character of Jesus in ourselves, allowing our lives to be shaped by him. Obviously this is a process, not the work of a moment, and it begins to happen as we submit to his will. John tells us that Jesus said:

> I do nothing on my own but speak just what the Father
> has taught me.... I always do what pleases him. (8:28–29)

Just as Jesus was submissive to his Father, so we enter into the same relationship of submission. Jesus submitted to his Father to accomplish a specific task—our salvation. So to pray in Jesus' name is to cooperate in that task: dying as Jesus died, being raised from death as Jesus was raised by the Father.

When we pray in submission to God's will, our prayers are no longer our own prayers, made from our point of view, but are made from Jesus' point of view within us. Because of our fallen humanity, this does not fully happen to us yet, but it will be true for us after death. Only then will our misunderstanding of Jesus and our estrangement from him be overcome. We will be one with him, as the Father and the Son are one. This hope of transformation is the goal of our whole lives.

THE WAY OF FAITH

Prayer is a way of faith, because through it we grab hold of realities that we cannot yet see or experience for ourselves. These realities are unknown to the world of secular psychology or to the world at large, but the hope of them plays a substantial part in our lives. However, this way of faith is a demanding road to travel. I have found it to be a journey through nausea, over a fearful abyss. This is because Jesus leads us through the dark tunnel of our childhood fears, our guilty secrets, and the many other things we have tried to forget and repress.

Afraid of the sea, I had to be ducked in it in my father's arms. Afraid of faith as a way of life, I had to be stripped of professional tenure. Afraid of failure, I had to be broken in public disgrace. Each of us has to go through the way of nausea.

The way of prayer is to become reparented by God in faith toward him alone. So to meet with Jesus as the disciples did is simply to "follow him." We can trace this process in the way the first disciples met Jesus at the beginning of John's gospel.

John the Baptist, when he saw Jesus, exclaimed, "Look, the Lamb of God, who takes away the sin of the world!" It is this that stops us in our tracks and makes us follow him. The disciples then asked Jesus, "Master, where are you staying?" We ask this because we simply want to go with him and be wherever he is. Jesus replied, "Come and see." We never know in advance what awaits us on this journey into faith. We need to beware of talking about "faith" as though it were just one of many commodities which we can take off the shelf and buy. In contrast, John's gospel talks about "believing." This word expresses an ongoing, dynamic relationship of friendship with Jesus. He is the way of believing, dynamic faith. We do nothing without Jesus: seeking only him, living only for him. This way of faith means to be saturated with the consciousness of his presence all the time.

THE WAY OF OBEDIENCE

Jesus gave a very simple, but very sharply observed, definition of what friendship with him means. He said,

> You are my friends if you do what I command.

To love is to obey, and in loving God, we love our brothers and sisters too. As Jesus said,

> A new commandment I give to you, that you love one
> another.

No one can be the friend of Jesus without having many other friends. No one can have the spirit of prayer without a willingness to submit on behalf of others in praying for them.

This friendship which expresses itself in obedience is illustrated for us graphically in several stories from John's gospel. Mary and Martha were friends of Jesus who submitted to him in different ways. Mary is shown serving him with great love, anointing his feet with oil in worship. Martha is more blunt with Jesus. When her brother Lazarus died and Jesus was slow to arrive, she came straight to the point on meeting him: "Lord, if you had been here, my brother would not have died." But then she added, submitting to him: "But I know that even now God will give you whatever you ask." Both Mary and Martha obeyed Jesus, in their own way.

John the Baptist is described as "the friend of the Bridegroom." He enjoyed his closeness to Jesus, like the best man at a wedding. But John's friendship with Jesus was marked by willingness to obey him. John told his group of disciples, "I must decrease and he must increase." This was a hard lesson for John, but he accepted it as a true friend of Jesus. The way of obedience for John was in selfless contraction, to allow the spotlight to leave him in darkness as it focused on Jesus.

At the opposite extreme is Nicodemus, the Pharisee who came to see Jesus at night. He was completely self-possessed, with his scholarship, his status, his official respectability, and sense of righteousness. Jesus told him, not surprisingly, that he needed a new birth. As we identify with him, we too need to pray:

> Take thy way: for sure thy way is best:
> Stretch or contract me, thy poor debtor;
> This is but tuning of my breast,
> To make the music better.
> —GEORGE HERBERT

Imagine if everything you had read so far in this book had been put into effect in your life. Even then you would not want to be congratulated as a woman or man of great prayer. Our aim is not to become a new style of Olympic champion—a prayer champion. If the changes we need are so radical that we need a new birth, then the implication is that our life is to become Jesus' life in us, and his prayers become our prayers also. This is his achievement, rather than ours. This is what lies ahead of us, and we anticipate what he will make us with joy and hope.

THE TRUTH THAT ILLUMINATES

We now turn to Jesus as the truth of prayer. As we think about ourselves apart from God, we can see how we naturally try to conceal the darkness inside from ourselves. Against our self-deception and blindness, Jesus declares:

> I am the light of the world. Whoever follows me will
> never walk in darkness, but will have the light of life.

Jesus shines a powerful, searching light into our inner darkness, bringing life to our death. However, this does not mean that from now on we will live without problems and uncertainty because of our "advanced" prayer life. But the light Jesus brings does help us to see ourselves more clearly and not to be fooled by what is hidden inside.

John's gospel has a powerful awareness of darkness. Darkness is expressed in all the opposition to the presence and work of Jesus. The truth always provokes darkness, which appears in many different forms. Jesus' enemies had the darkness of envy, because the religious leaders would have loved to have had half the popularity that Jesus enjoyed. Some of them lived in the darkness of hypocrisy which feared exposure and went on the attack, accusing others for the guilt felt inside. There was also the darkness of locked-up lives, which were closed and barred to the truth. They attacked Jesus' teaching, denying the possibility that he might be who he said he was.

All these different darknesses only reveal more sharply the contrast between light and darkness.

THE TRUTH THAT LIBERATES

To pray in Jesus' name means to be freed from ourselves. We become a person in Christ, no longer with our own personality, but freed to belong to Jesus, and Jesus alone. This sense of belonging is a powerful medicine against despair.

At one time, I felt very isolated and life seemed to have lost all its meaning. I was on an aircraft and, looking out of the window, pictured myself outside. I imagined myself falling through the deep blue without a parachute and realized that this captured my feelings of despair. I could do nothing except to trust in God that he would save me from my despair and from death.

For someone else, it might be as though the continent beneath their feet is sinking beneath the sea. As it disappears under the limitless waste of the sea, it leaves them floating alone. It is at these moments of sheer despair that we can discover the freedom of God. Jesus once spoke to our despair by saying, "Without me you can do nothing."

Many people have this experience of despair and insignificance when they realize the loneliness of their own uniqueness. They become aware that they are different from everyone else, and feel forever cut off from the rest of the human race. When this happens we either commit the knowledge and the destiny of our personal identities to God, or else we are doomed to wander the desert for the rest of our existence, unknown and unknowable. Truths like these jolt us out of our cheap securities to trust only in God. This frees us, because we no longer feel possessive about ourselves. Fear is an index of our possessiveness—the more self-possessed we feel, the more fearful we become. But if I no longer possess myself, but have given myself wholeheartedly to God, then I am both fearless and free.

We also gain our liberty by reading and listening to the teaching of the Bible. Jesus said:

> If you hold to my teaching, you are really my disciples. Then you will know the truth, and the truth will set you free. (John 8:31–32)

An old Scots preacher, John Brown of Haddington, used to pause now and again in his preaching, as if listening to a voice. Prayer is a constant listening to the voice of Jesus, and then meditating on his words. This is how we begin to experience how the truth sets us free. Prayerful meditation on the Bible frees us from many fears and weaknesses: the fear of other people's opinions, persistent habits of sin, personal weaknesses and self-indulgence. Praying in Jesus' name, we are set free in our inner lives to take on the identity of Jesus as the Son of God.

After we have been given our light and freedom in prayer, Jesus then directs us clearly and specifically. We need his direction because we can so easily go overboard with our freedom, seeing the potential for prayer in unbalanced ways.

Praying in Jesus' name means praying that his will be done in us. The primary purpose of prayer is therefore not for our own needs to be met, nor for our own desires to be satisfied, but to glorify God in the way we pray and live. Jesus said:

> I tell you the truth, anyone who has faith in me will do
> what I have been doing. And I will do whatever you ask in
> my name, so that the Son may bring glory to the Father.

The Father is glorified when Jesus his Son is surrounded by other people who are like-minded and like-spirited.

Prayer is also directed by our need to live in God. Jesus pictured this living in God as the branch of a vine—living in the vine, drawing its life from the vine. It is only by living in the trunk of the vine that the branch is able to grow and produce fruit. He told his disciples:

> I chose you to go and bear fruit—fruit that will last.

This picture shows us that our prayer life is always drawn from Jesus, and it is meant to provide for other people as well as for ourselves. As the sap is given to the branch to produce fruit, so we are given Jesus' teaching to bear fruit in our lives. Because of this, Jesus told us to pray in the realization that "if you remain in me, and my words remain in you, ask whatever you wish and it will be given you."

Jesus calls us for a specific purpose: that we should be fruitful. All our prayers are subservient to this clear objective. Jesus calls us his friends for a reason. We are called to share with other people the joy of our relationship with him.

We have looked at Jesus as the way and truth of prayer. We now turn to look at him as the life of prayer.

Unlike the other three gospels, John tells us very little about the way in which Jesus prayed. In the other gospels Jesus talked about some of the characteristics of true prayer, often by using parables. Prayer should be made persistently, like the man who kept knocking on his friend's door at night until he got up to give him bread. It should be humble and not proud, like the tax-man who prayed for God's mercy in the temple. Jesus also said that prayer should be marked by an awareness of what was happening, and by trust and expectancy.

In John's gospel, the emphasis is different. Jesus tells us about prayer simply by being the Son of God. When Jesus told his disciples, "I am the way and the truth and the life," he was assuring us that he is prayer, made before the Father. We have already seen that prayer means to live in Jesus as God's Son, sharing in his trust of the Father. What is true of the life of Jesus should also be true in our experience of prayer.

Jesus' life was marked by hiddenness. It was not that he was ashamed of his mission. He lived the life of a spy hidden behind enemy lines, preparing for the invasion of the kingdom of God, which would happen at his death and resurrection. Jesus remained hidden because what he had come to do was so against human nature that he was always open to misunderstanding. On a number of occasions in John's gospel, Jesus literally hid himself: "When he had finished speaking, Jesus left and hid himself from them."

If we take prayer seriously and begin to identify ourselves with the life of Jesus, then we must expect that a large part of our life will be lived incognito. We cannot expect to live with secret desires for public recognition. The extraverted life of showbiz is not what Jesus came to bring us! Instead, we should be prepared to spend time in what the Puritans called "closet-prayer" with God. As Jesus said:

> When you pray, go into your room, close the door and
> pray to your Father, who is unseen. Then your Father, who
> sees what is done in secret, will reward you. (Matt. 6:6)

This secret life with God is an important hallmark of prayer. Accepting identity with Jesus has a reverse side. It means rejecting identity gained by the approval of the crowd.

Jesus spent many hidden, silent years in Nazareth—an obscure town, not noted for anything significant. When one of his disciples first heard where he came from, he asked, "Can anything good come out of Nazareth?" Those years spent in Nazareth have come to symbolize an obscure, monotonous life, lived out faithfully. It was confidently stated that no prophet could ever come out of Galilee, and Jesus' own brothers rejected him as mad when he started his work. Cold shouldered by them, Jesus was left out of their world. He lived without the facilities to study, so that the Pharisees were surprised by his teaching: "How is it that this man has learning when he has never studied?" Jesus' life was clearly a hidden life, almost wholly misunderstood.

The secret life of prayer is also hidden from those who consider themselves to be wise or to have "made it" in the world. The mysteries of God are only revealed to those with simple, accepting hearts, and who have spiritual understanding. Jesus once prayed:

> I praise you, Father, Lord of heaven and earth, because
> you have hidden these things from the wise and learned,
> and revealed them to little children. Yes, Father, for this
> was your good pleasure.

THE LIFE OF DEPENDENCE

Prayer cannot flourish without hiddenness, but it is also paralyzed without dependence. The modern spirit of autonomy, of self-rule, is completely alien to the life of prayer. John's gospel is striking for its picture of Jesus' dependence on his Father for everything.

There are two important ways in which Jesus depended on the Father. Both can teach us about our dependence in prayer. He depended on his Father for power:

> The Son can do nothing by himself; he can do only what he sees his Father doing. (John 5:19)

In the other three gospels, there are many mentions of Jesus praying before critical points in his life, or when he was preparing to work a miracle. John's gospel takes this a stage further by showing Jesus' miracles as signs that point to his identity as the Son of God. The signs were evidence that the Father was working through him.

Prayer puts us into a dependent relationship with God, especially in giving us the energy we need for life. If we operate from our own natural energies, we can actually work against ourselves and experience what has come to be known as "burn-out." We need to depend on God in prayer for our strength, in the same way that Jesus did. We will then be able to say, as Jesus said, that what we do is not our work, but his work through us.

Jesus also depended on his Father for guidance. Sometimes we long to know what God wants us to do when we reach a point of chronic indecision. The guidance that Jesus received was very different. His whole life was a life guided by God. He was single-minded in pursuing God's will for the whole of his life, rather than just for the important decisions. John's first letter calls this radically different approach of Jesus, "walking in the light." We might crave magical signs from above, but Jesus insisted that guidance was a matter of living our whole lives in God's light. As Jesus told his disciples:

> Walk while you have the light, before darkness overtakes you. The man who walks in the dark does not know where he is going. (John 12:35)

Jesus depended on his Father in a rich, deep, continuous

relationship. His approach is a world away from our tendency to "say our prayers" at times of trouble. Jesus' relationship, like the best of our relationships, was permanent and sustained. He did not even have frequent times of prayer, but a way of life with God. Praying in his name means to be drawn into the same dependent relationship with God the Father.

THE LIFE OF HUMILITY

Even in our limited experience of God, we already know that we can only be humble in his presence. But we also need to live our whole lives in humility before him. Humility is the indispensable foundation for a life of true prayer. In this, as in all the other aspects of prayer, we follow the example of Jesus' life. Paul wrote about Jesus' amazing humility, using the words of an ancient hymn:

> He made himself nothing,
> taking the very nature of a servant,
> being made in human likeness.
>
> And being found in appearance as a man,
> he humbled himself
> and became obedient to death—
> even death on a cross.

Paul prefaces these striking words by calling on his readers to have exactly the same attitude themselves. Humility does not come to us easily; we need the help of Jesus himself to change. Two stories from John's gospel show us this need.

Nicodemus, whose story appears in John chapter 3, was a religious leader who had arrived at the top. He came to see Jesus by night, suggesting that it was beneath his dignity to be seen talking with him by day. Like many people, he thought that his knowledge about religion was all-important, instead of seeing that he needed a true relationship with God. With the pride of a man in charge, he was shocked by Jesus' replies to him. Jesus told him:

> I tell you the truth, unless a man is born again, he cannot see the kingdom of God.

Nicodemus responded with a sarcastic comment, which shows us how threatened he was:

> How can a man be born when he is old? Surely he cannot enter a second time into his mother's womb to be born!

What Jesus said was a fearful challenge to our fallen humanity. The possibility of a radical change of temperament and personality is painful. Think of the personal shame, the professional inconveniences, and the emotional obstacles of being so exposed. Our masks of personality would have to go forever. Yet this is the depth of humiliation demanded of us all.

The second story is about a Samaritan woman who met Jesus while she was drawing water at a well. Her story is in John chapter 4. When Jesus asked her for water, she proudly mocked him, a Jew, for asking her, a Samaritan, for a drink. The two races were in conflict. Jesus then told her that really she should ask him for living water. The woman adopted the same sarcastic tone as Nicodemus:

> You have nothing to draw with and the well is deep. Where can you get this living water?

Jesus gradually broke down her pride by revealing to her that he knew she had been married five times. She eventually brought all her friends to meet him.

The poet William Blake tells us that "we are put on earth for a little space that we may learn to bear the beams of light." Thankfully, they are also beams of love that shine within us, helping us to explore the abyss of our own nothingness, to remove the masks of our self-deception and the wasteland of our solitariness. This can only happen for us when we have determined in humility to make our lives a life of prayer.

Come, my Way, my Truth, my Life;
Such a Way as gives us breath:
Such a Truth as ends all strife:
Such a Life as killeth death.

Come, my Light, my Feast, my Strength:
Such a Light, as shows a feast:
Such a Feast, as mends in length:
Such a Strength, as makes his guest.

Come, my Joy, my Love, my Heart:
Such a Joy, as none can move:
Such a Love, as none can part:
Such a Heart, as joys in love.
        —George Herbert

9

THE DEEPENING FRIENDSHIP OF FATHER AND SON

*The discussion of prayer is so great that it requires the Father
to reveal it, his firstborn Word to teach it, and the Spirit to enable
us to think and speak rightly of so great a subject.*

—Origen

*I am convinced that when a Christian rightly prays the Lord's Prayer
at any time ... his praying is more than adequate.*

—Martin Luther

The fatherhood of God is challenged today by a growing number of feminists. Feminist Christians call on the church to cease praying "Our Father ..." because, they claim, it implies that God is male. How can we face this issue for ourselves?

On one hand, we could easily be sidetracked from praying at all simply because we are too busy thinking through the issues. At the other extreme, we could ignore the issues altogether and get on with praying to God as "Father." Both these extremes are unhelpful. There are many women and men who are caught between radical feminism and indifferent conservatism, with very little to guide their thinking or their praying. Just as our temperaments and personalities need to be transformed by a life of prayer, our minds too, chauvinist or feminist, need transformation.

The Fatherhood of God in a Fatherless Society

The Old Testament does not often talk about God as Father. It has been argued that there are good reasons for this. Many of the pagan religions of the ancient Near East called their gods "father," and said that human beings were their offspring. This view is in marked contrast to the Old Testament faith. On the few occasions where God is called "Father" in the Old Testament, it is clear that he was Israel's Father only because he had chosen the nation to be his son. Also, the prophets saw Israel as God's unworthy, rebellious son because the people constantly turned away from true faith in him. One of the prophets, Hosea, even went so far as to say that God told Israel "you are not my son," and "you are not my people."

The New Testament paints a far more positive picture of God's fatherhood. Jesus constantly talked about God as Father, and this teaching is consistently highlighted throughout the New Testament writings. Not only was God the Father of Jesus in an exclusive sense, but the privilege of sonship is extended to all those who are part of the kingdom of God. The call to rewrite the New Testament to remove its teaching about God's fatherhood is therefore a profoundly serious threat that cannot be ignored.

The Wounds of Fatherlessness

Fatherlessness is a strong feature of modern life, hardly noticed until this century. The novelist Franz Kafka wrote in his angry *Letter to My Father:*

> I was a mere nothing to you ... in front of you I lost my self-confidence and exchanged it for an infinite sense of guilt.

In his novel *The Castle*, Kafka describes this fatherlessness as the intense experience of having an absentee landlord, never visible, never trusted.

The way in which children see their parents deeply affects their understanding of God. George Bernard Shaw described his father as a "stuck man"—an unsuccessful gardener who escaped to play cricket in the afternoons and to drink in the evenings. Meanwhile, his mother was "a distressed and overworked little woman." Shaw said that "she realized more and more acutely as the years dragged on, without material alleviation, that our Father and Lord on whom, to begin with, she had perhaps counted unduly, was also playing perhaps at his sort of cricket in some remote quarter of the starry universe." Because of this view of God, Shaw decided to forget him as completely as he forgot his father.

The Danish philosopher Søren Kierkegaard also inherited a distorted image of God from his father. His father deflected so much real and imaginary guilt onto his son that Kierkegaard's own understanding of God was permanently guilt-ridden. He once said, "To pray to God is to feel guilty."

The English author Edmund Gosse, in his autobiography, *Father and Son,* tells us how as a child he watched his father pray:

> My father prayed in private in what I may almost call a spirit of violence. He entreated for spiritual guidance with nothing less than importunity. It might be said he stormed the citadels of God's grace, refusing to be baffled, urging his intercessions without mercy upon a Deity who sometimes struck me as inattentive to his prayers or wearied by them.

Gosse naturally reacted "against any religion in a violent form." He protested that it could never be seen as "a wholesome or valuable or desirable adjunct to human life," but rather as "harsh and void and negative." Tragically, many sons and daughters have reacted against their parents' God with bitterness and cynicism.

These reactions are natural to fallen humankind, and have happened for centuries. One ancient proverb, circulating in Israel over twenty-five hundred years ago, expressed the same idea:

> The fathers eat sour grapes, and the children's teeth are set on edge. (Ezek. 18:2)

This proverb is quoted by the prophet Ezekiel (18:3–4), who also records God's response:

> As surely as I live, declares the Sovereign LORD, you will no longer quote this proverb in Israel. For every living soul belongs to me, the father as well as the son—both alike belong to me. The soul who sins is the one who will die.

An earlier prophet, Jeremiah, also affirmed this principle of personal accountability for one's own life:

> Everyone will die for his own sin; whoever eats sour grapes—his own teeth will be set on edge. (31:30)

Clearly, we all have to make our own moral choices and personally vouch for them, in spite of our fathers. Our rebellion against God and our lack of prayer are our own responsibility before God. As someone has dryly pointed out, "If my parenting is responsible for 90 percent of my character and my life-choices, that means I must be only 10 percent alive!" To use New Testament language, it means that we are still "dead in our sins."

Modern feminism challenges us to realize that God is not the god of our fathers, a human projection into the sky. This is the reversal of God's creation, where he created humankind in his image and likeness, before sin entered the world to spoil that image in us. The biblical symbol of God's fatherhood is not a reflection of the patriarchal society of the ancient world. God's fatherhood is not based on the absentee American or Australian father, nor the rigid German father, the fiery Italian father, the formal, cold English father, the African father, nor indeed any other human model. God is above and beyond all imperfect human fathers.

God is a not a father in the human sense. He is a creator, not a procreator. He is God and not a man. As the Father of Israel and the Father of Jesus Christ he is not male or female—he encompasses and transcends both human sexes. In the Bible, God is never seen as a male figure. We can never load the symbolism of his fatherhood with uniquely male characteristics. The Bible balances any tendency men may have had to see God as male by stressing his motherly qualities. One of the psalms says:

> I have stilled and quieted my soul;
> like a weaned child with its mother,
> like a weaned child is my soul within me. (131:2)

The prophet Isaiah compares God to the constancy of a mother's love:

> Can a mother forget the baby at her breast and have no
> compassion on the child she has borne? Though she
> may forget, I will not forget you! (49:15)

These images of the character of God were never intended to be used as a compensatory argument for feminism. So it is clearer to say that we should give zero consent to the human figure of father, before we dare to invoke God as Father. For in addressing God as "holy Father," Jesus revealed a unique reality of deity that transcends all human projections of fatherhood. Literally, he is "Father"—beyond any human fatherhood. This term distills the essence of Christian faith. To say "holy Father" is to acknowledge "the buck stops here," cosmically and eternally. The Father is the ultimate source and authority behind all the powers that be—the originator of all creation, the love beyond all loving.

Much of the modern confusion and hostility toward fatherhood arose out of Sigmund Freud's book *Moses and Monotheism.*

This book introduced the idea of the "Oedipus complex." Freud speculated that the whole idea of morality arose out of an inner guilt over the desire to murder our father so that we could have our mother to ourselves. This inner guilt, Freud argued, generates the source of authority and conscience. So the death of Moses at the hands of his own people generated the powerful Israelite morality, summed up in the Ten Commandments. And the death of Jesus did exactly the same thing for his followers.

Freud's theories released an anti-father and an anti-parent movement, with the destructive effects that we see in modern family life. His theories legitimized the darkest feelings in the human psyche—rivalry, rebellion, and hatred—between parents and children, men and women, husbands and wives. Everyone began to claim their rights in a godless world.

These elements of war between the sexes and between the generations are completely absent from the New Testament. The passage that stands out most strongly against these raging feelings was written by the apostle Paul in his letter to the Christians in the Greek town of Philippi. In the same ancient hymn quoted in the previous chapter, Paul writes:

> Who, being in very nature God, did not consider equality with God something to be grasped, but made himself nothing, taking the very nature of a servant, being made in human likeness. And being found in appearance as a man, he humbled himself and became obedient to death—even death on a cross!
>
> Therefore God exalted him to the highest place and gave him the name that is above every name. (2:6–9)

There was no rivalry between Jesus and God the Father. He submitted himself to what his Father wanted him to do. Jesus revealed God the Father's character of love, rather than human fallenness and sin. The relationship of the Father and the Son was whole and complete, which speaks volumes to a world of broken relationships between children and parents.

LIVING IN A SCHIZOPHRENIC SOCIETY

Before we refocus on the biblical revelation of God as our Father, we need to explore further the despair of the modern world. The Russian philosopher Nicholas Berdyaev has sensitively described the isolation of his own childhood:

> My inner life has the likeness of a desert, a bare waste-land ... The happy moments of life have continually escaped my grasp. I was an absentee even when present in life ... I frequently thought in this connection of the feudal lord sitting in his castle with the draw-bridge up and shooting at everyone who attacked him ... This nonacceptance of the world may have been my first metaphysical cry at being born into it.

This description is reminiscent of the experience of many modern novelists and philosophers, and of countless ordinary people who cry out against the schizophrenia of modern life. Our alienation from God has led to an alienation within ourselves and within society. The biochemical breakdown that characterizes schizophrenics is symbolic of the deficiencies we all suffer as part of the human race.

These deficiencies can be summed up in this way: We lack identity. Because we are not called by God and we do not know ourselves as God knows us, our own identity mocks us in uncertainty. This leads to unstable relationships and actions. The New Testament implies that the double-minded man is unstable in all he does (James 1:8).

We also lack a fundamental certainty about life itself. We become prey to many fears: loneliness, being trapped by fate, meaninglessness, or the deep darkness within ourselves. We lack reality. When we are so unsure about ourselves, we find it difficult to distinguish between fantasy and reality. We begin to worship things instead of God. We lack community, and become isolated from the love and understanding of others around us.

Finally, we lack redemption and hope. We experience the mockery of being a person, made for relationships, and yet being alienated from others. There seems to be no way to reverse the forces that seem to be pushing us on to the end of life. Anger, cynicism, and despair fill the whole horizon.

This bleak description of a parentless society matches a description given by the apostle Paul in the New Testament. He described such people as being "without hope and without God in the world" (Eph. 2:12). We are adrift without the God and Father of Jesus Christ. We live in moral chaos—with disaster and death looming ahead of us, without God's presence.

I will never forget my first impression of the Sahara Desert, which I saw from an oasis in southern Algeria in the early 1950s. Outside the small oasis, the emptiness and vastness of the desert overwhelmed me. The sand was never still, but was constantly drifting before the wind. There was only one redeeming element in that whole landscape—a great slab of mountain, thrust up by geological forces. On its shadow side, the oasis had formed. The mountain provided shelter from the sun and from the drifting sands, and springs burst from the base of the rock to irrigate the oasis gardens. The rock was literally the *raison d'être* of the oasis, providing stability and life. This pattern is repeated many times in the Sahara. Wherever there is rock near surface water, oases are able to grow.

Our parenting is like that rock in the desert. It gives us identity, shelter, legitimacy, assurance, and hope. Without parenting, the sands of our drifting emotions would never be stabilized, and we would never know the fertile effects of love. We all need "rocks" to shelter us and to provide the water of life. Psalm 89:26 use exactly this imagery in describing God:

> You are my Father, my God, and the Rock of my
> salvation.

God is the one fixed point in the middle of drifting morality, the one green spot in the desert of spiritual barrenness.

Without God, we live in the wasteland of boredom and non-commitment to each other. We have no motivation to love and no sense of direction. The poet T. S. Eliot reminds us, as we watch faces in the street or commuters in rush-hour traffic:

> The desert is not to be found in southern climes, but in the tube-train, in the neighbour next to you.

THE FATHERHOOD OF GOD

The good news of Jesus Christ is that we can turn from the despair of our alienated society to discover God as our own Father. However, before we can do this, we need to realize that God's fatherhood should never be confused with the woundedness of our human relationships. As one young woman said to me:

> I have had it drilled into my head that if someone says they love me, I must believe it, even when I can't actually see much evidence of that love. My relationship with my parents illustrates this. They are good people, who have provided for my physical needs. Although they don't actually say they love me, nor hug me closely, I have to believe that they love me. With friends, my experience again is that they tell me they care, but I still see little evidence of that care. So I come to God without seriously believing that he can or will give me the kind of emotional support and the experience of being loved that I long to be able to rest in. My temptation is to suppose that my need has to be a mighty big one before God will be bothered with me.

This woman still depends on the god of her fathers, rather than truly experiencing the reality of God, the Father of Jesus. This is where St. John of the Cross and other Christian mystics have seen clearly that we need to go through what has been called "the dark night of the soul" in order to discover God. We need to be stripped and cleansed of mere emotional experiences of prayer. This is because it is not our own spirit that determines how we relate to God, but God's Spirit.

What does God's fatherhood mean for us? The Bible reveals a number of dimensions of God as Father. In his letter to the Romans Paul writes that God's Spirit enables us to recognize God as our Father for the first time:

> You did not receive a spirit that makes you a slave again
> to fear, but you received the Spirit of sonship. And by
> him we cry, "Abba, Father." (8:15)

One of the Old Testament prophets, Jeremiah, expressed the same insight when he spoke on behalf of God to God's rebellious people:

> I thought you would call me "Father" and not turn away
> from following me. (3:19)

The problem is that like the Israelites we too are rebellious people. We can only discover God as our Father through what Jesus has done. God's fatherhood is open to everyone who turns from that rebellion toward Jesus.

The New Testament use of the Aramaic word Abba for "Father" tells us a great deal about God's fatherhood. This was the word used by very young children when addressing their "daddy." It is an intimate, personal word used between a child and its father. The use of Abba has no parallel in all religious prayers, including the prayers of the Jewish faith, because it grows out of Jesus' own relationship with God as his Father, in the mystery of the Holy Trinity. Abba expresses Jesus' unique relationship with God, as the unique Son of God.

The biblical God is a Trinity of three persons in one God. Each person in the Trinity—the Father, the Son, and the Holy Spirit—is distinct from the others, and yet they live in harmony. In his very being, God expresses a dynamic relationship where love is eternally given and received. The Father loves the Son. The Son receives the love of his Father. The Holy Spirit shares the love of the Father and the Son, making their presence real to us. Our competitive relationships are replaced by the interrelation of the Holy Trinity. (We will be looking at this in greater depth in the next chapter.)

A final aspect of God as Father is that he is the Father who acts for us. Unlike the absentee fathers we may have known, God is present with his people and works to save them. This picture of God as the active Father is grounded firmly in the Old Testament. He brought his people out of slavery in Egypt. And in the New Testament he sent his only Son to save us from slavery to sin and to ourselves.

Through the work of Jesus in dying for us, we are adopted as "children of God." All the effects of sin in our lives are put into reverse. God calls us, giving us a new identity in him. We are renewed in the image and likeness of God, we become part of the family of God, with all that this means for our relationships. And we are given the hope of an eternal inheritance. It is as if all the schizophrenic traits of alienated humankind, fatherless and fallen, are responded to by the Father. Paul expressed this wholeness of God's fatherhood toward us in his great hymn of praise in Ephesians:

> Praise be to the God and Father of our Lord Jesus Christ,
> who has blessed us in the heavenly realms with every
> spiritual blessing in Christ. (1:3)

A New Way of Praying to the Father

Jesus made it clear to his disciples that this dynamic relationship between himself and his Father was to be shared with them, too. His Father was also their Father. This is the true gift of prayer.

We can imagine something of how Jesus told this to his followers. As godly Jews, they attended the synagogue regularly each day—at dawn, at 3:00 p.m., and at sunset—listening and worshipping in the ceremonial prayers. The disciples knew that John the Baptist had taught his disciples a particular prayer in which they expressed their discipleship to John. They had seen how Jesus prayed—not just in the synagogue, but out on the hills at night, and among the crowds by day. So one disciple, after watching Jesus praying, asked him why he had not given them a prayer.

Jesus responded by teaching them the prayer that is the signature of his discipleship. We know this prayer as "the Lord's Prayer." The early church took the prayer very seriously. Only baptismal candidates were taught the prayer, which was kept secret from the outside world. The prayer therefore became a mark of their new commitment to the Christian faith and the Christian community. This practice was the opposite of what happens in many churches today, where the prayer has become a formality, repeated automatically instead of with understanding of its meaning. The Lord's Prayer should in fact bind believers together in the love of God, the grace of Jesus, and the companionship of the Holy Spirit, in ever-deepening and ever-enlarging horizons.

The Lord's Prayer, as it appears in Matthew's gospel, clearly grew out of Jewish roots. Its opening, "Our Father in heaven," rings with the sound of a Jewish congregation at worship in the synagogue. But the prayer also contains elements that were not present in Judaism.

First, there is the astonishing reality of speaking to God personally as Abba. Then there is the idea that prayer is no longer something to be done in a synagogue. Jesus said,

> Go into your room, close the door and pray to your
> Father, who is unseen. (Matt. 6:6)

This secret, personal side to prayer was also new. Jesus was clearly opening up a whole new world of prayer that was not possible before he came. His relationship with God opened a new way for all people to relate to God—as their Father.

The Lord's Prayer symbolizes how we learn about being a child, relating to the Father through his Son, Jesus Christ. The six prayers within the Lord's Prayer show us that by knowing the Father we also learn the basic needs of our humanity from him.

OUR FATHER IN HEAVEN:
THE INTIMACY OF THE FATHER

This opening prayer tells us about the intimacy of the Father. Intimacy is the expression of true prayer, as we have seen. It is based upon God's initiative in calling us from our brokenness to be with him. We dare to call God Abba. For Jesus, this was the heart of the message he had come to bring. He once said to the disciples:

> No one knows the Son except the Father, and no one knows the Father except the Son and those to whom the Son chooses to reveal him. (Matt. 11:27)

Only Jesus can help us to know the Father. Once we know him, then our knowledge and our love for him grows. One of the early Christian writers, Ignatius of Antioch, said that once we have the possibility of knowing God, it is like the trickle of water heard as a refreshing murmur in the desert that says, "Come to the Father, come to the Father...." This invitation is echoed throughout the Gospels.

This intimacy can only be shared, which is why we pray "our Father." No child of God can live in isolation, even though we need the solitude of our hearts to make room for God's presence. It is this inner solitude that makes it possible to relate to other people. We cannot afford to live in community if we do not draw our resources from the Father in solitude. The same works in reverse. We cannot be in solitude with the Father unless we enjoy and share the life of community. "Our Father" demands both dimensions to our lives.

This intimacy with God is also about the life of heaven. To turn to the Father, we also turn toward heaven, the place where he lives. We turn away from the attitudes and values of the modern world to God, shedding our earthly ambitions and desires. In fact, once we begin to pray to "our Father in heaven," we become exiles on earth. Adopted by the Father as spiritual children, we can no longer give shelter to impure motives and fleshly lusts.

Hallowed Be Your Name: The Holy Father

The whole spirit of prayer is determined by the holiness of the Father. But how can we "hallow" (or "make holy") God's name? A name is intended to be symbolic of the whole character of the person whose name it is. We hallow God's name when we recognize the character of the Father, as shown us by Jesus. We certainly do not hallow it if we project our own prejudiced views onto God—whether they are racist, sexist, or reflect the way in which we see our earthly fathers. When this happens, we only reveal how little we know of God's true character.

But what does this word "holy" mean? As a holy God, the Father is "wholly other," as the Christian thinker Karl Barth put it. The Old Testament expresses this by saying "[his] thoughts are not [our] thoughts, neither are [our] ways [his] ways" (Isa. 55:8). The prophet Isaiah received a glorious vision of God in his holiness, recorded for us in the sixth chapter of his prophecy. He saw the Lord in the Jerusalem Temple, with his coronation robes filling the entire building, attended by angelic beings, the seraphim, who called out to one another: "Holy, holy, holy is the Lord Almighty; the whole earth is full of his glory" (Isa. 6:3).

Isaiah was dismayed by the vision because he realized at once his own sinfulness in God's presence. His sin was cleansed by a symbolic coal taken from the altar, where a sacrifice had been made. An angel touched the coal on Isaiah's lips and he was made clean. In the same way, we too approach this holy God through a sacrifice—the sacrifice made by Jesus, dying on the cross. As our own sin is cleansed, we can offer God the sacrifice of praise as we hallow his name. As we do this, our lives are reorientated to live for God. The way in which we live and relate to other people begins to reflect the character of the Father's holiness.

YOUR KINGDOM COME: THE FATHER'S KINGSHIP

Jesus once said, "the kingdom of God is within you" (Luke 17:21). To pray for the coming of God's kingdom means to accept his rule for ourselves. Such prayer brings the rule of the Father into the very texture of our persons. We are no longer possessed by our natural temperament and personality, but are instead completely possessed by the Father, just as Jesus was. Jesus spoke about this:

> If anyone loves me, he will obey my teaching. My Father
> will love him, and we will come to him and make our
> home with him. (John 14:23)

In practice this means altering our thoughts and feelings so that they focus on God. We order our whole being for the Father's rule, so that we can become like Jesus in the way we live. Paul wrote, "Do not let sin reign in your mortal body so that you obey its evil desires" (Rom. 6:12). The kingdom of sin cannot coexist with the kingdom of God, just as light cannot exist alongside darkness.

Because the door of prayer is also the door into our hearts, we need to pray this prayer constantly. "Your kingdom come" becomes the prayer: "Come into my heart, into the core of my being." It is this prayer that overcomes our alienation and despair, our loss of assurance and our need for his power to overcome the world inside us. We pray this prayer, in the words of Paul, "without ceasing." So we become permanently conscious of the Father's rule over us.

Your Will Be Done on Earth as It Is in Heaven: The Will of the Father

The Bible tells us that God is surrounded by an army of angels who willingly obey him. As God's will is carried out in heaven, we are called on to mirror this willing response on earth. We pray that our small desires for God will flow like streams, emptying into a vast Amazon and the ocean beyond, into the unimaginable purposes of God. Like the ocean, God's will is secret and unpredictable, because God is God. He answers to no one. But like the stream, God's will is also revealed to us by his Spirit. Once we have begun to relate to God, the Holy Spirit opens our eyes to understand things about God that were completely closed to us before.

With his Spirit and the Bible to guide us, we can pray knowing something of what God intends. John's letter expresses it in this way:

> If we ask anything according to his will, he hears us.
> And if we know that he hears us—whatever we ask—we
> know that we have what we asked of him.
> (1 John 5:14–15)

This is a vital principle of prayer. As we seek to do what the Father wants, we encounter his Spirit praying on our behalf that we will know what God's will is, through our own prayers.

Some people might fear that this prayer is an invitation for God to destroy our own selves. However, this part of the Lord's Prayer follows on from the previous part: "Your kingdom come." By praying these two parts together, we are saying, in a paraphrase of the words of Psalm 73:25 (NASB):

> Whom have I in heaven but you?
> And being with you, I desire nothing on earth.

When God's kingdom is embedded in our hearts, we will

want nothing else but God's will. This prayer looks forward in time to when God will fully bring his kingdom and his will upon earth. The comparison of God's kingdom on earth now to how it will be then is exactly like the difference between the tiny stream and the vast ocean. We pray that God's will should be done on earth one day as it is done now in heaven. God's will is the sole reality of heaven. But on earth, it is still disputed and denied. Prayer is therefore to anticipate the time when God will remove all the human contradictions on earth.

GIVE US TODAY OUR DAILY BREAD: THE FATHER AS PROVIDER

The Lord's Prayer up to this point opens our hearts to God, freeing us from being constricted by anxiety. This part of the prayer now tackles our basic anxiety head on. On the same occasion that Jesus taught his disciples this prayer, he also told them, "Do not be anxious about tomorrow" (Matt. 6:34 ESV). To belong to God's kingdom means losing a legion of anxieties: what clothes we wear, what we do with our outer appearance to make us more attractive, even what height we try to give ourselves! Instead, prayer helps us to keep our whole lives in proportion. Prayer is more realistic, not less, than our anxieties.

Jesus told his followers that they should go into a room to pray, shutting the door behind them. Some people have suggested that this door was the pantry door. If this is true, then to go in and pray was actually to go into the storehouse to see what was there. If it was empty, then they should indeed pray for daily bread. If it was full, then they should remember Jesus' own hunger in the wilderness and how he refused to turn stones into bread because it was more important to do the will of God. We should remember that it is prayer that rules our hearts and not food that rules our stomachs.

Our ruling passions need to become trust and dependence

on God for our daily needs. When this is true for us, then we can pray the words of an Old Testament proverb:

> Give me neither poverty nor riches,
> but give me only my daily bread.
> Otherwise, I may have too much and disown you
> and say, "Who is the Lord?"
> Or I may become poor and steal,
> and so dishonor the name of my God. (30:8–9)

A different translation of this part of the Lord's Prayer reads: "Give me today the bread of tomorrow." This would be a prayer for eternal life, the bread of tomorrow that we can enjoy now today. Our life with God in the future spills back over into the present, enabling us to enjoy a foretaste of the joy and glory to come. So while we eat and drink today, we pray that we may also be aware of God's presence with us now, and for our future hope too.

In the daily, simple needs of life, we should live as people who belong to God's kingdom, seeing life for all its significance. This is exactly how Jesus himself lived:

> Look at the birds of the air; they do not sow or reap or store
> away in barns, and yet your heavenly Father feeds them.
> Are you not much more valuable than they? (Matt. 6:26)

Every time we sit down to eat with prayerful thanks, the kingdom of human needs is merged into the kingdom of God's ultimate purposes.

FORGIVE US OUR DEBTS AS WE ALSO HAVE FORGIVEN OUR DEBTORS: THE FORGIVENESS OF THE FATHER

The prayer about daily bread is about our physical needs. This prayer refers to the reality that we are persons living in relationship to other persons. It is in the nature of persons that we make claims on each other. We can never fulfill all the claims made upon us, or see all our own claims on others fulfilled. God too has claims on us, and it is these that we most often fail to meet. In failing to reply to all our letters in time; in failing to complete what we have agreed to do; in simply not being sensitive enough to the feelings of others—let alone fulfilling those desires others may have secretly had about us—we can only ask God for forgiveness. This spirit of humility is most clearly shown in one of Jesus' parables, in which a guilty taxman creeps into the temple and simply prays, "God, be merciful to me, a sinner."

There is a strong connection in this prayer between receiving God's forgiveness and in forgiving others for the wrong they have done to us. Without God's help, we find it impossible to forgive other people. As I struggle to forgive someone else, which I cannot do, I am forcibly reminded that I have so much more to be forgiven by God. As I realize how much God has forgiven me, I am also given the spirit to forgive the other person.

If I nurse bitterness and unforgiveness toward another person, it only demonstrates to myself that I have not truly experienced the reality of God's forgiveness at all. And if I am unwilling to forgive another person, then I cannot expect God to forgive me. God would never support such a contradiction in my heart, and nor does he help us in our sinning.

This fundamental experience of forgiving to be forgiven tells us about our character as persons. We are relational beings. God has not created us simply for ourselves alone. Selfishness and the inward curvature of pride and narcissism are anti-creational. The modern cult of self-fulfillment actually destroys our selves. Instead, we are healed by healing others; we receive by giving; we are loved by loving. The popular "Peace Prayer" (which was not written by Francis of Assisi, but which reflects his spirit) captures this principle perfectly:

Lord, make me an instrument of your peace:

Where there is hatred, let me sow love;

Where there is discord, harmony;

Where there is injury, pardon;

Where there is error, truth;

Where there is doubt, faith;

Where there is despair, hope;

Where there is darkness, light;

Where there is sadness, joy.

O Divine Master, Grant that I may not so much seek

To be consoled, as to console;

To be understood, as to understand;

For it is in dying that we receive;

It is in forgetting self that we find ourselves;

It is in pardoning that we are pardoned;

It is in giving that we are born to eternal life.

The healing we give to other persons in turn heals our own persons. In the same way, we destroy ourselves when we hold grudges and nurture hidden anger within ourselves. If we withhold from others what God does not withhold from us, we will damn ourselves.

Jesus told a story to illustrate this. He described a servant who had been forgiven a vast debt by his master, only to go out and have someone who owed him a small sum of money thrown into prison. When the master heard of it, he had his servant imprisoned for his merciless attitude. Sin makes debtors of us all, but our indebtedness to God dwarfs any debts others owe to us.

Refusing forgiveness will ultimately lose us our personhood unless we are brought back to our senses. This can only happen when we experience the true forgiveness of God and are given the freedom to forgive others. God reveals to us his innermost being.

If we shut ourselves to that life-giving relationship, then we are fools indeed.

And Lead Us Not into Temptation, but Deliver Us from the Evil One: The Deliverance and Protection of the Father

If we are mortal in our physical needs, and personal in our relationships, then as moral agents we are highly temptable. This is why in Matthew 26:41 Jesus warned his disciples to be wise in their praying:

> Watch and pray so that you will not fall into temptation.

Some people are surprised by the sheer magnitude of the temptations they face. But we should not be shocked as we realize the moral responsibilities in our relationship with God. The more we know the friendship of God, the more sensitive we become to the reality of evil and its effect upon us.

Our own version of schizophrenia means that there is usually a great gulf between what we ought to do and what we actually do. But at the same time, the awareness of this brings into sharp focus the fact that we really do desire the Father's kingdom and the Father's will to be done on earth as it is done in heaven. Temptation can therefore be the agent of its own destruction as it brings us a greater realism about God, driving us closer to him for strength. This process can be seen in these two quotations, from Psalms 26 and 139:

> Test me, O Lord, and try me,
> examine my heart and my mind;
> for your love is ever before me,
> and I walk continually in your truth.
>
> Search me, O God, and know my heart;
> test me, and know my anxious thoughts.

See if there is any offensive way in me,
and lead me in the way everlasting.

We are surrounded by the mystery of evil. If chaos had to be overcome by God even in the very act of creation, so intrinsic is its presence in the nature of things, what hope have we to overcome it in our own hearts without praying to the Father for help?

So we cry out to the Father: Lead me through all the evil tendencies of my heart! Help me to overcome the temptations of my temperament. Change inside me the evil tendencies of my own personality as it relates to other people. Protect me from the temptations of my own age group in the phases of life: passionate when young, cynical when middle-aged, self-pitying when old and lonely. Save me from the temptations of our culture, the modern world in which we live. For in all these realms, and above all to my sinful heart, I am seducible.

Satan tempts us to destroy us. The Father tests us to help us grow as persons and to know his will. So this final part of the Lord's Prayer asks for two things. Deliverance from evil is a desperate need, like being rescued out of a lion's mouth. This means being rescued from ourselves, because the Devil is located and expresses himself in the shadow side of our self. We pray for the ultimate destruction of evil as well as for deliverance in the here and now.

However, temptation is also a process of testing by God the Father. His testing helps us to mature through our suffering and temptation. This form of temptation is God's way of bringing us to maturity; showing us how his will is to be done on earth as it is in heaven. From God's point of view, temptation is a necessary experience for us to triumph over, just as it was for Jesus. Seeing temptation in this way shows us that this painful experience is related to the whole of our life and growth as a person.

Temptation is not a solitary experience. This is why we

pray, "Lead us not ..." We suffer temptation alongside Jesus, and alongside all the Christians who have ever struggled with evil. The community of those who are tempted should therefore be the most understanding community, knowing each others' weaknesses and bearing each others' burdens. In its traditional form, there is a short verse of praise to close the Lord's Prayer. The prayer has expressed some desperate needs before the Father, and their answers provoke thanksgiving and worship. Thankfully, we can exclaim: "Yours is the kingdom...." The kingdom does not belong to evil; it is the Father's kingdom. Through the life and death of Jesus, this kingdom has come to earth, like a bridgehead between D-Day and V-Day.

Nothing but the power of God can accomplish all these prayers. This is why we add, "the power and the glory." The power makes possible the glory that is to come.

"Amen" is the final response of the community that lives the life expressed by this prayer. "Amen" literally means "so be it," affirming the truth of what has been said in the three tenses of past, present, and future. To say "amen" means in effect, "it has been so, it truly is so, it shall yet fully be so."

We cannot hope to carry this cosmic obligation by ourselves. Only Jesus Christ can do so. He is the "Amen" who can and will turn the thoughts and hopes of the prayer into reality. The final book of the Bible, the book of Revelation, speaks of Jesus as the "Amen":

> These are the words of the Amen, the faithful and true
> witness, the ruler of God's creation. (3:14)

No wonder Martin Luther could dryly point out that "when a Christian rightly prays the Lord's Prayer at any time ... his praying is more than adequate"!

Dear Father, may your name be hallowed in us. I confess that I have dishonored you, and with pride and the seeking of my personal honor and glory I blaspheme your name. Help me therefore by your grace that I may become nothing; so that you alone and your name and honor may be in me. Amen.

O Father, let me not fall to the doing of my own will. Break my will more and more. Whatever happens, let not my will but yours be done, for so it is in heaven. There is no self-will there. May that also be true on earth. Amen.

Almighty God, grant us the forgiveness of all our sins that we, being full of grace, virtue and good works, may become your kingdom. May we with heart, soul, mind and strength, inwardly and outwardly, submit to all your commands and do your will. Amen.

Father, lead us not into temptation. I do not desire to be free from testings for that would be more terrible than ten temptations. But I pray that I may not fall and sin against my neighbour or you. Amen.

Dear Father, may we be delivered entirely from Satan's dominion. If it please you to leave us longer in this world of misery, grant us your grace, that your realm may begin to be increased in us, while the Devil's dominion is retarded and destroyed. Amen.

Help us, O God, to receive the fulfillment of all our requests. Let us not doubt that you have heard and will hear them; that the answer is certain, not negative nor doubtful. So may we say cheerfully that the outcome is true and certain. Amen.

—A Prayer of Martin Luther

10

FRIENDSHIP
WITHIN THE
HOLY TRINITY

O eternal Trinity! O Godhead! You are a deep sea, into which the deeper I
enter the more I find, and the more I find the more I seek.

—Catherine of Siena

We ended the previous chapter with a meditation on the Lord's Prayer. This prayer is central to the Christian life. From Martin Luther on through John Calvin, the Puritans, the Pietists, and the Reformers all saw clearly that this prayer is the basis for Christian ethics. It teaches and motivates us to learn the practices of the friends of God's kingdom. Can we get any nearer to God than that?

Yes, audacious as it may seem, we can. A hymn writer spoke of "a place of quiet rest, close to the heart of God." This place is found in contemplating another prayer of Jesus, which he made in the Upper Room, the night before he died.

But before we come onto that prayer, we need to consider the important style of praying known as "contemplative prayer." Contemplative prayer means drawing close to God, so that we are in his presence simply to listen, and be drawn close to his love. This is part of the many-sided experience of prayer.

Prayer can be an elusive subject. It is no good approaching prayer as we approach many other aspects of our lives, with a "how to" attitude. This is because prayer is more concerned with a relationship than with using the correct techniques.

Prayer is more a matter of openness, faith, attention, and love in self-abandonment to God. This is how we make progress in prayer. We do not have to enter a monastery to be serious about the contemplative life. If we entrust our very persons to God's own life and love, we can plumb all the depths of prayer in the middle of a busy career, or as a mother with young children, as an unemployed person, or in whatever situation we live in. It is all a question of how we direct our inner lives toward God.

As we saw earlier, William Blake wrote in one of his poems, "We are put on earth for a little space that we may learn to bear the beams of love." This tells us that we have eternal longings that only God can satisfy. Bernard of Clairvaux expressed this in the words of the well-known hymn:

> We taste thee, O thou living bread
> And long to feast upon thee still:
> We drink of thee, the fountainhead
> And thirst our souls from thee to fill.

To walk the contemplative road is to recognize that Christ alone can satisfy our longings; everything else is empty in comparison. Peter once realized this when he said to Jesus, "Lord, to whom shall we go? You have the words of eternal life" (John 6:68). We are eventually convinced that Jesus Christ is truly the way, the truth and the life, as he said he was.

It is only by dying to ourselves and by being brought to new life "in Christ" that our lives are given ultimate satisfaction. "The beams of love" we experience then lead us into an even greater longing for God. Many different Christians have written about this:

When the three-personed Deity dwells within the saints and is known and felt to be present, it is not the fulfillment of desire, but the cause and beginning of a much greater and more fervent desire.

—Symeon the New Theologian

When we have tasted this in the very depth of our souls it makes us sink down and melt away in our nothingness and littleness. The brighter and purer the light shed on us by the greatness of God, the more clearly we see our littleness and nothingness.... For it is the Divine God shining into our very being.

—Johann Tauler

We can draw three conclusions from the contemplative experience of God. First, we are opened to a taste, a desire, a mystery, which introduces us to new perceptions of God. We respond to this experience with our whole being. We may never have experienced the use of mind-expanding drugs, but we can understand the deep desire of people who want to integrate their whole being into something happier and greater than the material dreariness of modern urban life. We can also understand the sense of "flatness" which many Christians, who have a very small sense of God, feel when their activism leaves them stale. Contemplative prayer is for those who are discontented with secondhand descriptions of God, and who want to experience the intimate presence of God for themselves.

Our second conclusion is that we are willing to give up everything of ourselves for this kind of "walk with God." We are willing to change within ourselves, regardless of the cost. We come to see that prayer, rather than being another activity in our lives, is the force that changes everything else in us and about us.

Our third conclusion is to recognize that the mystery of God is like an infinite ocean. He is not in the end approached through our logic or reason, but he is inexpressible, inexhaustible, immeasurable. Despite God's overwhelming nature, we begin to live comfortably with his mystery, making our hearts a space for him to live in, knowing that no space can possibly contain him.

We reach these three conclusions when his love dwells in us, calling us on in pilgrimage and freeing us from everything that slows us down from coming to God. Life can never be boring for the contemplative Christian. The sense of awe, wonder, and thanksgiving will forever fill the worshipper with delight and gratitude.

Despite this, friendship with God has its own terms. It is costly to our egos. It is not something that is cheaply bought. Instead, it contradicts all the false expectations of worldly friendship, so that the apostle John can say that to be friends with the world is to make an enemy of God.

When Jesus told his disciples at the last supper that he was now calling them his friends, and no longer servants, he revealed a relationship that we have largely lost today. This friendship spoken about by Jesus is not performance-oriented; it does not set itself up in leadership; it does not seek "success" or "fame" or any other type of self-focused life, but is happy to be hidden "in Christ." It is willing to live on its own in the desert, so that no other presence may distract us from God's presence, no other love may compete with his love. So what does this friendship with God involve?

AN UNPRETENTIOUS FRIENDSHIP

Even in human friendships it is a relief to "let our hair down" and do together the simple, unpretending things that set us at ease with each other. True friendship does not seek the spotlight, looking for titles, awards and recognition from the outside world. It is not seen in all the right places, and does not go around namedropping at every opportunity. Friendship with

God does not seek or receive the applause of the world. Instead, the friends of God may more often be treated like the person who was sneeringly known as "the friend of sinners." If Jesus risked his own reputation by associating with the despised of his day, he is hardly going to enhance our own egos in knowing "the right people."

Encountering the friendship of Jesus for the first time can be a painful as well as a joyful experience, as we see ourselves in a true light, possibly for the first time ever. When this happened to Peter, he said to Jesus, "Go away from me, Lord; I am a sinful man!" (Luke 5:8). Entering into a personal friendship with God means that we recognize our own sorry state and throw ourselves on God's mercy. This is a humbling experience, but it leads to an honest, unpretentious friendship.

A true friend can never have a hidden motive for being a friend. He can have no hidden agenda. A friend is simply a friend for the sake of friendship. In a much greater way, love for God is love for God's own sake. Bernard of Clairvaux wrote that our natural inclination is to love for our own sake. When we first learn to love God, we still love him for our own sake. As we grow in friendship with God, we come to love him not just for ourselves alone, but also for God's sake. At last, we may reach a point where we love even ourselves for the sake of God.

It was this quality of love that motivated Abraham in the Old Testament to be willing to sacrifice his son Isaac to God. This heightened consciousness of God's love, which makes us willing to sacrifice everything to him, also gives us the willingness to know God and be known by him. It is what the medieval contemplatives called *affectus,* the dominant desire to know and be known by God, regardless of the cost.

True love frees us to be ourselves. This can be hard to accept, because we experience so little of true love in our lives. Perhaps I grew up assuming that my mother loved me completely, only to discover later that there was an element of false motives in her love for me. Perhaps she needed compensatory love from me because my father neglected her. In many different ways we discover things that have gone wrong in all our relationships—with our parents, our friends, our children. We can spend all our lives looking for relationships where love is freely given to us.

Only the love of Jesus Christ truly frees us to be ourselves. Jesus once said, "If the Son sets you free, you will be free indeed" (John 8:36). In his life, Jesus was completely unpossessive, not demanding anything for himself. He was able to say:

> Foxes have holes and birds of the air have nests, but the Son of Man has no place to lay his head. (Luke 9:58)

Because of his unpossessiveness, he alone is the friend who liberates us simply to "be" before him. A contemplative Christian enjoys a measure of self-freedom, finding in Jesus the source of his or her personal significance, security and identity.

A Transforming Trust

With a true friend, we can afford to relax, let down our guard, and allow our friend to see something of our inner life. The Puritans spoke about having "a comfortable walking with God." Our relationship with God allows us to be completely open and honest, because we know that we can trust him not to take advantage of us. We can relax without fear of being exposed, ridiculed, or condemned. We gain a new inner confidence in God that we have never known before. We are known by God and this is infinitely more wonderful than the limits of our knowing. All our human needs—emotional, physical and spiritual—are covered by the trust we now enjoy in God.

We learn to trust God with our inner selves, so that the management, defense, and guidance of our whole lives are in his keeping. Since God knows me better, far more intimately than I can ever know myself, this trust has a transforming effect on my life. The prophet Jeremiah pictured it like this:

> Blessed is the man who trusts in the LORD,
>   whose confidence is in him.
> He will be like a tree planted by the water
>   that sends out its roots by the stream.
> It does not fear when heat comes;
>   its leaves are always green.
> It has no worries in a year of drought
>   and never fails to bear fruit. (17:7–8)

The book of Proverbs tells us that "a friend loves at all times." Jerome, one of the church fathers, wrote in one of his letters:

> A friendship that can cease to be never was a friendship.

Aelred of Rievaulx, the twelfth-century writer, once read the reflections on friendship penned by the classical writer Cicero. Although he found Cicero's ideas noble, he said that they were as "straw" compared with what he had experienced of Christ's friendship. He wrote a beautiful book called *Spiritual Friendship* and came to this conclusion:

> I am convinced that true friendship cannot exist among
> those who live without Christ.

Aelred lived in the royal court in Scotland. He saw that:

> Worldly friendship which is born of a desire for temporal
> advantage or possessions is always full of deceit and
> intrigue; it contains nothing certain, nothing constant,
> nothing secure.

By contrast, the friendship of Jesus Christ is based on his promises to us: "I will never leave you nor forsake you" (Heb. 13:5 ESV). It is a love that lasts forever.

It is remarkable that friendship has been so undervalued by the Christian faith. This may be because we choose our friends selectively, while the gospel calls us to show self-giving love to everyone. Bishop Jeremy Taylor, in one of the rare pieces of writing on spiritual friendship in Christian history, said:

> Christian charity is friendship to all the world; and when
> friendships were the noblest things in the world (that is,
> in the classical world of ancient Greece and Rome), char-
> ity was little, like the sun drawn in at a chink, or his
> beams drawn into the centre of a burning-glass; but
> Christian charity is friendship expanded like the face of
> the sun when it mounts the eastern hills.

The more we share in the love of friendship, the better we are, the greater our friendships are, and the closer we will be to God. Jeremy Taylor advised:

> Let them be as dear, and let them be as perfect, and let
> them be as many, as you can; there is no danger in it;
> only where restraint begins, there begins our imperfection.

Perhaps our understanding of real friendship should be drawn from the mystery of the triune God himself. Of human friendship we sometimes say, "Two's company, three's a crowd." Or we may more cynically add, "Two's friendship, but three's politics." Yet as we explore more deeply into the friendship of God, we discover to our amazement that the eternal character of God's love is that of love given, love received, and love shared. For the love of the Father "begets" the Son; the bye of the Son is that of "the Begotten"; and the love of the Holy Spirit is to share and make the Father and the Son known to us, and realizable within us. To live out our relationships in the light of such a transforming model is radical indeed for mere mortals.

Our contemplation of God, in Christ, through the Holy Spirit, is the heart of our friendship with him. Indeed, it is the primary reason why we are alive in this world. It is there that we "learn to bear the beams of love."

It is in John's gospel that we see most clearly what this

friendship with God involves. John chapter 17 records for us an intensely revealing prayer made by Jesus to his Father in the hours before his arrest and death. This chapter closes by looking at how Jesus prayed to the Father. But before we can look at the prayer of Jesus, we need to ask: how can we prepare ourselves to contemplate this communication between the Son and the Father? How do we learn to share in his love?

To Contemplate Is to Be a Person-in-Christ

Albert Einstein once observed that the single most important question one could ask was, "Is the universe a friendly place?"

The Bible's response is that it is, because behind the universe is a God who loves. Contemplation with God is the celebration of this essential friendliness of the universe. We can see this in action in the Genesis account of how God made human beings:

> Then God said, "Let us make man in our image, in our likeness...."
>
> So God created man in his own image, in the image of God he created him; male and female he created them. (Gen. 1:26–27)

It is no accident that this passage talks about "us" and "our" in referring to God. In the Old Testament this "our" and "us" relate to the Hebrew title "Elohim," which can equally be translated "God" or "the heavenly council." In his vision, Isaiah saw this heavenly council of seraphs gathered around the throne of God. From this perspective God is viewed as eternally surrounded by a divine community. But it is in the New Testament that we see more clearly that God himself is to be described as this "us" and "our," for it is his own intrinsic character that he is Father, Son, and Holy Spirit. From all the Scriptures we learn to recognize how mysteriously and profoundly relationships undergird the whole of reality. God in his own relational being, and surrounded by the angelic beings, is the source of all relationships, human and celestial.

We were not made to be alone. We were made not just for relationships, but to become people "in Christ" relating to God. As we abandon ourselves to God, moment by moment, our significance and identity will be in his hands; they become his responsibility, not ours. For as we reflect on our lives, we begin to recognize that our own uniqueness is something that we do not handle very well. It is difficult to know how to compare myself to other people, although I am constantly tempted to do so. I have no Greenwich mean time from which to travel around the world of people in the quest of my own identity.

This is why I oscillate between pride and anxiety: pride that I am not you (thank goodness!), and anxiety that I am alone with my uniqueness. This quest for ourselves, which is so obvious in the narcissism of our society, makes us jump through all sorts of hoops on the assumption that what we do, what we look like, what we achieve, and what we earn determines who we are.

This scenario is vividly brought to life in the words of John chapter 9, where Jesus gave a blind young man his sight. Three types of people figure in this story. The religious establishment, represented by the Pharisees, cannot accept the evidence of the miracle. In their arrogance of status, they repeatedly use the words "we know" as they cross-examine the young man. They refuse to acknowledge any other interpretation than their own.

Then there are the simple, ordinary people, who had known the young man from birth. They are intimidated by the "experts" and are afraid to give a personal opinion of what has happened. Like the Pharisees, they too have no basis for contemplating who Jesus really is.

The young man himself represents the third group. He not only sees physically, but spiritually too. In the climax of the story, he tells Jesus, "Lord, I believe," and worships him. This is the only way in which we can experience God for ourselves. It is the way described in one of the psalms:

Those who look to him are radiant;

their faces are never covered with shame. (34:5)

One girl had suffered a low self-image since childhood, brought on by eczema. Because of her affliction, she came to hate herself. It was only as she gave herself to Christ, to become a person-in-Christ, that her affliction was changed to become her greatest asset. Through her redeemed suffering she received a new inner beauty, the radiance of the Spirit shining through her.

When we personally meet with God, we leave theories behind us. When we enter into the presence of God and feel the reality of his companionship with us, we leave descriptions behind us. We are invaded and overwhelmed by a reality greater than anything we have known before. Adjectives fail, words become shallow, descriptions cease.

Then we begin to see for ourselves the sheer absurdity of all explanations made from the outside. We see how foolish we were to theorize about what we had not experienced for ourselves in Christ. At the last supper, recorded for us in John chapter 14, the disciples seem to have forgotten all that they had experienced by being with Jesus, and instead wanted to get their theories straight. They became the kind of people who wanted to read the "right books" that would give them the "right instructions" about what to do next. This is a warning to us not to substitute our living relationship with God for the comfort of "how to" books, prayer manuals, or even books of factual knowledge about the faith. All these things are important and have their place, but the most important thing of all is simply to be with Jesus.

So when Thomas anxiously asks Jesus a "how to" question—"How can we know the way?"—Jesus simply responds: "I am the way and the truth and the life." And when Philip asks for solid evidence—"Lord, show us the Father, and that will be enough for us"—Jesus rebukes him by saying, "Don't you know me, Philip? Don't you believe that I am in the Father, and that the Father is in me?" (John 14:5–6). Each time, Jesus leads them back to see that they need to know him, rather than know about him.

Christian meditation is impossible if God is just an idea, an impersonal God with whom we can have no personal contact. We need the personal presence of Jesus to bring us the personal presence of God the Father.

To Contemplate Is to Abide in God

Jesus then led his disciples on by teaching them what it means to live in him. In John chapter 15 he gave the well-known parable of the vine and the branches. This picture was often used in the Old Testament to symbolize Israel's experience of God. But here, Jesus uses it to picture his relationship with the disciples and with his Father:

> I am the true vine and my Father is the gardener.... I am the vine; you are the branches. (John 15:1, 5)

Just as the branch must live in the vine to produce fruit, so Jesus said:

> If you remain in me and my words remain in you, ask whatever you wish, and it will be given you. This is to my Father's glory, that you bear much fruit, showing yourselves to be my disciples. (John 15:7)

In this way Jesus emphasized the relational character of the Christian life. This life originates with the Father, who gives the disciples to his Son. The Son faithfully ensures that they bring forth fruit; fruit that expresses the character of God himself. Paul also showed that this harvest is full of the qualities that can only be found in relationships. He described it in relationship words in Galatians 5:22–23:

> The fruit of the Spirit is love, joy, peace, patience, kindness, goodness, faithfulness, gentleness and self-control.

This emphasis of being "in Christ" as Christ is "in the Father" is consistently expressed in John's gospel. Jesus does not even take the initiative to pick out certain men to make them his disciples. No, it is the Father who gives disciples to the Son, and in response the Son reveals the Father to them.

In the same way, Jesus says he is the good shepherd: "I know my sheep and my sheep know me...." But the basis for this relationship is: "... just as the Father knows me and I know the Father" (John 10:14–15). This imagery vividly tells us that our character as Christians is derived from the very being of God, from the Father and the Son. So when Jesus begins to talk to his disciples at the last supper, the book of John tells us that Jesus knew "he had come from God and was returning to God" (13:3).

We can never share with others the reality and experience of contemplation simply by talking about it, or by giving lessons on how it is done. There is no point in attempting to get other people excited about our special friend if they have never met him. Breathing exercises, yoga positions, and even "interiorizing" one's self will not bring God into existence. We are more likely to bring others into the reality of contemplative prayer when they can see that we have been with Jesus for ourselves. To do this, we have to withdraw from talking and reasoning about contemplation, to witness how Jesus prays to the Father.

This we will now do by looking at John 17.

LISTENING TO THE FATHER THROUGH THE SON

This prayer has been called many things: the High Priestly Prayer, the Prayer of the Departing Redeemer, and other names. The diversity of names may reflect its unique character in the Bible.

The closest analogy to it is the farewell prayers used by some of the Old Testament patriarchs. Just before his death, Jacob gathered his twelve sons around him and blessed each of them. Moses too blessed the twelve tribes of Israel before he died. And so Jesus, in the hours before his death, gathered his disciples around him to express in prayer the character and purposes of his Father.

As we listen in awe to the contemplation of the Son with the Father, we might well respond with the thought of Francis of Assisi:

> We should make a dwelling place within ourselves,
> where he can stay, he who is Father, Son and Holy Spirit.

Only God—not we ourselves—can make this happen, so we listen to the prayer of Jesus.

After speaking to the disciples in the upper room, John tells us:

> After Jesus said this, he looked toward heaven and
> prayed. (John 17:1)

Jesus oriented himself toward the source of supreme authority for his life, and now also for his words of prayer. Just as navigators at sea locate their position by the stars, so Jesus plots his course by the Father. He starts by praying:

> Father, the time has come. (John 17:2)

The climax of Jesus' incarnation, his passion, is now about to be entered. As long as Jesus remained hidden, as a human being, the time was always in the future. But his death on the cross was about to finalize what he had come to do. He prayed:

> Glorify your Son, that your Son may glorify you. For you
> granted him authority over all people that he might give
> eternal life to all those you have given him. (John 17:2)

Jesus, speaking earlier in John's gospel, said, "No one can come to me unless the Father has enabled him" (John 6:65). So all the disciples of Jesus are the gift of the Father. The Father has given authority to us to be adopted as the children of God. This is in Jesus, the source of endless life, which he goes on giving. John 17:3 states,

> Now this is eternal life: that they may know you, the
> only true God, and Jesus Christ, whom you have sent.

Eternal life is to recognize who God is. Our insight, vision, and growing relationship with God is the source of all life for us. This is the true God, for he can be personally known. All else are ideas or idols that have no true existence. Jesus continues,

> I have brought you glory on earth by completing the
> work you gave me to do. (John 17:4)

One of the strongest themes in John's gospel is that Jesus brings glory to the Father by his life and actions. His character as God's Son is to do the things which please the Father. Jesus' death and resurrection will now reveal the Father's glory in the fullest way.

> And now, Father, glorify me in your presence with the
> glory I had with you before the world began. (John 17:5)

In this sentence, Jesus jumps forward in time, across the abyss of being forsaken by God on the cross. He prays that the eternal union he had with God from before the existence of the world will be resumed. And yet it is not simply a resumption of the glory that the Father and the Son had before. Jesus brings a greater glory, because he brings with him many sons and daughters to glory so that they too will enter into the eternal embrace of the Trinity.

WHY JESUS PRAYS FOR HIS DISCIPLES

Jesus had brought the disciples into the community of God's friends. So he now enlarges the circle of his prayer to include them before the Father:

> I have revealed you to those whom you gave me out of
> the world. They were yours; you gave them to me and
> they have obeyed your word. (John 17:6)

The disciples were the gift of the Father to the Son, and in turn the Son showed them the Father. The Father gave them to the Son so that they could learn the relational life of the Trinity. Jesus continues,

> Now they know that everything you have given me
> comes from you. (John 17:7)

The disciples were learning that nothing the Son has is his own. Everything comes from the Father. This includes not only all the gifts we receive from God, but also the Son of God himself, who was "begotten by the Father." The Holy Spirit too was "sent forth from God." It is God's character to give, by his Son and through his Spirit.

> For I gave them the words you gave me and they accepted
> them. They knew with certainty that I came from you,
> and they believed that you sent me. (John 17:8)

The disciples believed because they saw Jesus' own obedience to the Father. As a result, they too believed and obeyed. Their acceptance was based on the overwhelming quality of Jesus' life, which showed them exactly what God was like. Jesus now turns the focus of his prayer on the disciples:

> I pray for them. I am not praying for the world, but for
> those you have given me, for they are yours. (John 17:9)

Jesus will pray for the world later, and in a different way. Here he prays for the disciples, given to him by the Father. It is not enough that we should pray for ourselves. Underneath all our prayers, holding us up, is the prayer of Jesus for us. By praying for the disciples, Jesus is simply completing what the Father has already begun in giving the disciples to the Son. Jesus' prayer rings with the confidence that his followers already belong to the Father. This is the basis for all our confidence in prayer.

> All I have is yours, and all you have is mine. And glory
> has come to me through them. (John 17:10)

Prayer is an unconcerned, fully trusting relationship, where Father and Son share the same concerns for the disciples, just as a united father and mother share concern for their children. Such prayer expresses the mutual interests of the Father and the Son. But glory has come to Jesus through the sharing of his love with the disciples. This means that there is now a wider circle of love within the Godhead. The reason why Jesus is praying for the disciples is now made explicit:

> I will remain in the world no longer, but they are still in
> the world, and I am coming to you. Holy Father, protect
> them by the power of your name—the name you gave
> me—so that they may be one as we are one. (John 17:11)

The world in which the disciples are about to be left is alien to the character of God. This is obvious in the modern world, with all its evidence of self-love, hatred, and all the forces of evil that are anti-personal and anti-Christ. The disciples need protection from these evil forces, just as we do today.

Everything the disciples were becoming they owed to the character of Jesus, and to the character of the Father who had given them to his Son. It was this character (or "name") of God, his holiness, which would go on protecting them in godliness. Jesus himself had this name, this character of God, and the purpose of his coming was that he would make the disciples one, just as the three persons are one God. So Jesus prays that the unity of the disciples would reflect the character of the one God. He then prays:

> While I was with them, I protected them and kept them
> safe by that name you gave me. None has been lost

> except the one doomed to destruction so that Scripture
> would be fulfilled. (John 17:12)

Jesus prays to the Father to go on doing what he did while he was in the world. Even the tragedy of Judas, who betrayed Jesus to his enemies, was not outside God's plan. The Scriptures had already anticipated this tragedy before it happened, and foresaw its purpose.

The prayer now moves into a new phase. Jesus is now returning to the Father. But instead of seeing this as a deprivation for the disciples, Jesus can only see the joy they will soon have:

> I am coming to you now, but I say these things while I
> am still in the world, so that they may have the full
> measure of my joy within them. (John 17:13)

Leaving his disciples in the hands of the Father brings Jesus the greatest joy. For himself, Jesus longs for his reunion with the Father, just as the Father longs to receive him too. The disciples will also benefit from the reunion of the Father and the Son in receiving a full measure of joy. They could never experience this joy while Jesus was with them on earth. But in his physical absence, they will have Jesus' own joy within them. Unlike an emotional form of ecstasy, this joy springs out of God's own words:

> I have given them your word and the world has hated
> them, for they are not of the world any more than I am
> of the world. (John 17:14)

Because the disciples share in God's character, they do not have the character of the world, which is in opposition to God. The world will hate them for this, and they will experience some of the rebellion against God, which reached its climax at the cross. This hatred is in sharpest contrast with Jesus, who gave his disciples the life-giving words of God. God's Word brought creation into being and men and women into friendship with him.

Once we receive that Word, there is full scope for us to grow in faith, hope, and love. Jesus also prays that the disciples' relationship with God will be preserved. So the prayer continues:

> My prayer is not that you take them out of the world but that you protect them from the evil one. (John 17:15)

All Jesus' disciples need protection from Satan, for the Devil depersonalizes all who go near his evil influence. The Devil is capable of great destruction. He can destroy all our relationships with God and with other people. The disciples must remain in the world to keep it genuinely human, but they need the protection of Christ who prays for them to the Father. In John 17:16, Jesus goes on to emphasize even more clearly that the disciples do not belong to the world:

> They are not of the world, even as I am not of it.

That is why prayer is so vital for the Christian. It gives us a lifeline to another realm, the realm of the Father and the Son, where we truly belong. We can only be protected from the world as we live in prayer, bonded to Christ and the Father. We also need prayer to make us holy—that is, to be like God:

> Sanctify them by the truth; your word is truth. (John 17:17)

To "sanctify" means to be restored to the image and likeness of God, as the Creator originally intended us to be. Prayer restores the relationship that we were always meant to have with God.

These words give us one of the few allusions to the Holy Spirit in this prayer. The "word of truth" can also be seen as the "Spirit of truth" who penetrates our inner being and shows us what the truth of God is. He changes us from the inside to enable us to live out this truth. This then is truly a transforming friendship. Just as Jesus' mission reflected his character, so now he prays for the disciples' mission in the world to do the same thing:

> As you sent me into the world, I have sent them into the
> world. For them I sanctify myself; that they too may be
> truly sanctified. (John 17:18–19)

Prayer must lie at the heart of our service if it is to be like the service Jesus gave, and for his glory. Jesus "sanctified himself" (or "made himself holy") by putting himself entirely at the service of the Father. Our process of becoming holy is based entirely on Jesus, and on the way in which he submitted himself to the Father on our behalf. In his own pure, perfect holiness, the life and ministry of the disciples becomes pure and perfect too.

THE WIDENING CIRCLE OF GOD'S FRIENDS

In his parable of the vine, Jesus had spoken not only of the branches on the trunk, but also of the fruit growing on the branches. So now the circle of Jesus' prayer widens still further to include all those who will hear and believe the gospel:

> My prayer is not for them alone. I pray also for those
> who will believe in me through their message, that all of
> them may be one, Father, just as you are in me and I am
> in you. May they also be in us so that the world may
> believe that you have sent me. (John 17:20–21)

Jesus had often spoken to his disciples about the union between the Father and himself. He could say truthfully that "I and the Father are one." Here Jesus prays that his followers will know this same unity—the unity of a flock under one shepherd, or of branches in one vine. He had already told them that as he loved them, so they should love each other. So in the same way he now says that as they are one in him, they should be one in each other.

Only this can make the gospel credible to an unbelieving world. For a divided church is expressive of a divided faith which, in the unity of the Father with the Son, is wounding indeed. Yet such union is not the result of human organization, nor of political or ecclesiastical ecumenical projects, but is the consequence of personal dependence on and corporate relationship with God himself.

> I have given them the glory that you gave me, that they
> may be one as we are one. (John 17:22)

It is the glory of the Son to belong to the Father, to share in his eternal life and to radiate his love. Jesus brought this same glory down to earth to be shared in the community of God's people. The apostle Peter later expressed this same thought by saying that we have become "partakers of the divine nature" (2 Peter 1:4 ESV).

> I in them and you in me. May they be brought to com-
> plete unity to let the world know that you sent me and
> have loved them even as you have loved me. (John 17:23)

God can only be revealed to the world when we love others with the love of God. When we are divided by suspicion, anger, and every other evil that destroys relationships, we obscure the love between the Father and the Son, which was given on our behalf. Just as the Father is always in Jesus, Jesus is always in us, bringing about love and unity among all God's people. It is only by seeing this that those who are outside God's people will be brought in.

Jesus' prayer now moves to its conclusion. He uses the personal name "Father" for the last time. But now his language becomes urgent, demanding, as the coequal of the Father, that his followers will share in his glory:

> Father, I want those you have given me to be with me
> where I am, and to see my glory, the glory which you
> have given me because you loved me before the creation
> of the world. (John 17:24)

What is this glory? This is the glory of his eternal Sonship, which was hidden when he came to earth as a human being. But

Jesus now wants all his followers to see his eternal Sonship that also glorifies the Father.

Jesus has now come full circle in his prayer. At the beginning he had prayed, "Father, glorify me in your presence with the glory I had with you before the world began." That prayer is now extended to include all those who believe in his name (John 17:25):

> Righteous Father, though the world does not know you,
> I know you, and they know that you have sent me.

The Son knows the Father, but he does not keep this knowledge to himself. He shares it with the disciples. They now know the righteous, loving, forgiving character of God, because Jesus has shown it to them. John 17:26 states,

> I have made you known to them, and will continue to
> make you known in order that the love you have for me
> may be in them and that I myself may be in them.

Jesus had made the Father known to the disciples. In the final words of his prayer he assures the Father that they will go on knowing him. The purpose is that the Father's love will live in them, and that Jesus himself will be within them.

The Christian life is a process which is not complete until this prayer of Jesus is finally realized in our lives. It is a revelation of the life of God, growing fuller and fuller as it progresses. Jesus knows that he is pouring upon us the fullness of his love, and our receptacles are too small to contain it. We find it almost inconceivable to live in a life that is only love, so this prayer continues its work among us, just as Jesus is among us.

The infinite God dwells in us! This is a life that explodes everything we have ever experienced, so that we remain forever in contemplation of God.

The prayer of Jesus is over, but our contemplation continues.

It is this that gives our lives their energy and vitality. But how can we ensure that our relationship with God in prayer continues to be this source of life for us?

LIVING IN CONSTANT AWE AND HARMONY

Any serious look at prayer will show that it implies a belief in an infinite God. Prayer sets us on an endless journey in search of God, and awe is the dynamic of this journey.

Jesus saw prayer as a way to tap limitless power. The apostle Paul entered an unlimited realm in prayer, where length and breadth, height and depth no longer had any meaning. As an old Latin hymn expresses it:

> Who taste thy goodness hunger still,
> who drink thee cannot drink their fill.

When our lives are focused on God, awe and wonder lead us to worship him, filling our inner being with a fullness we would never have thought possible. Awe is fundamental to all human beings of whatever religious (or nonreligious) persuasion. Awe has been recognized as the starting point in the human quest for religion. Awe encourages us to think of God as a transcendent presence: someone outside and beyond our own small concerns and our own vulnerable lives. Awe opens us up to the possibility of living always on the brink of mystery. Awe helps us to be truly alive, fully open to new possibilities we had not envisaged before. Above all, the life of the Trinity, as we have already seen it, fills us with awe, praise, and worship.

Awe prepares the way in us for the power of God, which transforms us. The opposite of awe is arrogance, where we are inwardly bent upon ourselves in self-exaltation and pride. The Russian contemplative, Theophan the Recluse, once described the selfish person as being "... like a thin shaving of wood, curling up around the void of his inner nothingness, cut off alike from the cosmos and the creator of all things." Instead, awe points us toward a life filled with gratitude rather than bitterness. This is why Paul the apostle could encourage his readers:

> Be joyful always; pray continually; give thanks in all circumstances. (1 Thess. 5:16–18)

He could also share the secret freedom of his heart by saying:

> I have learned the secret of being content in any and every situation, whether well fed or hungry, whether living in plenty or in want. I can do everything through him who gives me strength. (Phil. 4:12–13)

This transformation of our inner attitudes can only take place when awe leads us in turn to wonder, admiration, reverence, surrender, and obedience toward God.

A prayerful life is also filled with what Augustine once called "the harmonious sounding together of all the parts." This harmony comes about when there is harmony in ourselves. Our humanity is restored and healed, so that in our lives there is a consistency between being and doing, thinking and acting, prayer and friendships. Only a life of awe in God's presence can empower us to live harmoniously, responding to the work of the Holy Spirit within us. Without a sense of awe at God, and harmony with him, we lose our sense of God's presence with us, for days or even years of our lives.

Awe and harmony are really the north and south poles in God's character, which are united in us.

Awe tells us about God being God, about his vastness and the fact that he is "wholly other." Awe tells us that we can only bow before God, that he knows us through and through, and that we should give ourselves to him in love and worship.

Harmony tells us about God becoming man, coming to our level to make his home with us. This is the distinctively Christian character of God: God in Jesus, who became one of us so that we might be brought safely home to God.

In prayer, we experience both poles: God's majesty and his humility, his otherness and his nearness. True prayer is to recognize that he is both above us, calling for our worship, and walking alongside us, understanding us completely.

This harmony of life in Christ is the secret of my own inner harmony. It enables me to have compassion on others, to live at peace with my friends and to be filled with joy and happiness. It helps me to live in gentleness, patience, firmness of purpose, stability, and inner freedom. It helps me to have a life that is in tune with my friends and with my God.

LIVING IN SELF-ABANDONMENT

A life of self-abandonment is what it means to be a person-in-Christ. It implies that we are open to God's Spirit, detached from other attachments, whether they are addictive, habitual, enslaving, or just plain fascinating. All these obscure our vision of God. If we truly want to live in awe of God, and to enjoy harmony with him, we will need to become detached from ourselves. We need to take the contemplative stance of the listener before him.

Self-abandonment has been a strong theme among contemplatives throughout the history of the Christian faith. Jean Pierre de Caussade saw that every moment was radiant with promise and power when life was lived in dependence upon God throughout the day. His love—which fills, lifts, moves, and surrounds me—motivates me to offer my whole self to him in prayer.

Then an amazing paradox begins to dawn upon me: that I am never more truly myself than when I have given myself up to God. My actions are never more authentic than when they are the Spirit's actions through me. I am never more genuinely human than when I am most godly. The more harmoniously God lives within me, the more freely I live. God has the most glory before the world when I am most genuinely human.

Perhaps there is an echo of Jesus' final prayer here, that the

Father is glorified in the Son, and the Son is glorified in those the Father has given him. As the early church writer Irenaeus recorded:

> The glory of God is a living man; and the life of man consists in beholding God.

Left to ourselves, we can never handle our own uniqueness. We have to give the burden of "being me" to God's care and nurture. But in doing this, we discover more of the greatness of our loving Father. For if God is indeed God, then he has a separate perception and thought for every thing that exists. Every creature at every moment is specifically known and sustained by him. An infinite love has an infinite attention to loving each creature in its own specific way. As Jesus said, not a hair of our head goes unnoticed by our heavenly Father.

Because of this, it is no idle pretence or false arrogance on our part to believe that each one of us has a unique journey to make in the company of God. It is this profound individuation of our whole life before God that gives substance to the reality: He loved me; he gave himself for me.

Our distrust, our discontent, and our disbelief of his eternal friendship actually robs God of his glory; for it is his glory that he can and does love each one of us in such a way that we are most ourselves when we give ourselves to him.

So we can see that being contemplative, in stillness and silence, as well as being surrounded by the noise of need all around us, is more than a possibility. It is our greatest gift and calling. Then we can understand the meaning of the words of Irenaeus, already quoted:

> The glory of God is a living man; and the life of man consists in beholding God.

It is, says the poet:

A condition of complete simplicity,

(Costing not less than everything)

And all shall be well and all shall be well

All manner of things shall be well.

—T. S. Eliot

Such is the life of men and women before God that Jesus can assure us, "Not a hair of your head will perish" (Luke 21:18). And he says elsewhere, "The very hairs of your head are all numbered" (Luke 12:7).

So in one of his lovely prayers, Michel Quoist thinks of a man with a bald head: a fitting symbol for the simplest need with which we can come to the Father, through the Son, by the Holy Spirit. We conclude with his prayer:

It's true, Lord, that you are always thinking of us.

It's true from the beginning of time, before we existed,

Even before the world existed,

You have been dreaming of me,

Thinking of me,

Loving me.

Not on the assembly line, but unique,

The first one so made, and the last,

Indispensable to humanity.

It's true that you have an eternal plan for me alone,

A wonderful plan that you have always cherished in
    your heart,

As a father thinks over the smallest details in the life of
    his little one still unborn.

It's true that, always bending over me, you guide me to
    bring your plan about, light on my path and strength
    for my soul.

It's true that you are saddened when I stray or run away,
    but that you hasten to pick me up if I stumble or fall.

Lord, you who make bald heads, but above all beautiful
    lives,
You, the divine Attentive One,
the divine Patient One,
the divine Present One,
See that at no time I forget your presence.
I don't ask you to bless what I have decided to do, but
Give me the grace to discover and to live what you have
    dreamed for me.

Lord, living in your grace, let me share a little, through
    the attention I give to others, your loving care for us.

Let me, on my knees, adore in them the mystery of
your created love.

Let me respect your idea of them without trying to
impose my own.
May I allow them to follow the path that you have
marked out for them without trying to take them along
mine.
May I realize that they are indispensable to the
world, and that I can't do without the least of them.
May I never tire of looking at them and of enriching
myself with the treasures you have entrusted to them.
Help me to praise you in their journeyings, to find
you in their lives.
Grant that not an instant of their existence go by,
Not a hair of their heads fall,
By me, as by you, unheeded.
—Michel Quoist

Part Four

PRAYER IN GOD'S COMMUNITY

11

PAUL'S LIFE OF PRAYER AND FRIENDSHIP

Do not reduce your prayers to words,
but rather make the totality of your life a prayer to God.

—Isaac of Syria

When we have had a peak experience in our lives, the aftermath can be very disillusioning. The ups and downs of our lives show us how important is sustained, consistent friendship.

We need two kinds of friendship: the friendship of God as Father, Son, and Holy Spirit, and also the human friendships that encourage spiritual life in the common flatness of daily living. Richard Rolle, an English mystic who lived during the fourteenth century, recognized just how important this "soul friendship" could be:

> Holy friendship truly is of God, that amid the wretchedness of this exile, we'll be comforted with the counsel of friends until we come to him.

Friendships such as these link us with God's friendship. A soul friend can encourage us to continue in the Christian faith, and allows us to embody the qualities of faith that can only be expressed in relationships with other people.

However, the Christian church has not always been too happy to identify the value of friendship with the spiritual life of the Christian. This has mainly been because the New Testament uses two quite different Greek words to distinguish between friendship and Christian love.

The word used for friendship *(philia)* is a preferential love. We choose our friends and even pursue friendships if they admit us to a magic circle of "special" people. Christian love *(agape)* is radically different. It expresses a love that is open to everyone, mirroring the love of God that sent Jesus to die on the cross for those who did not love him. Compared with agape, philia is a pale kind of love.

Apart from the monastic writings of the twelfth century, such as Aelred of Rievaulx's *Spiritual Friendship,* friendship has never been a central theme of Western Christianity. In contrast, the ancient Greeks and Romans made friendship central to their societies. Jeremy Taylor, a seventeenth-century writer, said that "when friendships were the noblest things in the world, charity was little." In other words, when the preferential love of philia dominates relationships, then agape love is overshadowed completely.

All this seems to suggest that friendship is a suspect love, not capable of helping us in our spiritual growth. However, the modern world is very different to the world of Jeremy Taylor. Friendships are no longer "the noblest things in the world." Instead, our careers are the integrating bond of society, giving many people their sense of identity and status. Put more bluntly, the pursuit of money and power underlies a great deal of what goes on in the modern world. In this hostile environment, true friendship becomes a spiritual value, challenging the most deeply held obsessions of our society.

The disintegration of friendship is a very serious challenge for the credibility of the Christian faith. This is why we should defiantly insist that friendship and prayer together truly reflect the character of God as Father, Son, and Holy Spirit.

The connections between friendship and prayer come to the surface clearly in the life of the apostle Paul. His warm friendship encouraged many people in his time to pray more deeply—and he encourages us in the same way. The rest of this chapter looks at the friendship and prayer of Paul.

ENCOUNTERING PAUL'S FRIENDSHIP

Paul (whose original name was Saul) grew up to become a Pharisee, teaching that the Jewish Law should be strictly kept in every area of life. Soon after the crucifixion of Jesus, he became a violent persecutor of the first Christians, championing the cause of those who were stamping out the new faith. It was while he was on his way to Damascus in order to arrest Christians that he had an experience that was to disrupt his life forever in Acts 9:3–5:

> As he neared Damascus on his journey, suddenly a light from heaven flashed around him. He fell to the ground and heard a voice say to him, "Saul, Saul, why do you persecute me?"
>
> "Who are you, Lord?" Saul asked.
>
> "I am Jesus, whom you are persecuting," he replied.

Saul was led into Damascus, blinded by the great light. God then told Ananias, a Christian living in the city, to go to see Saul. The description given to Ananias is striking: "Ask for a man from Tarsus named Saul, for he is praying" (Acts 9:11). It was as if Saul's own prayer on the Damascus road had found a permanent place inside him: "Who are you, Lord?"

For the rest of Paul's life, his work and his friendships were shot through with prayer. His letters, in which he wrote passionately, affectionately, and prayerfully, reveal this dynamic between prayer and friendship. Paul cared deeply that his many converts to the faith should live out the reality of the good news he had preached to them. He combined tenderness and empathy with a stern authority that guarded the truth of the Christian faith. Brilliant and quick to focus on the essentials in any argument, his mind was on fire for God.

Paul was also always on his knees before God. In his own life, prayer and teaching were integrated, and he never encouraged others to separate the two. He told the Christians of Thessalonica to "pray without ceasing" (1 Thess. 5:17 NASB), and the Ephesians to "pray in the Spirit on all occasions with all kinds of prayers and requests. With this in mind, be alert, and always keep on praying for all the saints" (Eph. 6:18).

His faithful prayers for others were also made in a wholehearted way. In 2 Timothy 1:3–4, he told Timothy in Rome,

> I constantly remember you in my prayers night and day.

Through his unbroken relationship with God, Paul gave to his friends.

While Paul prayed for others, he also prayed three times that a personal affliction, which he called his "thorn in the flesh," be removed by God. However, when God told him that his "thorn" was there for a good reason, Paul knew when to stop praying and to accept God's grace. In this way, Paul knew the difference between insistent, continuous prayer, and submitting to the will of God without wrestling against circumstances.

The key feature of Paul's prayer life is that it dominates all his relationships with other people. His style of writing is saturated with the spirit of prayer in all its forms: pouring out love to God, asking God, giving thanks, praising God for his goodness. His greetings, his farewells, his travel plans, his tellings-off, his hopes and concerns, his communication of the truth—all are cast in the mold of a man who was jealous that the glory of God should become obvious in the lives of his converts.

Paul's entire personality was shaped by his abiding sense of God's presence. For us, he embodies all that it means to be a prayerful person, no longer operating from the impulses of our natural temperament, nor the instincts of a natural personality.

GREETINGS WITH PRAYER

Paul began many of his letters with the words "Grace and peace to you ..." This was a customary form of greeting, rather like our "Dear John ..." But unlike phony e-mails and text messages that we receive today, Paul carefully personalized the greetings to match each situation he was writing to.

Philemon is a letter to a particular friend in which Paul makes a personal request. Ephesians is a circular letter to a group of churches. The books of 1 and 2 Thessalonians, 1 and 2 Corinthians, and Philippians are all written to individual churches that were well-known to Paul. In these letters, Paul does not greet anyone by name, unless they are fellow workers with him. It seems that he knew everyone in these churches well, and did not wish to pick anyone out for specific mention.

On the other hand, to the churches he had not yet visited, such as Rome and Colossae, Paul sent numerous greetings to individuals he had already met. For example, he lists twenty-six people in his letter to Rome. This personal approach is a world away from the later emphasis on teaching in the church. In the Middle Ages, Christian truth became abstract, as scholars attempted to present the Christian faith in a systematic way. There was no reference to prayer or personal relationships. This approach is remote from the spirit in which Paul and the other Christian pioneers taught in the early days of the church.

Paul's letter to the Christians in Rome shows us most clearly his ties of friendship. In addressing individual people, he gives his reasons for remembering them and encourages them by frequent thanks and prayer:

Greet Priscilla and Aquila, my fellow workers in Christ
Jesus. They risked their lives for me. Not only I but all
the churches of the Gentiles are grateful to them.

Greet also the church that meets at their house.

Greet my dear friend Epenetus, who was the first convert
to Christ in the province of Asia.

Greet Mary, who worked very hard for you.

Greet Andronicus and Junias, my relatives who have
been in prison with me. They are outstanding among
the apostles, and they were in Christ before I was.

Greet Ampliatus, whom I love in the Lord.

Greet Urbanus, our fellow worker in Christ, and my dear
friend Stachys.

Greet Apelles, tested and approved in Christ.

Greet those who belong to the household of Aristobulus.

Greet Herodion, my relative.

Greet those in the household of Narcissus who are in the
Lord.

Greet Tryphena and Tryphosa, those women who work
hard in the Lord.

Greet my dear friend Persis, another woman who has
worked very hard in the Lord.

Greet Rufus, chosen in the Lord, and his mother, who
has been a mother to me, too.

Greet Asyncritus, Phlegon, Hermes, Patrobas, Hermas
and the brothers with them.

Greet Philologus, Julia, Nereus and his sister, and
Olympas and all the saints with them.

Greet one another with a holy kiss.

All the churches of Christ send greetings. (Rom. 16:1–16)

What a list of friends! Paul clearly loved all these people who
had helped and served him, who had risked their lives for him
and in one case had even mothered him!

This same quality of friendship comes across in Paul's letter to the Christians in Philippi. Paul wrote this letter from his prison cell, either in Caesarea or in Rome. Half the Mediterranean Sea separated him from the Philippian Christians. But they had heard of his imprisonment and sent a companion, Epaphroditus, to be with him. But Epaphroditus was taken ill while he was in prison with Paul, and this news was carried back to Philippi. Paul heard that they were anxious about the health of their friend, so when Epaphroditus had recovered Paul sent him back to Philippi with a letter full of affection for them, promising that he would soon visit them. This is what friendship meant to Paul.

Paul made time for the commitment of friendship, even though he might have been weighed down with his ministry to all the churches that depended on him. His letters were an integral part of his work, and he needed close companions to act as his letter carriers. In this way, Paul's friendships went hand-in-hand with the spreading of the Christian message.

PAUL'S SPIRIT OF THANKSGIVING

The introductions to Paul's letters are characteristically full of thanksgiving to God for the life and witness of his converts. He was deeply concerned for those to whom he was writing. Even his most condemning letter, to the chaotic church in Corinth, opens with words of gratitude to God for their enrichment in the faith. In his letters to Philemon and the Philippians, where there was more reason for thanksgiving, Paul pours out his joy and warmth of feeling.

Throughout these letters, Paul's language constantly crosses the border into praise as he speaks with joy about the grace of God that has so transformed the lives of his readers. They have been brought out of darkness into God's marvelous light. The letters contain this attractive mixture of prayer, teaching, and thanksgiving.

In the midst of his own sufferings, Paul's life was marked by constant thanksgiving. Humanly speaking, he had every reason not to be thankful. As he catalogs the list of sufferings he has endured, it has been reckoned that his life contained the suffering of ten people, and yet he did not succumb. It is astonishing that he did not die under all that he suffered physically, let alone the constant "care of all the churches," which was also a great burden on his mind and spirit. Prayer and suffering were intertwined in Paul's life.

He prayed and suffered over the Jewish people's rejection of Jesus Christ. With great longing, just as Jesus wept as he prayed over Jerusalem, Paul longed for his people to accept Jesus:

> I speak the truth in Christ—I am not lying, my conscience confirms it in the Holy Spirit—I have great sorrow and unceasing anguish in my heart. For I could wish that I myself were cursed and cut off from Christ for the sake of my brothers, those of my own race, the people of Israel.... My heart's desire and prayer to God for the Israelites is that they may be saved. (Rom. 9:1–4; 10:1)

Paul also suffered physically, as he was flogged, stoned, shipwrecked, hungry, and fatigued on his many journeys. He was given the dreaded lashing, stretched on a beam in the torture chamber, when suddenly he saw the Lord standing beside him. "Take courage! As you have testified about me in Jerusalem, so you must also testify in Rome." His prayer was again answered, and in quiet confidence Paul prepared himself for this new stage in his work. He had learned that when he was weak, then he was made strong (Phil. 4:13 NKJV):

> I can do all things through Christ who strengthens me.

This was not the boasting of an aggressive, self-made man, but the assurance of a person who had discovered God's strength through great pain and weakness. This was why Paul lived a deeply thankful life. He had abandoned himself to the will and providing help of God at all times. His thankfulness was the dominant climate of his whole life.

PAUL'S CERTAINTY IN ASKING

Paul's many travels, trials, and sufferings gave him an excellent opportunity to test out the reality of prayer. He was able to discover whether his prayers and his experience of God were merely subjective or whether they were a genuine transaction between himself and God. His letters tell us that prayer is the supreme experience of the Christian life. For Paul, prayer was unthinkable without an encounter with the personal, living God. He lived in the many different dimensions of prayer, including praise, confession, and meditation. But it was in "asking" that Paul excelled, showing us the communicative nature of prayer.

However, we should not think that Paul neatly categorized his prayers. The thirty or forty prayers which he wrote in his letters cannot be divided into types or categories. He moves easily from thankfulness into teaching, into prayer, into warning. His letters include prayers of blessing; thanksgiving for prayers that have been answered; thanksgiving mixed together with requests, greetings, and teaching; prayers made for the needs of other people; and prayer requests for his own needs. All this indicates the scope and density of Paul's daily experience of God. The list could also include his bursts of praise to God, the early hymns he includes in his letters, and his quotations from the Old Testament psalms.

Paul's life of prayer drew its roots from prayer in the Old Testament, especially in his use of prayers of blessing. Paul recognized that the fruitfulness of life, both biologically and spiritually, came from the vitality given by the Creator himself. This approach to God is seen clearly in the book of Psalms (especially in Psalms 103 and 104) and also in the Beatitudes of Jesus in Matthew chapter 5.

God is a God who "blesses" (or gives life) to those he loves.

The prayer, "Blessed be the Lord" is as old as all human relationships with God. This is what Noah prayed after the flood, and what Abraham's servant prayed after finding a wife for his master's son Isaac. Prayers of blessing are a regular feature throughout the Old Testament, and they played an important part in the life of the local synagogue.

Paul drew from this rich tradition, with its celebration of God's love and faithfulness to his people, in his own prayers of blessing. Our own prayer life needs to be rooted in the truth of God as the one who "blesses" us, giving us new life as he has done for all his people through the ages. In some traditions, such as the Anglican use of the prayer book, the continuity of prayer and its corporate expression has shaped those who use it to a distinctive style of devotion that is much needed in today's secular world. We need to follow in the great traditions of prayer.

The prayers of blessing in the Bible can enrich our prayer life. There is the prayer of Zechariah, the father of John the Baptist:

> Praise be to the Lord, the God of Israel, because he has come and has redeemed his people. (Luke 1:68)

In one of his most personal greetings, Paul bursts out in praise:

> Praise be to the God and Father of our Lord Jesus Christ, the Father of compassion and the God of all comfort, who comforts us in all our troubles, so that we can comfort those in any trouble with the comfort we ourselves have received from God. (2 Cor. 1:3–4)

In the majestic opening verses of Paul's letter to the Christians in Ephesus, he begins by praising God for our new status in Christ:

> Praise be to the God and Father of our Lord Jesus Christ, who has blessed us in the heavenly realms with every spiritual blessing in Christ. (1:3)

This is why Paul was so sure that God heard and answered his prayers. He was confident in the character of the God who blesses his people. Paul's life and his prayers complemented each other. His on-the-road ministry, interrupted by periods in prison, provided the personal needs that fueled his prayers asking for God's help. Paul's letters reveal that his hopes and disappointments about his travel plans played a significant role in his life of prayer. At a critical decision in his life, Paul had a vision of a man from northern Greece appealing to him, "Come over to Macedonia and help us." Paul concluded that God had called them to go into Europe, and so he got ready and left at once.

Paul's journey decisions involved real struggles in prayer. He once wrote to the Christians in Rome:

> I urge you brothers, by our Lord Jesus Christ and by the love of the Spirit, to join me in my struggle by praying for me. Pray that I may be rescued from the unbelievers in Judea and that my service in Jerusalem may be acceptable to the saints there, so that by God's will I may come to you with joy and together with you be refreshed. (15:30–32)

The urgency of this plea was not mere rhetoric. When we read in the book of Acts about the turmoil caused in Jerusalem by Paul's arrest and torture, we can start to understand what he was up against. On that occasion, the commander of the Roman garrison where he was taken was afraid that "Paul would be torn to pieces" (Acts 23:10) by the violent mob outside. Small wonder then that Paul wrote in such strong terms to the Christians in Rome.

At another time, Paul wrote to the Christians in Thessalonica:

> When we were torn away from you for a short time (in person, not in thought), out of our intense longing we made every effort to see you. For we wanted to come to you—certainly I, Paul, did, again and again—but Satan stopped us. (1 Thess. 2:17–18)

Later on in the letter, Paul added:

> Night and day we pray most earnestly that we may see
> you again and supply what is lacking in your faith. (3:10)

It is ironic that other friends do not always see our predicaments in the same way that we do, because they are not with us when disasters happen. We can see exactly this situation in the pages of the New Testament. Luke, writing his account of Paul's travels in the book of Acts, coolly records that Paul, journeying through modern-day Turkey, was "kept by the Holy Spirit from preaching the word" (16:6). Luke was not with Paul at the time, so he could afford to write in this rather detached fashion. But this is not at all how Paul saw it! "Satan hindered us," was his explanation (1 Thess. 2:18 NASB). Luke could chronicle the events from afar, but Paul was in the middle of intense frustrations. Nor was this an isolated event in his travel plans. He told the Roman Christians: "I have often been hindered from coming to you" (15:22).

So we can see how Paul's prayers were very much a part of his ministry and his travels. Significantly, his prayers focused around frustration, weakness and helplessness, as all true prayer must do. It is out of our helplessness that we pray best, because self-confidence robs our incentive to pray as we should. When we reach a point of utter helplessness, we discover, as Paul did, that "we do not know what we ought to pray for, but the Spirit himself intercedes for us with groans that words cannot express" (Rom. 8:26). It is out of this sense of weakness that we can approach God for the strength we need.

Paul's teaching has great depth and character partly because of his own experience in prayer and suffering. His frustrations, doubts, and despair, coupled with his passionate concern to declare the gospel and his thankfulness, are all used to give his teaching such richness, personal conviction, and power. Paul speaks about all this in chapter 8 of his letter to the Romans.

Exuberantly he expresses the joy of the Holy Spirit, living in the life of every Christian, enabling us to cry out to God as our Father. But as the chapter progresses, Paul's mood shifts to stress personal suffering, weakness and dependence upon God.

All this points toward our need for a deep trust in God in every imaginable dimension of threat and need. Paul concludes this section of his letter by saying that "neither height nor depth, nor anything else in all creation, will be able to separate us from the love of God that is in Christ Jesus our Lord." The secret of Paul's powerful ministry was in his own relationship through prayer with God the Father, Son, and Holy Spirit.

THEOLOGY MIXED WITH PRAYER

Paul excels in his remarkable intermingling of theology (teaching about God) and prayer. He realized that it is only by growing in our understanding and our experience of God that we become mature in the faith. So he frequently uses terms like "fullness," "growth," and "fruit" to get across the spiritual progress that he looked for. He prayed that the knowledge his new converts had received would be embodied in life itself, working out toward a practical expression of blessing for other people too. All this kept him in constant prayer on behalf of those he taught.

The climax of Paul's teaching ministry focused around the city of Ephesus. He spent two years there, lecturing in the Hall of Tyrannus. The book of Acts tells us that during this time "all the Jews and Greeks of the province of Asia heard the word of the Lord" (19:10). One ancient manuscript tells us that Paul used the hall between 11:00 a.m. and 4:00 p.m., which was siesta time. It must have been quite a feat to capture an audience during the hottest time of the day when most people were sleeping at home!

And yet the teachers who were taught there by Paul went on to spread the Christian message throughout the Roman world.

There was Timothy, who accompanied Paul on many of his journeys. There was Tychicus, who was frequently sent by Paul to encourage the young churches he had planted. There was Epaphras, originally named by his pagan parents after the Greek goddess of love, but who became a true servant of Jesus Christ.

After Paul had left Ephesus, he wrote a letter to be sent around to the churches in the towns near the city. This letter to the Ephesians marks his high point in blending prayer and theology. Paul uses a link phrase that appears three times in this letter, the phrase "for this reason." He uses it to connect what he has taught with the prayer that springs naturally from his teaching. So at the end of the great hymn of praise in 1:15–17, he writes,

> For this reason, ever since I heard about your faith in the Lord Jesus and your love for all the saints, I have not stopped giving thanks for you, remembering you in my prayers. I keep asking that the God of our Lord Jesus Christ, the glorious Father, may give you the Spirit of wisdom and revelation, so that you may know him better.

The second time he uses the link phrase is to relate his own personal circumstances as a "prisoner of the Lord" for the sake of the message he was called to preach. His third use of "for this reason" has added force. He gathers up his whole teaching in the first three chapters of the letter to pray that his readers may be able "to grasp how wide and long and high and deep is the love of Christ, and to know this love that surpasses knowledge" (3:18–19).

This whole projectile of ardent and powerful prayer can be illustrated by the modern achievement of the Voyager 2 space probe. The journey of Voyager 2 into deep space was made possible by the discovery of a *syzygy*—the synchronization of the four giant planets of our solar system into a straight line. This event occurs only at rare intervals, and will not happen again until the twenty-second century. Voyager 2 was launched toward the first planet in line and used each planet's gravity in turn, like a sequence of sling shots, to speed itself deeper into space. Voyager 2 passed Jupiter in 1979, Saturn in 1981, Uranus in 1986, and Neptune in 1989, sending back its signals to Earth.

Paul's understanding of the mysteries of faith in Ephesians 1 are like this use of the *syzygy*. His thanksgiving in prayer is swept out into space as he contemplates God's purposes in redeeming humankind. He begins the chapter by saying that we receive our new life from the Father of Jesus Christ.

It is because we are "in Christ" (a phrase that Paul uses 164 times in his letters), united with him, that God has blessed us. The life we receive from God is life in the spiritual dimension, which comes from the Holy Spirit. It is because we are "in Christ" that we receive a continuous flow of blessings from God the Father: adoption as his sons, the forgiveness of our sins, and his deliberate resolve to be our friend. He also gives us wisdom and understanding, which allows us to see into the heart of things and to act wisely in life. All this is possible because God chose to reveal himself to us.

Paul then moves on to the Holy Spirit, who is given to us as "a seal," a final proof that we truly belong to God's circle of friends. The Holy Spirit is the outward sign of God's work that goes on inside us. He sets us free from slavery to become the children of God. This then is the first *syzygy* that hurls us out toward a greater awareness of the cosmic purposes of God. Paul immediately follows this by plunging into prayer, showing that prayer is the most appropriate response to receiving a new understanding of God.

This pattern of teaching and prayer is repeated at the end of chapter 3 as Paul prays what must be the New Testament equivalent of Jacob's dream of a ladder going up into heaven (Gen. 28). But while a Jew would stand in prayer, Paul bows prostrate before God in prayer. He is before God, the Father of all, the One alone in whom fatherhood is seen in perfection. He prays that his readers "may be filled to the measure of all the fullness of God" (Eph. 3:19).

What It Means to Call God "Father"

Paul's prayer (which appears in full at the end of this chapter) tells us what it means to experience God as our Father.

First, Paul prays that God "may strengthen you with power through his Spirit in your inner being" (Eph. 3:16). We are equipped with the dynamic power that makes our prayer life, and our love and knowledge of God, fully effective. The purpose of this is to help us to stand firm as Christians, to serve Jesus loyally. None of this could possibly happen without the presence of the Holy Spirit inside us. Paul prays that our prayer life will itself express the permanent presence of God's Spirit in our hearts, strengthening and controlling us. This takes place at the seat of our personalities, so that our temperaments can grow to full maturity in prayer. Only the strength and the power of God can bring about such a transformation of our personality.

To experience God as Father also means to be "rooted and established in love" (Eph. 3:17). Like a tree with strong roots or a building with solid foundations, we are to be so deeply rooted in the love of Christ that we can stand up to any emotional earthquake, storm, or any form of discouragement. Knowing God as our Father also means to "grasp how wide and long and high and deep is the love of Christ, and to know this love that surpasses knowledge" (Eph. 3:18–19). We both experience the love of Christ in our own lives and begin to love him in return. We start to experience all that we have looked at in this book about the friendship of Jesus Christ in a more personal way than we have ever known it before.

This is where many of the Christian writers of the past often had a deeper insight than the people of today. For they saw that true love for God takes us up to God as we contemplate him and long for him, instead of dragging God down to our level, as the rationalistic faith of today tends to do.

The love of Christ has many dimensions, which Paul here describes in terms of width, length, height, and depth. This understanding of love belongs to the ecstatic experiences of life before

God, and they demand our contemplation. This love takes us beyond rational thinking into the pure experience of God as our Father.

Significantly, Paul prays that we may grasp this limitless love of Christ in company with "all the saints." We need to read the great classics of the Christian faith in order to understand how other Christians have grasped this same love of Christ. So the writer of *The Cloud of Unknowing* actually explores the "width, length, height, and depth" of Paul's prayer. We rob ourselves if we do not learn to live with Augustine, Thomas Aquinas, Teresa of Avila, John of the Cross, Martin Luther, Jonathan Edwards, and the whole host of saints who have truly been friends of God. This love for the people of God, which characterized Paul's own life, should mark us out too. We will pray much more richly when we pray "with all the saints."

A final consequence of experiencing God as our Father is to be "filled to the measure of all the fullness of God" (Eph. 3:19). This is the climax of all prayer. This desire to be filled with God eclipses any other desires we will ever have in the life of prayer. Some people have interpreted this verse to mean that we are filled to what we are capable of receiving. So that if I am a mere thimble, and my friend is a bucket, both of us are filled in different measures with God's presence. However, the meaning of the Greek words used by Paul suggests something greater than this. We are not simply to be filled to our own limits with God's fullness, but actually filled to the limit of God himself.

It is a staggering thought that I should ever dare to ask God to fill me with all his fullness. It implies that my prayer will be a never-ending process. So now I set myself an agenda before God that will never be completed as long as I live. This is a desire that will carry me throughout my life until it is drawn up to see God face to face, to be transformed fully and completely into his image by the love of Christ. No other prayer, desire, or friendship could ever match up to this vision of my relationship with God. This prayer leads me forward, in communion with all the saints, to heaven itself.

We saw earlier how this prayer is like the ladder that Jacob saw in a dream, connecting earth with heaven. Jesus promised his disciples that they would see greater things than this:

> You shall see heaven open, and the angels of God ascending and descending on the Son of Man. (John 1:51)

This is what we see in this prayer. No prayer has ever been so bold or adventurous as this. All that we have explored about our difficulties in prayer and our need for understanding about God pale into insignificance beside Paul's great prayer for us. But can we really ask God for what this prayer suggests?

This was the personal dilemma for the writer C. S. Lewis. He said that he observed two conflicting patterns of prayer in the New Testament. The first teaches that whatever we ask for in faith will be given to us. The second pattern teaches us that all prayer should be qualified by the clause "your will be done"—just as Jesus prayed in the garden of Gethsemane before his arrest. Lewis suggested that most Christians never experience this second pattern of prayer. Modestly, he confessed that he was on the foothills of the life of prayer; he did not have a head for heights, unlike the mountaineering mystics!

Perhaps the resolution to this problem is that we tend to see our prayers for help as a conflict of wills: my will versus God's will. Some people still tend to think of prayer as asking God for things. If we do not get beyond this stage, then our prayers will die out. We will soon get discouraged if our prayers are merely a way of expressing our self-will in the presence of the sovereign God. Instead of pitting our wills against God, true prayer happens only when our lives have been disorientated away from ourselves to become oriented on the will of God. Then we will begin to want the will of God for which we pray.

Modern communication theory recognizes that real communication only takes place when the two parties are oriented toward each other. We turn our concentration and concern to focus on the other person's perspective, which opens up the lines of communication between us. This is what Jesus did when he prayed to his Father in the garden of Gethsemane. But then, his whole life had been oriented toward God.

This is the life of God the Trinity: each person focused on the others. We enter into the experience of that life when we are oriented upon the will of God, just as Paul prayed so movingly in his letter to the Ephesians. Knowing that we are turned and focused on the will and heart of God, we can approach him with the same boldness as the apostles. One New Testament writer said:

> Let us draw near to God with a sincere heart in full
> assurance of faith. (Heb. 10:22)

Yes, we can even pray that we may be filled with all the fullness of God.

PRAISE: THE CONCLUSION OF PRAYER

The conclusion of all prayer is praise. Paul's great prayer leads us to recognize that the true friend of God expresses praise that runs over like an overfilled cup. This is exactly how Paul's prayer ends. He shows us how God is able to do many things for us when we pray.

Unlike false gods who can do nothing, God is alive and active, in spite of what some theologians have said about him! He is able to do what we ask. God hears and answers prayer as our true friend. God is also able to do what we imagine. He reads our thoughts and can interpret the thoughts and feelings we cannot express as we cry out to him in distress. God is able to do all that we ask or think. He is the King of kings and Lord of lords. He knows everything and can complete the work he started in us.

But Paul's prayer goes even further. God is able to do more than what we ask for in our desires and prayers. His thoughts are way beyond us and he longs to give us what we have not even dreamed of. Finally, Paul says that God is able to do very much more than all this. He is able to do immeasurably more than all that we can ask or think. He is the superlative God, for no limits can ever contain him.

This infinite ability to work for us beyond our wildest prayers and dreams is made possible by "his power that is at work within us."

Paul ends with a simple, breathless prayer of blessing. He prays that God would receive glory—the glory which Jesus prayed would be revealed by his death and resurrection, and passed down to all those who believe in his name. "To him be glory in the church and in Christ Jesus," Paul prays (Eph. 3:21). This glory encompasses both the bride and the bridegroom, the body and the head, in a transforming and one day wholly transformed friendship. Amen. So it has been, so it is, so it shall ever be, forever and ever. Amen.

> For this reason I kneel before the Father, from whom his whole family in heaven and on earth derives its name. I pray that out of his glorious riches he may strengthen you with power through his Spirit in your inner being, so that Christ may dwell in your hearts through faith. And I pray that you, being rooted and established in love, may have power, together with all the saints, to grasp how wide and long and high and deep is the love of Christ, and to know this love that surpasses knowledge—that you may be filled to the measure of all the fullness of God.
>
> Now to him who is able to do immeasurably more than all we ask or imagine, according to his power that is at work within us, to him be glory in the church and in Christ Jesus throughout all generations, forever and ever! Amen. (Eph. 3:14–21)

12

PRAYER BY THE
FRIENDS OF GOD

*The lives of the saints; what are these save practical illustrations of the
gospel? The difference between the Word and the saints' lives is like that
between music in score and the same music sung by living voices.*
—Francis De Sales

As I write this book I have the happy option of choosing to work in two very different rooms. Downstairs in my basement study I am enclosed by four windowless walls. However, these walls are lined with bookshelves that hold the books I like best. They remind me vividly of what is called "the communion of saints." This is the friendship of Christians whose insights into life with God I treasure so much, because they have helped to change my own life. Upstairs, I can work in a room with picture windows that open onto a panoramic view of the city of Vancouver, with its magnificent setting in the mountains on the rim of the Pacific Ocean.

These two perspectives are symbolic of our lives. Downstairs, in the cellar, we have the space of inwardness that can be frightening or even imprisoning for people whose lives are messy, lonely, or desperate. Alternatively, we can experience inner spaciousness for God by reflecting on him, and by relating to him and his friends. Upstairs, we live out our public life, with its many relationships and activities.

Prayer takes place in both these dimensions, inward and outward, personal and social. The balance of our lives lies in the use of solitude with God to enrich community with our friends, and the use of community to deepen our solitude with God. As Dietrich Bonhoeffer, the twentieth-century writer, once remarked, none of us can afford solitude if we do not live in community, nor can we have real community without solitude. That is why so many people who live without prayer are so superficial with others; and why people who appear to be very religious are suspect because of the intense individualism of their faith.

The analogy between the two rooms and our lives can be pushed further. The view from my upstairs room shows the great port of Vancouver, the focus of many lines of communication across Canada and the Pacific. Yellow mounds of sulphur have been brought here from the ancient lake beds of Alberta. Grain elevators are full of grain harvested in the prairies. The fishing docks load salmon from the coastal waters. All this display of wealth and activity feeds the economic life of Vancouver as well as many other communities across the world. Downstairs in my study there is also a wealth of resources stored on my shelves. The books are full of thoughts and reflections that help to enrich my life and enable me to communicate to others.

For most of us, prayer will be the most important resource of all.

PRAYER AND THE COMMUNION OF SAINTS

The Bible's resources for a life of prayer are vast and deep. We now want to extend ourselves further by reflecting on the explorations of God's people in the different traditions, or families, of prayer. Some of these traditions are more adventurous than others, but they can all help to enrich our own life of prayer.

As we saw in the last chapter, the apostle Paul prayed that we would make our own explorations in prayer "with all the saints." If we simply concentrate on ourselves in prayer, our introspection can mislead us, or even damage our spiritual lives. We need instead to walk with God's people, past and present, learning from the experiences they share with us.

At the same time, it is sad that in some traditions superstition about the saints has clouded our appreciation of them. Prayers made to the saints instead of to God, and adoration of the saints, has caused great confusion in the minds of ordinary Christians. We do not need the saints to pray to God for us when God is our Father, Jesus is our mediator, and the Holy Spirit helps us to pray even when we cannot express our feelings. So why did this strong emphasis on prayer made to the saints arise in the first place?

In the early centuries of the Christian church, there was a strong emphasis on the glory of martyrdom. Dying for your faith in Jesus was seen as the greatest possible expression of love and loyalty toward him. Those who had died for their faith were venerated, and gradually people began to pray for them and to believe that they prayed for us to God.

A few voices of dissent were raised against the growing belief that the saints interceded in prayer for the living, but they were overruled by a succession of powerful church leaders. Leaders such as John Chrysostom, Ambrose, and Augustine upheld the right of the faithful to pray at the tombs of saints and to venerate their relics. These practices were tempered by the teaching of theologians, such as Ambrose, that Jesus occupied the central position in praying for us to God:

> He is our mouth, through which we speak to the Father; he is our eye, through which we see the father; he is our right hand, through which we offer ourselves to the father. Unless he intercedes, there is no intercourse with God, either for us or for all the saints.

Much later, in 1523, Martin Luther quoted Ambrose's words as the reason why the worship of the saints should be eliminated altogether. Another reformer, John Calvin, also attacked the saints' ability to pray for the living:

> They do not abandon their own repose so as to be drawn into earthly care; and much less must we on their account be always calling upon them!

If there is any virtue in remembering the saints, it is for their example rather than for their prayers. Bishop Hall of Norwich, in the seventeenth century, summed up a position that probably reflects the views of many people in today's church:

> O ye blessed saints above, we honor your memories as far as we ought; we with praise recount your virtues; we magnify your victories; we bless God for your happy exemption from the misery of this world, and for your estating in that blessed immortality; we imitate your holy examples; we long and pray for a happy consociation with you. We dare not raise temples, dedicate altars, direct prayers to you; we dare not, finally, offer any thing to you which you are unwilling to receive, nor put anything upon you which you would disclaim as prejudicial to your Creator and Redeemer.

If theologians have a hard time trying to vindicate the long-held superstition of prayers to the saints, modern culture has undermined the whole practice by turning its back on the relevance of the past. Modern life has a short memory, with very little sense of history. The Christian faith cannot afford to forget the past, because the events of the past are central to its whole meaning. Our faith depends on the fact that Jesus Christ lived, died, and was raised from the dead in a series of historical events.

Christians who lived in the past also link us with the purpose of God, as we see the way in which he has worked throughout time. If we lose our sense of history, we amputate a vital part of human existence and cut ourselves off from a greater sense of God at work.

The communion of saints therefore implies two great realities. The first is that prayer can never be divorced from a right way of living. We can learn this by looking at the way in which Christians before us lived.

Prayer expresses our whole lives before God. To pray is to ask God to transform our lives. Worship that does not seek this transformation of life is not true worship. It is because many people are unwilling to face a radical change in their attitudes and actions that worship is at such a low ebb today.

The second implication is that prayer cannot be divorced from the historical traditions pioneered and followed by the Christians of the past in their own friendship with God. By looking at their high standards of faith and devotion, we can be lifted out of the prejudices and blind spots of our own culture to become more aware of the limitations of our own age. We can learn to lose the complacency about prayer that is so much a feature of our culture, and start to take prayer more seriously.

Until we read Augustine's *Confessions* we may have no idea of the honesty we can express before God. Until we read the writings of Teresa of Avila we may not appreciate the passionate love for Christ we can cultivate in our prayer life. Until we read the devotional writings of the medieval mystics we may remain completely unaware of the depths of the life of contemplation.

If our own emotional experiences with God lack a sense of history and an understanding of the Bible, then our emotions can lead us a long way from the truth. We need both a transformed life and a knowledge of Christian teaching and history to give us stability. With these two guiding lights, we do not need to fear the adventure ahead of us—a deepening life of prayer.

However, there is also a third element that we should add as we exercise the communion of the saints. This third element is to become aware of the church worldwide. We need to read across all the living traditions of the Christian faith, as well as the traditions in the past.

When we do this, we begin to realize how much richer is the experience of prayer than the attitudes we have been taught to accept. We will also be challenged to accept changes in our understanding of prayer and of our life before God. Just as a human friendship can never be static, so our relationship with God in prayer cannot remain a static, unchanging series of habits. A living faith grows and changes as our relationship with God develops.

LIVING IN ALL THE SPHERES OF PRAYER

A number of traditions in prayer have marked different periods in the history of the church. These traditions, or styles of worship, are still alive and form the living experience of God for different groups of Christians. These diverse spheres of prayer are open to us in our own personal growth. The traditions are summarized in the diagram on the next page.

As the diagram illustrates, we approach God's presence with mind and heart, more readily thoughtful, or more moved emotionally. We can also be attentive to God through reading the Bible, or with other symbols that remind us of him. We speak of this as "attentiveness," as if in his absence we need reminders to help us describe him and be attentive to him—we know, mentally at least, that he is always with us.

But we also experience God as unknowable, as Moses found when a cloud hid God from sight. Then we focus in awe and wonder upon the great mystery of God. Paradoxically, it is at times when we sense his great mystery that he seems to be present with us in the most intimate way possible.

We can now develop the diagram further in distinguishing four quadrants, expressing four types of prayer.

We begin with the exercise of verbal prayer, where we are using our minds most vigorously, and expressing ourselves in "attentiveness" before God, with the symbolic use of language.

This kind of prayer is most typical of the "Reformed" tradition. Meditative prayer is less articulate with words, and so it has more to do with the feelings than the mind. But both verbal and meditative prayer are on the "attentive" or descriptive side of the celebration of God's presence.

However, there are times when words or even thoughts are unnecessary, even an intrusion. For we sense that we are in the presence of God in such an intimate and personal manner that nothing else is needed: Heart communes with heart. It is like the experience of two lovers holding hands. If asked, what did you say to each other? Nothing. What did you do? Again, nothing. What then happened? Everything! So likewise in contemplative prayer, the heart is mightily affected in the presence of God, yet the experience is wordless. It is not something actively sought or worked up by the person praying, but rather comes as a gift from God.

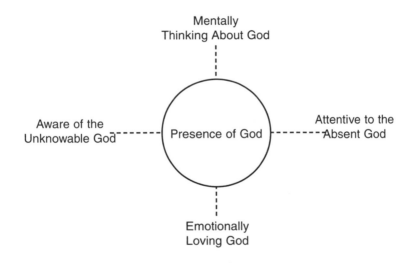

Such a convicting sense of God's presence, such an "awareness," requires no words. The mystics call it the "prayer of quiet." In turn, contemplative prayer may lead to ecstatic experiences of prayer, when literally we seem "taken out of ourselves," as the word "ecstasy" actually means. Such experiences will naturally challenge us to use our minds all the more, to seek what is the meaning of such workings of God's Spirit in us.

The second diagram illustrates how each of us can experience one or more of these four types of prayer, though the verbal form is most common among us today. (See below.) This is probably because we live in such a strongly rationalistic culture. It became characteristic of the church after the Protestant Reformation. But throughout the Middle Ages meditation was much more normal, certainly in the monastic way of life.

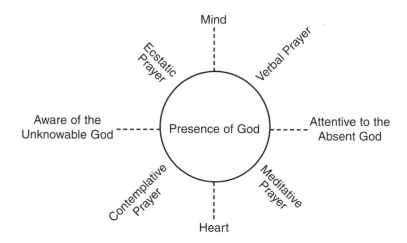

Perhaps contemplation was at a high point in the fourteenth century, when the great mystics were practicing prayer. Ecstatic prayer has always been a brief, momentary type of experience, though certain traditions, such as the charismatic movement today, have placed strong emphasis on it.

VERBAL PRAYER

The Bible is rich in examples of verbal prayer. Many Old Testament characters pray long prayers, and the book of Psalms is full of all types of prayers expressed to God. The New Testament also is rich in verbal prayer, especially in the letters of Paul, as we saw in the last chapter. This emphasis on verbal prayer has been followed by Christians throughout history.

In the Gospels, the story of blind Bartimaeus has sustained a strong tradition of verbal prayer in the Orthodox churches.

Bartimaeus cried out, "Jesus, Son of David, have mercy on me!" (Mark 10:47).

This prayer forms the basis of the Orthodox "Jesus Prayer":

> Lord Jesus Christ, Son of God, have mercy on me, a sinner.

The Anglican practice of prayer is dominated by the *Book of Common Prayer* that arose out of the English Reformation after 1549. The prayer book was used to teach the common people the reformed approach to prayer and worship. The great emphasis of this tradition is the need to confess our sins before God in corporate prayer and praise.

George Herbert caught the twofold emphasis of confession and thanksgiving in his poem, which later became the hymn "King of Glory, King of Peace."

> Though my sinnes against me cried,
> Thou didst clere me;
> And alone, when they replied,
> Thou didst heare me.
>
> Sev'n whole dayes, not one in seven,
> I will praise Thee.
> In my heart, though not in heaven,
> I can raise thee.
>
> Thou grew'st soft and moist with tears,
> Thou relentedst;
> And when justice call'd for fears,
> Thou dissentedst.
>
> Small it is, in this poore sort
> To enroll thee:
> Ev'n eternitie's too short
> To extoll thee.

> Small it is, in this poore sort
> To enroll thee:
> Ev'n eternitie's too short
> To extoll thee.

Lancelot Andrewes is another great seventeenth-century teacher of the tradition of prayer as confession followed by thanksgiving. We pray, he argued, not simply to bring our personal needs to God, but because we are commanded to pray:

> So when Christ commands us to pray, he doth not leave it as a thing of our own choice, but binds us to the performance of it; for prayer is not only required as a thing supplying our need—for when we feel want, we need not be provoked to prayer ... but it is required as a part of God's service. Anna being in the temple, "served God by prayer"; by prayer the Apostles performed that service to the Lord.

To be a Christian is to be someone who prays. And in praying we need to watch what we say, as well as how we say it. The seventeenth century saw a controversy in England between those who championed written prayers read aloud, and those who would only allow spontaneous prayers, spoken straight from the heart. The important point was made, during the controversy, that the prayer book provided uneducated people with good Christian teaching for their prayers—something that spontaneous prayer did not do. The benefit of praying together, from the prayer book, was also recognized, as people expressed their agreed needs as a community to God.

John Calvin spoke about this need for balance in our lives between prayers said together in public, and prayer made on our own in private:

> We must consider that whoever refuses to pray in the
> holy assembly of the godly knows not what it is to pray
> individually, or in a secret spot, or at home. Again, he
> who neglects to pray alone in private, however unremit-
> tingly he may frequent public assemblies, there contrives
> only windy prayers, for he defers more to the opinion of
> men than to the secret judgment of God.

Calvin saw public prayer as the way to do everything "decently and in order," as the apostle Paul had commanded in one of his letters. He defended the use of written prayers by pointing to the Lord's Prayer, which had been given to the disciples by Jesus:

> From his goodness in this respect we derive the great
> comfort of knowing, that as we ask almost in his words,
> we ask nothing that is absurd, or foreign, or unreason-
> able; nothing, in short, that is not agreeable to him.

The Lord's Prayer is given to us as revealed truth about God and the way in which he responds to our needs. We could certainly never improve on this prayer in addressing ourselves to God.

Prayer is the way in which we expose our ignorance or our wisdom, our wrong or our right attitudes to God. True prayer always expresses reverence to God, a real sense of need, the suppression of pride and the confidence of being heard by God. Written prayers can help to educate us in understanding these different dimensions to prayer. But this education must also go hand in hand with a personal awareness that this is my own prayer that I am offering to God—and not simply a prayer that I am reading out loud. Prayer is both verbal and mental, coming from the heart.

Martin Luther also stressed that prayer is not an optional extra in the Christian life. It is the unique privilege and the chief work of Christians to pray. He said that just as a woman might prepare herself for the day by looking into three mirrors at her dressing table, so the Christian has a threefold devotion each day as he or she recites the Apostles' Creed, the Ten Commandments, and the Lord's Prayer. These teach us how to enjoy a right relationship with God, and call us to put it into practice. Luther saw that prayer essentially expresses our faith in God, by "a climbing up of the heart into God." By confessing our sins, asking him to meet our needs, and giving him thanks, our lives are offered up to God:

> Prayer is made vigorous by petitioning, urgent by supplication; by thanksgiving, pleasing and acceptable.
> Strength and acceptance combine to prevail and secure the petition.

Reciting the Lord's Prayer has always been seen as important from the very early days of the church. Cyprian, the Bishop of Carthage, said that in the Lord's Prayer "there is absolutely nothing passed over pertaining to our petitions and prayers." Origen, a Christian leader and writer in Egypt, compared the Lord's Prayer to a piece of writing that children copied in school to help them learn to do their own writing. Gregory of Nyssa, who wrote in the fourth century, said that all our vain desires and foolish requests are excluded when we are educated in the realities of the Lord's Prayer. The prayer then becomes a guide to keep us on track in our personal prayers. The value of the Lord's Prayer as an education was widely accepted, with the result that the prayer was taught to new converts as they prepared for baptism.

In the earliest reference that we have to the use of the Lord's Prayer, it is assumed that it will be recited three times a day. One hundred years later, Christian discipline called for the prayer to be recited at midnight as well. This was the ideal, but as now, there was always a gap between the theory and practice. Lack of prayer has always been a problem, which is why Gregory of Nyssa complains in one of his sermons:

> The present congregations need instruction not on how to pray but on the necessity of prayer to begin with.

All this suggests that verbal prayer is centrally important in the life of the Christian. It focuses around the educational importance of the Lord's Prayer, which sets the agenda for our own prayers and demands thought in thinking through and speaking out our prayers—even when they are spontaneous.

However, there is more to prayer than verbalization. "Saying our prayers" is simply not enough. The true Christian needs to devote his or her whole life to prayer. Clement of Alexandria, one of the earliest Christian writers outside the New Testament, expressed it in this way:

> Not in a specified time or selected temple or on certain festivals or days, but during one's entire life, the Christian in every place acknowledges his gratitude for the knowledge of the way to live. We cultivate our fields praising; we sail the seas hymning.

In the same way, the Eastern churches' use of the Jesus Prayer is more than a mere recitation of the words. It is a prayer of the mind, as the words are quietly reflected upon, as well as a prayer of the heart, as the whole person is caught up in prayer. Bishop Theophan, of the Eastern church, summed up the practice of the Jesus Prayer in these well-known words:

> The principal thing is to stand before God with the intellect and the heart, and to go on standing before him unceasingly day and night, until the end of life.

"Standing before God" suggests a permanent approach in our personal relationship with God. "In the heart" suggests that our whole person is transparent before God. "The intellect in the heart" suggests there is no opposition between the mind and the emotions, the head and the heart, in our prayers. "Standing unceasingly" suggests a continuous relationship.

In his first letter to the Thessalonians, Paul tells us to "pray continually" (5:17). In the Eastern tradition this has been interpreted as a whole reorientation of life rather than as a verbal recitation of prayer. This leads us into the second quadrant of prayer: meditation.

MEDITATION

To meditate means to reflect with our minds on the Bible and the truths of God, in order to love God more personally and to live as he wants us to. Meditation is a form of conversation with God, or before God, that is mental rather than verbalized.

Despite this emphasis upon the mental, many great Christian writers have fortunately written down their meditations for our benefit! In Psalm 1, meditation is a feature that points out the contrast between "the way of the righteous" and "the way of the wicked":

> Blessed is the man
>> who does not walk in the counsel of the wicked,
>> or stand in the way of sinners
>> or sit in the seat of mockers.
> But his delight is in the law of the Lord,
>> and on his law he meditates day and night. (vv.1–2)

This introductory psalm is probably the key to the whole book of Psalms, because the whole purpose of the psalms is to be a source of meditation for God's people. The psalms were originally written out of meditation before God, and they still provide the basis for all meditative prayer.

In the medieval monastic tradition, prayer and reading went together. Prayer was short and briefly expressed. It was followed by prolonged reading, which in turn prompted prayer once more. The monks were taught to see prayer and reading as inseparable and to give themselves to both activities. Between the two there was also meditation, which was seen as reflecting upon and memorizing Scripture after it had been read.

The idea was to avoid the shallow type of reading that we are so used to. They attempted to engage the whole person in reading. This called for admiration for what was being read; it prompted desire and aroused attention. It was a free exercise—quite unlike our reading—unbound by rules, a method, or length of time. It resulted in reverence and a love of the Bible, preparing the mind and heart for further prayer.

Unlike verbal prayer, which has often been seen as a form of discipline and a test of endurance during periods of spiritual dryness, meditation has always been a spontaneous delight and joy in wonder at the mysteries of Scripture, especially in its use of the psalms. It developed a sacred imagination, prompted a spirit of gratitude and a sharing of thoughts with others. Although the act of prayer was brief, the state of prayer was constantly sustained by a meditative spirit. As a result, the whole climate of the soul turned to longing and yearning for God. This climate of continuous longing broke forth from time to time in verbal prayer.

Two types of writing arose from this tradition of meditative prayer. There were prayers addressed personally to God (such as the prayers written by Anselm); and there were proposed themes for meditation (such as those written by William of St. Thierry, Bernard of Clairvaux, and Aelred of Rievaulx). The themes mainly focused around the mysteries of Christ, his suffering and death.

The monastic life, which included silence, fasting, vigils, purification of the heart, repentance, humility, and patience, made possible a climate of prayer that encouraged these meditations.

This great tradition has a great deal to say to us today, both to those who do not practice meditation, and to those who do. For those who have never learned to meditate, we learn that reading the Bible without meditation is barren, just as meditation unguided by the Bible is misleading, and can be destructive. In the same way, the tradition tells us that prayer without meditation is weak and powerless.

For those who do meditate, the medieval tradition lays down some valuable guidelines. It shows us that some modern forms of meditation can be dangerous. Meditation is being encouraged without reference to the Bible, and therefore not enough thought is being given to the subject-matter of meditation.

Meditation without reference to God is not true Christian meditation. We cannot take it up, as in the many secular forms of meditation today, simply to alleviate stress, in the same way that jogging promotes physical health. Christian meditators have always seen the vital importance of having a personal relationship with God and submitting to him in order to meditate appropriately.

This is where Christian meditation differs so sharply from transcendental meditation and its relations. We do not gain unaided access into the presence of God by breathing or sitting in the right way. We do not enter ecstatic experiences by the use of drugs, nor are certain gurus the "experts" in Christian meditation. All these devices are denied by the cross of Christ and our trust in Jesus' death and resurrection to bring us the salvation we need. All our meditation depends on the work Jesus did for us in giving us access to God's presence. Just as the writer of Psalm 1 delighted in the law of the Lord, meditating on it day and night, so all true meditation focuses on God's revelation through the Bible, and through Jesus Christ.

Francis de Sales, writing in the early seventeenth century, had many wise words to say on meditation, which was greatly neglected in his time. This is how he recommended people to meditate: Place yourself in the presence of God, he advised, and realize with keen intensity how present God is to us, not only because he is everywhere, but because he is also within our heart and spirit. It is his Spirit living inside us who animates us to meditate before God.

Having prepared yourself, now reflect on the humanity of Jesus. He looks on us from heaven with the deepest understanding of our human condition, with all its needs and distress. See that Jesus is actually present with you. Now think about an aspect of Jesus' life—his teaching, or an event from his ministry that grasps you and helps to change you as you absorb it within yourself. We need to guard against vague, generalized desires for God that do not specifically focus our attention on the areas in which we need to listen to and obey God.

Finally, thank God for the specific thoughts he has given you to meditate on. Devote yourself to making them come true in your life, asking God to give you the strength to do this. The whole point of meditation, said de Sales, is to see our lives changed in accordance with our meditations. Because of this we need to avoid finishing our time of meditation abruptly, but learn to withdraw slowly from our time spent before God. This long pause allows us to return to practical, everyday life, taking our thoughts with us.

The Puritans of England and New England saw meditation not as an exercise in itself, as we might tend to do today, but as part of the whole character of godliness. For them, meditation was not a kind of introspection, experienced when the mood takes us. Nor was it a vaguely defined series of "good thoughts," brought on after a good meal, watching a sunset, talking with old friends, or even after hearing a great sermon. Instead, meditation expressed our seriousness to become "heavenly minded" people.

A professional person takes his or her professional training and career with utmost seriousness. A sports person keeps fit and practices technique with the same concentration. Meditation has the same seriousness and dedication. Its preoccupation is with God and with "heavenly business." It is hard work, like climbing a mountain; it is lifelong; it demands humility of spirit; it views sin in our own lives with deep contrition and repentance, with a growing sense of its threat to us.

One of the Puritans, Richard Baxter, wrote a well-known classic on meditation called *The Saints' Everlasting Rest*. He saw meditation above all as "heavenly mindedness." For him, this meant seeing all the things around us in the context of God's presence, whether it be the soaring of a bird in flight, the sound of church bells, the daily routine of work, or the sights, smells, and sounds of the earth around us. All of this heightens our sense of living before God, in praise, thanksgiving and adoration.

Many writers on prayer confuse contemplation with meditation, or speak of them as if they were one and the same. So how are they different?

Meditation involves verbal and symbolic communication, where the mind is active, conscious of both our thoughts and feelings. In contemplation, God's presence is so intensely and intimately real that description of him gives way to the sheer awareness of his presence. Words and even thoughts are simply no longer necessary.

Many mystical writers describe their progress from meditation to contemplation in terms of going through a spiritual desert, or passing through an experience called "the dark night of the soul." This hard experience simplifies our trust, love, and desire for God, bypassing the senses.

The experiences of prayer narrated for us by Teresa of Avila may encourage us to move on from merely "saying our prayers" to enter more deeply into a life of prayer that experiences all four quadrants of the diagram we looked at earlier. Teresa's earliest recollection of prayer was that as a child she reflected on the passion of Christ every night before she went to sleep:

> I feel sure that my soul gained a great deal through this
> custom, because I began to practise prayer without
> knowing what it was.

This early pattern helped to set her on a life of prayer, so that "I was determined to follow the path of prayer with all my strength."

At first Teresa was pleased with her prayer life, but there soon followed a period of almost twenty years where she was prayerless and deeply frustrated because of it. She was surrounded by nuns in her convent who had no rules and no practice of personal, private prayer. She was also baffled about how she should practice meditation, when all she knew was verbal, public prayer. On top of all this, she found that when she did try to pray personally, she could not control her thoughts.

> In all those years, except after communion, I never dared to begin prayer without a book. For my soul was as fearful of being without it during prayer as it would have been should it have to do battle with a lot of people.

Teresa also confided,

> For several years I was more often anxious that the hour I had determined to spend in prayer be over than I was to remain there, and more anxious to listen for the striking of the clock than to attend to other good things. I would often have preferred to undergo any penance rather than recollect myself in the practise of prayer.

For Teresa, prayer became a battlefield for her tensions and her agonized conscience. She came to the conclusion halfway through her twenty-year struggle that it was more honest to give up prayer entirely than to continue the struggle. Then in a series of mystical experiences, she identified herself first with Mary Magdalene at the feet of Jesus, begging for his forgiveness, and later alongside Augustine in his *Confessions*. On both occasions Jesus came to her personally. From that point on, her growth in contemplative prayer became a series of experiences of finding herself in the presence of Jesus, whom she began to love passionately. She relates some of the stages of the intensifying sense of the presence of Christ in her book *The Interior Castle*.

Mystical prayer is therefore the deeply personal awareness of God's presence with us and in us. Teresa said that mental prayer (or meditation) "is nothing but an intimate conversation between friends; it means conversing frequently and alone with him who we know loves us." Then she adds:

> In order that love be true and the friendship endure, the
> wills of the friends must be in accord.... And if you do
> not yet love him as he loves you ... you will endure this
> pain of spending a long while with one who is so differ-
> ent from you when you see how much it benefits you to
> possess his friendship and how much he loves you....
> Oh, what a good friend you make, my Lord!

For Teresa, contemplation means to simplify the wonderful manifestation of friendship that prayer is. It is the essence of friendship, first in conversation (as verbal prayer is), then in the meditation of what such friendship means (as meditative prayer is), and then finally in actually experiencing the mutuality of such love in the presence of each other.

Teresa said that this friendship is activated by "conversing frequently and alone." We can take the initiative in this, by making the time to be alone before God. But the actual mystical experiences of God's presence comes from God's initiative. At that point, observes Teresa, we need not "a lot of thinking, but rather a lot of loving.... This does not require much strength, just love and habit."

We also need to be able to accept the tensions of our friendship with God. We have to learn to live with our own sense of unworthiness at having a friend whose love for us is so great that we can never give him the love he deserves. Yet contemplative prayer releases us from this guilt and frustration as we become totally absorbed with his presence and his love. We learn that we can relate to him more intimately and concretely than any human friendship we can ever have. His friendship sets the pace for all our other relationships, helping us to see why they are at best shadowy and inconsistent in comparison to the friendship of God.

The experience of contemplative prayer removes forever the temptation to assume that there must be some techniques or some methods that we need in order to develop in prayer. Instead, we discover that this friendship that is prayer is as remote from the controlling mind-set of technology as heaven is from earth.

ECSTATIC PRAYER

This chapter deliberately avoids any description of the various types of contemplative prayer as they were experienced by the Christian mystics. This is because the contemplative journey and its experiences are essentially personal rather than public. The goal of the journey is rapture, declaring as Paul the apostle did:

> I have been crucified with Christ and I no longer live,
> but Christ lives in me. (Gal. 2:20)

In his own suffering and weakness, Paul too had mystical experiences. "Whether it was in the body or out of the body I do not know—God knows" (2 Cor. 12:2). He did not draw attention to these experiences, but instead concentrated on their effect on his life, which had been to turn his sense of weakness into a new expression of strength in God. It is the state of love for God, the hallmark of contemplative prayer, that turns all sorrow into inexpressible joy. It helps to generate in our lives the dynamic of "love, joy, and peace" that Paul so often used in greeting his friends.

Ecstasy is the true climax of our friendship with God in prayer. The word *ecstasy* comes directly from a Greek word that literally means to be "taken out of ourselves." In English we still use this idea when we speak of people being "beside themselves" with joy, anger, or some other strong emotion. To experience ecstasy in prayer means that we are taken out of ourselves; we are no longer in control because the love of God controls us instead. We no longer live by human effort but by the power of God's Spirit living inside us. In this sense, our whole lives, controlled by God, become ecstatic.

The Holy Spirit produces in our lives the qualities that the apostle Paul called "the fruit of the Spirit," including love, joy, and peace. It is this fruit that restores to us our full humanity and the happiness that God has always intended for us. Paul said, "The kingdom of God is not a matter of eating and drinking"—the activities that we think will bring us happiness—"but of righteousness, peace and joy in the Holy Spirit" (Rom. 14:17). We can therefore use another diagram to show how the "fruit of the Spirit" is the dynamic expression of a changed life in our relationship with God, with other people, and with ourselves.

We are caught up in a life of prayer into God's own being as Trinity, relating to the Father, Son, and Holy Spirit. The upward pull of this new life leads us into a deeper quality of friendship with God in love, joy, and peace, and into more positive and creative relationships with others and with ourselves. "Gentleness" is a key element in the spiritual life; it encourages the stabilizing influence of faithfulness, which in turn produces self-control.

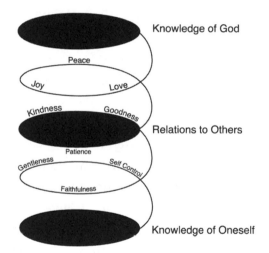

In this way, the upward spiraling of our lives extends outward to embrace others in this ecstatic experience, and moves deeper into our souls, so that all our relationships, lifting each other in turn, are transformed.

We might have a close friend or a marriage partner who seems to be becoming too "mystical," exploring the life of prayer way ahead of us. We do not need to be afraid of the consequences, because we will be one of the first to benefit from the change in our friend or partner! Be in love with God, and your love for your friends will be richer and greater. Be willing to be recognized by God, and all the fear of loneliness will be dispelled in the ecstasy of joy that you are known and accepted by God. Be open to release control over your life, abandoning it to God, and you will be protected by the one who gives us peace that "surpasses all understanding" (Phil. 4:7 ESV).

In turn, the patience, goodness and kindness that we show to other people will no longer be stoic and self-possessed, but relaxed and gifted, flowing endlessly from a hidden spring of life within ourselves. And in our own relationship with ourselves, we will see a transformation away from harshness toward ourselves, or inconsistency, or a lack of self-freedom. Instead, there will be gentleness, faithfulness, and self-control that prove the power of the transforming friendship of God.

Many people tend to jump from the exercise of verbal prayer into a charismatic experience of ecstatic prayer, genuinely believing that this is all they need for a dynamic experience of God's Spirit. Later, they may become disillusioned, discovering that the gifts they received for worshipping God have not been all that they expected. We can experience the gift of tongues or the gift of prophecy and still remain virtually unchanged as people, even though we started out by hoping for dramatic changes in ourselves. The same is true for those who have been through a powerful conversion experience. The experience may give us a flying start in the Christian life, but to rely on this experience without going forward in prayer also leads straight to disillusionment and frustration.

Because of this, it is far more realistic, and biblical, to expect that our transformation by God will be a gradual process, requiring sustained effort and discipline in prayer. We go forward in our journey by progressing from verbal prayer, through a deepening of our lives in meditation. The next stage of our journey will be to receive contemplative experiences of God's presence and love.

Finally, we will see the fruit of the Spirit in ecstatic prayer, producing transformation throughout our lives. We cannot speed up this process, although we can slow it down through a lack of desire and discipline. It takes time and gentleness, as well as consistent desire, to progress in the different experiences of prayer. This is a hard process, but one that brings joy.

The classic children's story book *The Wind in the Willows*, by Kenneth Grahame, may not seem a likely source of instruction for what we have been discussing so far! And yet it perfectly illustrates the spirit of what is needed. One of the Otter's children, Pordy, has gotten lost, and unable to sleep for worry, Rat suggests to his friend Mole that they go along the river in search of the child. Near daybreak, Rat hears music he never dreamed of:

> The call in it is stronger even than the music is sweet! Row on, Mole, row! For the music and the call must be for us.

At first Mole hears only the wind playing in the reeds, rushes, and osiers, but rowing steadily forward, he too hears the sound.

> Breathless and transfixed the Mole stopped rowing as the liquid run of that glad piping broke on him like a wave, caught him up, and possessed him utterly. He saw the tears on his companion's cheeks, and bowed his head and understood ...
>
> Then suddenly the Mole felt a great awe fall upon him, an awe that turned his muscles to water, bowed his head, and rooted his feet to the ground. It was no panic terror—indeed he felt wonderfully at peace and happy— but it was an awe that smote and held him and, without seeing, he knew it could only mean that some august Presence was very, very near. With difficulty he turned to look for his friend, and saw him at his side, cowed, stricken, and trembling violently. And still there was utter silence in the populous bird-haunted branches around them; and still the light grew and grew.

Perhaps he would never have dared to raise his eye, but that, though the piping was now hushed, the call and the summons seemed still dominant and imperious. He might not refuse, were Death himself waiting to strike him instantly, once he had looked with mortal eyes on things rightly kept hidden. Trembling he obeyed, and raised his humble head; and then, in that utter clearness of the imminent dawn, while Nature, flushed with the fullness of incredible colour, seemed to hold her breath for the event, he looked in the very eyes of the Friend and Helper ... saw, sleeping soundly in entire peace and contentment, the little, round, podgy, childish form of the baby otter. All this he saw, for one moment breathless and intense, vivid on the morning sky; and still, as he looked, he lived; and still, as he lived he wondered. "Rat!" he found breath to whisper, shaking, "Are you afraid?" "Afraid?" murmured the Rat, his eyes shining with unutterable love. "Afraid! of Him? O, never, never! And yet—and yet—O, Mole, I am afraid!"

Then the two animals, crouching to the earth, bowed their heads and did worship....

When they were able to look once more, the Vision had vanished, and the air was full of the carol of birds that hailed the dawn.

Following this numinous experience, the animals were only too eager to comfort the little otter who had been lost. For they had met with the Helper and Healer himself.

The communion of saints is a supportive friendship, a mutual love of God that helps us to walk his road. One group in the history of the church (in the Rhine valley during the fourteenth century) even called themselves "the Friends of God." They wanted to discover God's friendship in a closer way than the church encouraged. They tried to revitalize the spiritual life of the local communities through letter-writing, visiting people, and what they called "soul friendships." They became a great informal society, and were one of the great spiritual forces in Europe before the days of the Reformation.

Perhaps today we need the awakening of a similar movement of Friends of God, to work against the alienation that blights our lives with self-interest and the denial of community. To encourage each other as soul friends in the life of prayer could once more become a revolutionary force. In our divorcing culture, many people long for deeper, more satisfying relationships. Loneliness is another deep problem of our times. Prayerlessness also affects many people, both inside and outside the church. As books on spirituality become more popular, and the classics of faith and devotion are repackaged and reprinted, many people read widely without their lives being in the slightest way affected. Perhaps in such a climate we need to pray as Henri Nouwen has already prayed:

> O Lord, thinking about you, being fascinated with theological ideas and discussions, being excited about histories of spirituality and stimulated by thoughts and ideas about prayer and meditation, all of this can be as merely an expression of greed as the unruly desire for food, possessions, or power. Each day I see again that only you can teach me to pray, only you can let me dwell in your presence. No book, no idea, no concept or thing, will ever bring me close to you, unless you yourself let these instruments become the way to you.

13

THE COMMUNITY
OF PRAYER

The prayer preceding all prayer is "May it be the real I who speaks.
May it be the real Thou that I speak to."

—C. S. Lewis

Culturally and personally, we have struggled with prayer. Biblically perhaps, we have begun to see its possibilities grow within us, correcting and changing us in the process. Prayer expresses the heart of God, his triune Being. It becomes a cause for awe and for coming into harmony with God. A central emphasis of this book has been the inter-connection between prayer and friendship, which is really about the royal command, to love God and our neighbor.

It is good news today that many people are turning to prayer. This movement to rediscover prayer is not a passing fad, but something deep and real. Why has it emerged at this time?

Perhaps it is because in this era of rapid change there are so few features of modern life that stay fixed. Perhaps it is because of the intense sense of alienation in our culture, where people find themselves lonely, and relationships are shallow and superficial. Perhaps it is because of the artificiality of our society, which is shaped by science and technology. The spirit of our times is cold, rational and pragmatic, and our souls are starved of love and warmth.

Yet it would be too shallow to explain our need of prayer in these terms alone. We cannot explain the renewed interest in prayer simply on the cultural barrenness of our times. Deep down in all of us there is a need for friendship with God, as well as a desire to praise him. Humans are simply made that way, by a God who is himself eternal friendship, as Father, Son, and Holy Spirit.

Within God's own being, as three persons in one God, there is love and friendship given and received. Augustine, one of the great fathers of the church, tells us in his famous words:

> You have made us for yourself, and our hearts are restless until they rest in you.

We are drawn to God as iron toward a magnet, as friends are drawn in love to each other. To be human is to long for relationships and for love, and God is love.

However, all our longing for God is clouded by the fact that we have turned from him in rebellion. The sin that is deeply ingrained into each of us has had a domino effect on our understanding of ourselves, our relationships with others, and above all our relationship with God.

Far more significant than any intellectual confusion we may have about God is the disorder of our hearts before him. Our frustrated longing for God turns instead to a longing and a worship of other things, or other people. Misdirected love can easily grasp the gift instead of the giver, leading us into all the modern forms of idolatry: materialism, self-fulfillment, the drive to achieve status, and so on. This is why prayer is the reorientation of our affections, turning us back from the love of things to the love of God.

PRAYER IS FOR AMATEURS

Nothing punctures our smug efficiency or our confident professionalism more effectively than recognizing that we can never be experts in prayer. When we begin to see the infinite possibilities in our relationship with God, we have to admit that we are all beginners in prayer.

A negative tendency of medieval monasticism was to divide Christians into "the religious" (monks, priests, and so on) and "the laity" (Christians who did not hold church office), just as we distinguish between professionals and amateurs. This raises an important question. When a priest or a pastor prays for me, are his prayers somehow "better" than my own? Or is this just a cop-out, giving me an excuse from meeting with God for myself?

The New Testament tells us that "the prayer of a righteous man is powerful and effective." But these prayers are powerful not because the person praying them is an expert in prayer, but because he or she is righteous. It is not by expertise or professionalism that our prayers become effective. It is by our enjoying a true, deep relationship with God.

Many Olympic athletes are keen to preserve the amateur status of sport today. And yet we have seen how national prestige has crushed the spirit of sheer love for sport with the fierce spirit of nationalism. We have also seen how the use of steroids and other drugs has brought an atmosphere to sport that takes it away from amateurism.

What is happening in sport is a reflection of trends in the rest of our culture. The whole of life has been caned up by "experts," who are seen to hold the unique right to speak on their specialized area. The break-up of the family is now a specialized area, so that when John and Mary agree to split, the professionals move in and take over. The Third World suffers from "degree mania," as people desperately seek paper qualifications to escape the tyranny of poverty and of being "nobodies." In the midst of this cultural obsession with expertise, it is essential that the Christian life should be preserved with its proper amateur status.

Prayer is the greatest antidote to professionalism, because it expresses our friendship with God as Father, Son, and Holy Spirit. Yet the more the experts take over, the less incentive there is for prayer. Why pray if the experts can solve the problem for us? The more self-reliant we become, priding ourselves in our skills and abilities, the easier it is to practice atheism.

If we set out single-mindedly to pursue "success," then our life becomes mechanical. Our determination and self-interest will be like a juggernaut, smashing its way through our relationships as it heads straight for "success." It is only when we see life more mysteriously, giving our time and energy to relationships, that we will sense our need for God in prayer.

This leads us into a deeper issue that underlies the problem of professionalism in our culture. We have a tendency to praise educational achievements while playing down moral, emotional, and relational achievements. It has become more important that my child has a scholarship to Oxford or Yale than that he or she is a practicing Christian. The result is that our society is full of moral pygmies and technological giants.

The distortion of sin gives us the illusion that our emotional life is the junior partner in the human economy. By downgrading our relationships—pursuing instead a degree, a bigger salary, a better career—we doom ourselves to family breakdown, lack of personal identity, and ultimately to loneliness. Thinking is a poor substitute for loving, and without love there can be no genuine human existence. God intended thought to be a tool for us to enhance our lives—not to take the place of life itself.

Our capacity for deep relationships is what distinguishes us from the animals, so that prayer is at the heart of what it means to be human. The moral philosopher John MacMurray said, "Friendship is the fundamental religious fact in human life." This is why all of us need to press on with our journey into prayer, allowing God to make us more fully human.

PRAYER IN THE HEALING OF THE HEART

If our emotions lie at the heart of our being, our conversion to God is much more than the conversion of the mind; it is the conversion of our love. We now have the desire to please and serve God, and yet our old personalities stubbornly resist the rapid change we would like to see. What can we do when we feel stuck in this way?

We can only turn to God in prayer, seeking to deepen our relationship with him. Prayer broadens our horizons to see that God's will is far more important than our own. Prayer draws us away from the small and trivial to see things from his point of view. To begin with, we start to see ourselves with God's perspective.

We discover that our lives are defined by our loves. We give priority to the things we love, which determine how we spend our time and energy. Prayer remakes our lives by reshaping and refocusing our loves. The more progress we make in the love of God, the more evidence we (and others!) will see of radical change inside us. This is why it is vitally important to seek the healing of the heart.

Prayer is often the first thought of people who have been told they have a serious illness. If someone is told the terrible news that they have cancer, their almost instinctive response is to turn to God and pray. No one can dismiss the vital importance of praying for healthy bodies. One of the striking features of the life of Jesus was the way in which he almost constantly responded to sickness, healing the people who came to him for help. But in stressing the place of physical healing, we can easily overlook an even more basic human need. We need to experience God's healing at the heart of who we are, so that we can be re-created as people.

The letter of James in the New Testament tells us how prayer should be made for those who suffer:

> Is any one of you sick? He should call the elders of the church to pray over him and anoint him with oil in the name of the Lord. And the prayer offered in faith will make the sick person well; the Lord will raise him up. If he has sinned, he will be forgiven. Therefore confess

your sins to each other and pray for each other so that you may be healed. The prayer of a righteous man is powerful and effective. (James 5:14–16)

This passage should not be restricted by seeing it only in terms of physical healing. It is interesting that James does not simply talk about healing, but also about confessing sins, receiving forgiveness, and the power of righteous prayer. The passage echoes the times when Jesus both healed sick people and forgave their sins at the same time.

Of course, sin does not always lead to sickness, and sick people should not always be suspected of having some dark secret that explains their condition! But it is well known that our inner life affects our physical health. Some have even suggested that as much as three-quarters of modern illness would be better helped by prayer than surgery.

This is not to suggest that prayer should be used ignorantly or superstitiously. To say "let us pray about your illness" could mean a number of things: It could be an attempt to escape from genuine responsibility, or it could be used in a magical sense, or it could be "the prayer of a righteous man," as James puts it.

This righteous prayer, which brings the healing of the heart before God, can happen in various ways. We seek God's guidance over whether or not to pray for the other person's healing. We pray to know if the illness is psychosomatic, and if it is, how the person can be freed from it. We pray honestly, baring ourselves before God, understanding our motives in what we are doing. We surrender ourselves in complete trust to the power and love of God. We listen carefully to the distress of the other person—which may be half the battle in approaching the root of his or her suffering. This combination of right attitudes in prayer on behalf of others is powerful and effective, just as the passage from James tells us.

Our sexuality is a vast area in need of healing by prayer. We can be terrified of our own sexuality, especially if it was never affirmed in a healthy way in our childhood. Our sexual identity does not lie in certain sexual acts themselves, but in the way in which our love is directed—inward, toward ourselves, or outward, toward others and toward God.

Paul said that the sexual union of marriage was a symbol of Christ's love for us. God made us for friendship with himself, and when we deny this our love becomes introverted. Many people have never realized that their sexual problems are caused primarily by misdirecting their urge to need and love God.

Probably the most graphic illustration of this misdirected love can be seen in masturbation. The writer C. S. Lewis describes masturbation as a hell of self-love, a prison in which is kept a harem of imaginary brides:

> And this harem, once admitted, works against his ever getting out and really uniting with a real woman. For the harem is always accessible, always subservient, calls for no sacrifices or adjustments, and can be endowed with erotic and psychological attractions which no real woman can rival.

This love, turned in on itself, is destructive. It is quickly followed by feelings of self-revulsion, physical loneliness, and a lack of self-acceptance. This habit allows extreme self-love to take root in our characters, which can then lead on to homosexuality and many other types of broken sexuality.

True prayer always seeks to heal the whole of our emotional life so that we change from being neurotic persons to become whole, holy persons.

Quite apart from the pressure of daily needs, we need prayer simply to be a person. We need prayer to affirm our own uniqueness in a fallen world, and to protect us from allowing our sense of uniqueness to fall into loneliness, arrogance, anxiety, or simply a selfish way of life. We need prayer to surrender ourselves to God, offering him our will and our desires, our fears and anxieties, our virtues and talents, our relationships and our reputation.

We must be willing to be an offering to God, living a prayer-filled, prayer-directed, prayer-inspired life. We give up our old personality to allow God to remold and reshape us in the way he wants to. George MacDonald, the Victorian novelist, expressed it in this way:

> No less than thou, O Father, do we need
> A God to friend each lonely one of us....
>
> Lord, till I meet thee thus, life is delayed;
> I am not I until that morning breaks,
> Not I until my consciousness eternal wakes.

We look to God the Father for the assurance that no one else can give us. We look to Jesus Christ for the understanding, tenderness, and love that are quite alien to this world. We look to his Spirit for the wisdom, guidance, and direction that not even our closest friend can give. And as our prayers flow out from what we are not, so his answers will make us what we are "in Christ." As George MacDonald prayed:

> O Christ, my life, possess me utterly.
> Take me and make a little Christ of me.
>
> If I am anything but thy Father's Son
> 'Tis something not yet from the darkness won.
>
> Oh, give me light to live with open eyes.
> Oh, give me life to hope above all skies.
> Give me thy Spirit to haunt the Father with my cries.

At its deepest, prayer allows us to receive God into our hearts, to transform our lives. In this way we are drawn into the life of the three-in-one God, loving each person individually, and yet knowing their inseparable power. The Father penetrates the misdirected layers of desire within us to draw our attention to the love and beauty of Jesus Christ. And the Holy Spirit makes it possible for us to give ourselves, beyond our own strength, to God.

PRAYER IN SPIRITUAL DIRECTION

To make progress in the life of prayer, we need spiritual friends whose example and guidance will give us spiritual direction on our journey. To receive "spiritual direction," we form a relationship with a spiritually mature person who will show us how to live the life of the gospel.

In one of his letters, Paul wrote about his companion Epaphras: "He is always wrestling in prayer for you." The primary qualification for anyone who tries to help us deepen our lives with God is that they have a deep experience in prayer. Prayer will enable them to have insight into our thoughts and actions, and will show them how best to guide us.

We all need companionship and encouragement, and one of the best gifts of spiritual friendship is that our perspective on life is broadened. Even a passing comment from a true friend can transform the way we look at things. Sin always tends to make us blind to our own faults, but a faithful friend will see the destructive elements of our personality, and will help us to see them too. We need a friend to stop us from deceiving ourselves that what we are doing is not so bad after all. We need a friend to help us overcome our low self-image, inflated self-importance, selfishness, pride, our deceitful nature, our dangerous fantasies, and so much else.

A spiritual friend is someone with whom it is safe to take apart our shallow faith, our compulsive addictions, or whatever else might be under the surface of our visible lives. He or she will help us to exchange our weaknesses for a new source of trust, conviction, and desire that will help us to grow spiritually. We have been born into and grown up in a culture that is deeply alienated from God. So as we cross the border into God's kingdom, with its radically new attitudes and priorities, we will need all the help we can get from a spiritual friend who has made the same perilous journey before.

The way in which friends behave toward us can also help us to have faith in God. If friends really pay attention to me, listening to me and not just to my words, then I am encouraged to believe that God pays attention and listens to me in an even greater way.

It is not easy to believe in God if we live in an emotional vacuum. Many people have enjoyed relating with a spiritual friend, and have found the friendship vital to their life and growth as a person. Baron Friedrich von Hugel spoke in this way about his spiritual friend:

> There was the Abbé Huvelin—a rich and deep, a cultivated, above all an heroic soul, to whom I owe incalculably much. A man full of vitality, the strongest passions and the deepest affections, the life of deliberate, irrevocable lifelong celibacy, entered upon him in full manhood and with the clearest understanding of its meaning and range, was I am very sure, profoundly costly. Yet he willed, used and loved this renunciation as an instrument, condition and price of the tenderest love of souls in God and God in souls, right on to his end, in the seventies of his life.

Huvelin was soul friend also to Charles de Foucauld, who wrote to him:

> If it were possible I should come and ring your doorbell and have a talk with you. "And—your soul?" That would be your first question. It seems to me that it has not changed a great deal. It is still living on what you put into it. It still loves those whom it used to love—loving them more than formerly, not less.

Returning to Baron von Hugel, mystical writer Evelyn Underhill wrote about him:

> He is the most wonderful personality I have ever
> known—so saintly, so truthful, sane and tolerant. Under
> God I owe him my whole spiritual life, and there would
> have been more of it than there is, if I had been more
> courageous and stern with myself, and followed his
> directions more thoroughly.

What do spiritual directors, or spiritual friends, do for us? Primarily they should guide and encourage us to enjoy right praying for right living.

Spiritual friends also help us to identify our "Achilles heel," the place in our character where our emotions are bent and cause pain. Our Achilles heel determines our outlook and our relationships with others. There God will touch and heal us, making our weakness the point of contact for our greatest blessing and renewal. A spiritual friend will be able to see our inner injuries far better than we can see them ourselves, and will guide our praying to focus God's love and healing on them.

A spiritual friend will also show us where our life is unbalanced and how we can become more emotionally mature. Our lives are ideally made up of a whole series of balances. We enjoy many relationships, in a balance between those people who are closest to us, and those whom we relate to less often. We are grateful to help other people, giving freely of ourselves, but are also willing to receive help from them, which can demand humility.

Our prayers are a balance between a concern for ourselves and a concern for the needs of others. Even prayer can turn into a narrow existence of self-absorption if we let our self-concern turn into self-obsession. One of the great services a spiritual friend can do for us is to restore the balance to all the different areas of our lives.

Finally, a spiritual friend points us away from himself or herself to the God we worship. To worship God takes us beyond friendship with him, as we give him our love and adoration for his character.

One of the psalms says that we worship God for the beauty of his holiness. As we become absorbed in God's beauty, so our lives too become beautiful. This beauty of God, which we see in him and which grows in us, is the terminus of our journey. This is what we long for, turning away from everything else as we recognize that nothing else will do except God alone. Our friends in the Christian faith all show us something of God's character, in different degrees, but in the end it is God whom we want. The spiritual friend who keeps us faithful to the friendship of God is a friend indeed!

PRAYER IN COMMUNITY

Prayer is not simply a solitary activity; it is also an expression of the community of God's people. And yet in many modern churches, prayer is rarely expressed in this communal way. Even in the churches that do have a prayer meeting, the small group that gathers rarely represents the whole life of the congregation, but instead represents only two or three expressions of the community. The church needs to rediscover communal prayer and to make it a central feature of its life.

Community is so easily taken for granted. Like the soil, we hardly even notice that it is there. At the beginning of this century, 40 percent of the land in the country of Ethiopia was covered by trees. But over the years the trees were cut down, leaving only 3 percent of the land under forest. The country's rich soil, which had been held together by the trees, was simply washed away into the rivers. This damage, which helped to cause the devastating famines in the mid-1980s, will take many years to put right.

It takes centuries to build up a heritage of community, which can enrich the lives of so many people. But like the soil, once it is lost, the damage is very hard to put right.

Our culture has shed its community values almost overnight, casually exchanging these hard-won values for the modern cult of self-fulfillment. The church, which rightly lives in the world, but wrongly is so deeply affected by it, has also suffered in this stripping away of community.

Only prayer, practiced in an environment of spiritual friendships, can bring growth and fruitfulness back to our Christian lives. Without prayer and community, religious activism becomes sterile and deadly.

Today in North America, many people are waking up to the need for community values. They recognize that without the community, with its commitment to other people, there can be no basis for peace-keeping on the earth, or a return to home and family life. And yet, to call for community does not create community. Discovering techniques to organize community life only undermines what is left of community. In some churches, the minister may ask us to turn around to the stranger behind us to say "I love you." But this attempt to manufacture communal feeling only intensifies the phoniness of our relationships.

We cannot organize communities any more than we can manufacture friendships. So where do we begin to escape from the artificiality of church life? We need to start in a fresh way with God as Father, Son, and Holy Spirit, basing our lives on the mystery of the Holy Trinity. We start by praying, as the poet John Donne did:

Shatter my heart, Three-Person'ed God.

Unlike the gods of our own emotions, God, the Father of Jesus Christ, challenges us to the depths of our being, both shattering us and healing us, making us new persons. He does not only call us to be "born again." He calls us to move beyond that experience of new birth, to grow up and "live again." As our relationships are made richer and deeper through the gospel, so we will reach the possibility of becoming a living force in society.

What does Christian community mean? Community is letter writing to friends who need our spiritual encouragement. Community means visiting those who are depressed, bereaved, or wounded at heart. Community involves prayer and friendship, experienced in small groups and together.

The house church movement in some parts of the world, and the growth of small groups, meeting for Bible study and prayer, are new signs of communal growth among God's people. There is also a growth in retreat houses, and the widespread interest in prayer and spirituality. But the growth of true community is still organic, rather than organized. It will only happen as friendships and groups are transformed by prayer.

THE TRANSCENDENT PRESENCE OF THE HOLY TRINITY

Prayer is central to our lives because it reaches into the very core of our being, into the heart of human existence. In his *Confessions,* as we saw earlier, Augustine said that our central drive is our desire for God, whether we recognize this or not. We are not capable of generating our own happiness; we must go outside ourselves to find it. Augustine told his congregation:

> Men are not sufficient for their own bliss.

C. S. Lewis described this process as being "surprised by joy"—the sudden discovery that all our lives we were looking for something beyond our relationships, achievements, and successes. We were, in fact, looking for God, but we did not know it.

Only when all our drives and desires, hopes and loves are redirected toward God, do we become fully human. We were made for relationships, created to glorify God and enjoy him forever. The function of prayer is to bring these realizations to the surface of our lives. Prayer points us beyond ourselves, beyond our friendships, to the deepest realization of all: that God made us to be lovers of God. He is at the very heart of our hearts.

This is why the absence of God in our lives can feel so like an emptiness in our hearts. This is why we can experience such persistent feelings of aloneness when we are with others, even those who know us best. This is why at the moments of greatest triumph we can feel so discontented inside.

Complete joy, said Augustine, is "that than which nothing is greater: to enjoy God the Trinity in whose image we have been made." If we do not live for others (as the Father does for the Son, the Son for the Father, and the Spirit for the Father and the Son) then we will live discordant lives.

Our life will lack identity unless we are "in Christ." Our love will stay warped unless we direct it to God. We will stay in the confusion of sin and suffering until we accept the love of God which Jesus died to give us. We will stay alone in our uniqueness unless we allow the friendship of God to give us dignity. We will never know peace until the peace of Christ makes our lives whole. If we experience, as Paul did in 2 Corinthians 12:9, God saying to us, "My grace is sufficient for you, for my power is made perfect in weakness," then we can respond as he did:

> Therefore I will boast all the more gladly about my weaknesses, so that Christ's power may rest upon me. That is why, for Christ's sake, I delight in weaknesses, in insults, in hardships, in persecutions, in difficulties. For when I am weak, then I am strong. (2 Cor. 12:9–10)

With this attitude, Paul concluded the letter he was writing by praying:

> May the grace of the Lord Jesus Christ, and the love of God, and the fellowship of the Holy Spirit be with you all. (2 Cor. 13:4)

These three elements—grace, love, and fellowship—provide the dynamic for making prayer the central reality of our existence here on earth. They are given to help us in our struggles and temptation in this life. It is only in heaven that prayer will finally give way to uninterrupted praise, when our tongues will no longer be in discord with our hearts and when our prayers will no longer express need but our fulfillment in God. Until then, however, we persist in needing the grace, love, and fellowship of the Father, Son, and Holy Spirit. The final part of this chapter looks at each of these three gifts from God in turn.

THE GRACE OF CHRIST AS REVEALING TRUTH

Most of us think of the frustrations and suffering of our lives in negative terms. But although these experiences are painful, they can be allowed by God to help us in our growth as persons.

We can so easily fall into the danger of thinking that we know precisely what is good for us. Paul the apostle begged God three times to take an affliction away from him, but God refused. When this happens to us, we may think that God does not care about us. However, God's silence means that he is showing mercy toward us, rather than indifference. He is educating us in the school of prayer to become familiar with the way he works in our lives.

Jesus lived a fully human life, and went through all the temptations and struggles that we do. He hears our prayers, and he understands our needs. The fact is, he knows our needs better than we can ever know them ourselves. So we are going to learn far more about ourselves, and about our true needs, by a life of constant prayer than in any other way possible. A doctor who worked in a Swiss sanatorium used to pray two prayers as he went to see his patients:

> O God, if this person will glorify you more by being
> healed, use us here for his healing.
> O God, if this person will glorify you more by remaining
> sick, let him be sick.

That doctor saw the heart of the issue: Are we serving God, or are we using him merely for our advantage? In a society that wants only to be "healthy, wealthy, and wise," the scandal of illness seems intolerable. But there are deeper issues at stake than simply being healthy. When Jesus once healed a blind man, his disciples asked him why he had been born blind. Jesus replied:

> This happened that the work of God might be displayed
> in his life. (John 9:3)

This shows us that the glory of God is the true object of prayer, rather than trying to gratify our own short-sighted needs and desires. We have many things to learn from our relationship with Jesus in prayer, as this prayer shows, written by an unknown Confederate soldier:

> I asked for strength that I might achieve;
> I was made weak that I might learn humbly to obey.
>
> I asked for health that I might do greater things;
> I was given infirmity that I might do better things.
>
> I asked for riches that I might be happy;
> I was given poverty that I might be wise.
>
> I asked for power that I might have the praise of men;
> I was given weakness that I might feel the need of God.
>
> I asked for all things that I might enjoy life;
> I was given life that I might enjoy all things.
>
> I got nothing that I had asked for,
> but everything that I had hoped for.
>
> Almost despite myself my unspoken prayers were
>   answered;
> I am, among all men, most richly blessed.

It is a mark of the quality of Jesus' friendship with us that he firmly refuses many of the things we ask for in prayer. We begin to realize with horror what a judgment it would be on us if God did sometimes let us have the things we asked for! Instead, in prayer Jesus begins to show us the wider and deeper perspective of seeing our situations from God's point of view.

We also pray for "the grace of our Lord Jesus Christ" to help us forgive others. We ask for his grace and help to do this because only God can forgive sins, and only God can make it possible for us to forgive others. Only the power of his Spirit in us can make real the words of the Lord's Prayer: "Forgive us our debts, as we also have forgiven our debtors" (Matt. 6:12).

As he forgives us, he also gives us the grace to forgive others in turn. If we do not or cannot forgive the people who have hurt or wronged us, then this is a sign that we have not yet received his forgiveness ourselves.

Even more radically, Jesus also told us to love our enemies and to pray for those who actively work against us. His eight famous beatitudes in Matthew 5:3–10 demonstrate the force of this:

> Blessed are the poor in spirit, for theirs is the kingdom of heaven.
>
> Blessed are those who mourn, for they will be comforted.
>
> Blessed are the meek, for they will inherit the earth.
>
> Blessed are those who hunger and thirst for righteousness, for they will be filled.
>
> Blessed are the merciful, for they will be shown mercy.
>
> Blessed are the pure in heart, for they will see God.
>
> Blessed are the peacemakers, for they will be called sons of God.
>
> Blessed are those who are persecuted because of righteousness, for theirs is the kingdom of heaven.

THE PRAYER

It is only as our life is transformed by Christ that we can truly pray for our enemies. After we have become poor in spirit, mourned our brokenness, hungered and thirsted for God, become merciful, pure in heart and a peacemaker, then we can pray for those who persecute us.

Bishop Dehqani-Tafti of Tehran was able to pray these words after his son was murdered:

> O God, we remember not only our son but also his murderers—not because they killed him in the prime of his youth and made our hearts bleed and our tears flow; not because with this savage act they have brought further disgrace on the name of our country among the civilized nations of the world; but because through their crime we now follow thy footsteps more closely in the way of sacrifice.
>
> The terrible fire of this calamity bums up all selfishness and possessiveness in us. Its flame reveals the depth of depravity and meanness and suspicion, the dimensions of hatred and the measure of sinfulness in human nature; it makes obvious as never before our need to trust in God's love as shown in the cross of Jesus and his resurrection love which makes us free from hate towards our persecutors; love which brings patience, forbearance, courage, loyalty, humility, generosity, greatness of heart; love which teaches us how to prepare ourselves to face our own day of death, O God.
>
> Our son's blood has multiplied the fruit of the Spirit in the soil of our souls. So when his murderers stand before thee on the Day of Judgment, remember the fruit of the Spirit by which they have enriched our lives. And forgive.

A prayer such as this can only be explained by a whole life lived in prayer before God. A father cannot pray like this for the murderers of his son unless he does so in "the grace of our Lord Jesus Christ." Only then can this grace reveal the truth of the cross of Christ.

We have seen how the grace of Christ reveals the distortions of our emotions and desires, and how he gives us the ability to forgive beyond ourselves. But this grace also changes our personalities as we pray. We will find prayer a dangerous experience if we are unwilling to change. To pray is rather like joining an underground resistance movement in an enemy-occupied country. We fight back in prayer to overthrow the kingdom of darkness with the light of the gospel.

The problem is that the darkness is not simply all around us, but inside us too. So prayer becomes a weapon that can painfully turn in on us. Prayer opposes everything in us that is false, evil, and sinful. Prayer attacks all the indifference and moral complacency, all the conceit and selfishness within us. Prayer assaults our spiritual apathy and dryness. Because of this, prayer is constantly the means we can use to reassess our values and objectives before God.

Through prayer, we receive Christ's grace to question ourselves, to bring our lives up to the line of his teaching. Prayer changes us more than we would expect, or want. Accepting this is also the grace of Christ in us.

THE LOVE OF GOD AS AN ENFOLDING MYSTERY

How is the love of God different from the grace of Jesus Christ?

From our perspective, the grace of Christ does seem to have had a beginning in time. Jesus' life, death, and resurrection all happened on specific dates in time. Our own encounter with Jesus happened in time. His grace punctuates the experiences of our life with memorable events. In contrast, the love of God is eternal, having an absolute beginning in the Father outside of time, which reaches back into the character of God as Trinity. It was in that beginning that God loved us—before we existed, before the universe was made. It was then that he predestined and called us.

So our praise to God does not spring simply from what he has done for us in his Son. The work of Jesus restored and completed what God the Father had begun in creation, to make humans in his image and likeness. Paul the apostle expressed it in his letter to the Ephesians:

> He [the Father] chose us in him [Christ] before the cre-
> ation of the world to be holy and blameless in his sight.
> In love he predestined us to be adopted as his sons
> through Jesus Christ, in accordance with his pleasure
> and will—to the praise of his glorious grace, which he
> has freely given us in the One he loves. (1:4–6)

Our worship of God focuses on what he determined to do before the world began.

Prayer to the Father is therefore an exploration of his mystery and glory. The atmosphere of such prayer is bold and confident, open and hopeful, but at the same time full of awe, wonder, worship, praise, and adoration. All these qualities reflect the character of God in his love toward us.

Our contemplative prayer mirrors the love of God himself. This act of contemplating the love of God must be an act of the whole person, because it wholly absorbs, unites, and possesses us. It is not simply a part of our lives (labeled "the spiritual") that prays for the love of God. Instead, God's love reconciles our inner contradictions: our thoughts with our actions; our prayer with our life; our mind with our heart.

God's love enables us to do out of what we are. We are forgiven, so we forgive. We are healed, so we bring healing. We are redeemed, so we live as redeemed people. We are loved, so we love.

In turn, the mystery of God's enfolding love enables us to face life far more radically than when we were trying to control things ourselves. John of the Cross experienced the love of God as a "living flame of fire," where the soul is completely on fire in union with God. Francis de Sales likens the love of God to the radiance of the sun which bathes everything in light. George Herbert sees it as a genial host, welcoming the shy, unworthy guest to the banquet, meeting his every need. For François Fénelon, the reality of God's love transcends the need for anything else, turning life into a sacrifice made for God. Yet he also says,

> This detachment from self and from all you love, far
> from withering good friendships and hardening your
> heart, produces, on the contrary, a friendship in God,
> not only pure and firm, but completely cordial, faithful,
> affectionate, full of a sweet relationship. And we find
> there all the fullness of friendship which human nature
> seeks for its consolation.

The life of the lover of God therefore has two dimensions. There is a normality about it that enriches us simply to be good human beings with transformed relationships with those around us. And yet there lies below the surface a sweeping radicalism of attitude that can only be described in extremes of language: being swept into a great torrent; engulfed in flames; lost in the middle of a vast ocean. This is what it is like to allow the love of God to enfold you. So the lover of God travels incognito through his or her relationships on earth, recognized only occasionally by another lover of God as though an angel had just passed their window.

It is in the nature of love to live in peace in the love of the other person. So to know the love of God is to have arrived at a safe anchorage and forever to be there. This may seem to contradict the wild images of the last paragraph, but the reality of God's love tears us away from all our lesser loves, from all our flirtations, calling us to this peaceful rest only in God. In loving us, the Father does not give us some thing, he gives us himself.

This is why our response in prayer must mirror his action by giving him ourselves. There is nowhere else to go, and there is nothing more worthy of our being than to be with him. We were made for God: His character, and our character as he first created us, were intended for each other. One of the psalms says, "I am always with you; you hold me by my right hand" (Ps. 73:23). Each one of us, through our experiences and the convictions of our hearts, has to make the decision personally that, "as for me, it is good to be near God."

THE FELLOWSHIP OF THE HOLY SPIRIT AS AN INSPIRING LIFE

The lasting fellowship (or "companionship") of men and women is based on the love of God and the transforming grace of Jesus Christ.

One interpretation of this phrase, "the fellowship of the Holy Spirit," is that it means the company of people who have been redeemed by the death and resurrection of Christ. The Greek word for "fellowship," used by Paul in his letters, was *koinonia*. This rich word has many shades of meaning: sharing in common ownership, associating with others, showing generosity, being a full, active partner, working alongside others. All these are good descriptions of the way in which fellow Christians relate to one another. As God reveals his love for us in the death of his Son, we share together in the life of his Spirit.

As we saw in the previous chapters, the Holy Spirit is the person who enables us to experience God. It is because of his work in our lives that we are adopted as God's children, crying out to God, "Abba, Father!" So the "fellowship of the Holy Spirit" also has another meaning. The Holy Spirit draws us up more and more into the life of the three-in-one God. We participate in the whole life of the Trinity, which is eternally completed in the Holy Spirit. Just as the Spirit is the one who has the inside story on us, knowing us completely, so too it is the Spirit alone who "searches all things, even the deep things of God." In this way, the Holy Spirit connects the deepest parts of our being with the deepest parts of God—as much as we can bear. For this reason, no one can truly know God without receiving the Spirit. And unless our prayer is trinitarian, bound up with the life of the whole Trinity, it is not true prayer.

"The fellowship of the Holy Spirit" is very much needed today. Many people in the West have turned to the New Age movement, with its stress on pantheism. This belief states that God is everywhere and that we can be absorbed into this infinite being, losing our own identity in the process. This is not the work of the Holy Spirit. He does not abolish the distinctions between the Father and the Son, but unites with them as three persons in one God. In the same way, he preserves our identity as persons as we are drawn up into God. He lives within us, but it is still you or I who can contemplate God.

The whole possibility of prayer is based on the reality of God as Trinity. "The grace of our Lord Jesus Christ" calls for a response from our inner selves; "the love of God" draws us to the character of God the Father; and "the fellowship of the Holy Spirit" preserves our identity as persons in unity with God.

As we have seen:

> The Spirit helps us in our weakness. We do not know what we ought to pray for, but the Spirit himself intercedes for us ... in accordance with God's will. (Rom. 8:26–27)

The Spirit is on our side, but he is also God's Spirit. And yet, finite human beings maintain their true being before the infinite God. This is true friendship!

We have probably all seen powerful human personalities in action. Marriage partners who can only survive by crushing the personality of their spouse. Business magnates who enjoy cruel power games at the expense of their employees. But God is not a cosmic bully. He does not crush or absorb us as persons. Instead, we enjoy "the fellowship of the Holy Spirit."

The fruit of the union of a man and woman in marriage is the birth of a child. This can perhaps give us an image of the fruit of the union between a human being and the fellowship of the Holy Spirit within that person. We bear the fruit of the Spirit, described by Paul and explored at the end of the last chapter. Instead of being observers of God, watching him from the outside with a television cameraman's cool air of detachment, we are personally implicated in what God is doing. All our affections and the workings of our mind and heart are possessed and transformed by the Holy Spirit. We gain a new approach to life, a new principle of thinking, a new way of looking at the world. We desire holiness, seek to behave in holiness, and bend our wills to obey the Word of God, which is holiness.

A new nature is being formed within us. This is the heart transplant that God promised through the prophet Ezekiel (36:26–27) in the Old Testament, but which becomes our living experience today:

> I will give you a new heart and put a new spirit in you; I will remove from you your heart of stone and give you a heart of flesh. And I will put my Spirit in you and move you to follow my decrees and be careful to keep my laws.

Prayer, then, is called forth by the Father's love, made possible by the grace of Christ, and becomes our living experience in the companionship of the Holy Spirit. Since prayer has become such a transforming friendship with God the Father, Son, and Holy Spirit, the doctrine of the Trinity no longer remains a subject for discussion, but a new source of life and joy for every believer.

> No friend of the world will ever be the friend of God....
> Woe, O my soul, to those who desire the glory of men,
> for they will be stripped of the glory of God ...
> But you, O friends of God, hear the truthful and
>   amazing words
> which the mouth of the Lord has already spoken
> and is still now speaking to all!

"If you do not push aside glory,
if you do not cast aside your riches,
if you do not take off completely your vain pride,
if you do not become the least of men in all your works,
and in your reasoning, even in your thoughts,
and consider yourselves as the last of all,
you will not have the streams of tears
nor the purification of the flesh
nor will you see how these come about.
Therefore, weep for yourselves, therefore be repentant...."

"O Abba, O my Father!
For they have become as children of God
and with child-like confidence they know me
and see me and address me as a Father."

And he says to each one of them
who presently possess him truly within themselves,
"O children, do not fear! Behold, I, as I see you, am within you,
and I dwell within you and I am freeing you
once and for all from corruption and death.
And I am showing you my children and my friends;
look what I have made you to be!
Rejoice in the Lord!"

Therefore this is the true sign to me
that they have become sons and heirs to God
that they have received and really possess my divine Spirit
All these things are realized by faith and love, by Christ ...
and by this they really merit to be called Christians in truth
and in fact and not in name only....
—Symeon the New Theologian

14

PRAYING
TOGETHER

If the home, everyone's haven in the storms of life, affords no solid security, what shall one say of the civic community? The bigger the city is, the fuller it is of legal battles, civil and criminal, and the more frequent are wild and bloody seditions or civil wars. Even when the fracas are over, there is never any freedom from fear. The City of God, however, has a peace of its own, namely peace with God—in this world by faith, and in the world to come by vision.

—Augustine

Ecologists are alarmed by the vast destruction of our tropical forests, especially in the Amazon basin. It threatens the loss of a breathable atmosphere. Likewise the loss of community life is affecting the quality of modern society. People, like plants, need each other. We live in a web of inter-dependent relationships, whose destruction makes it very hard to sustain the proper environment for a humane way of living.

What is to blame for this breakdown of community? The mobility of an electronic age? The divorce between home and workplace? The rise of giant cities, bigger than anything Augustine could envisage? His historic diagnosis goes deeper:

> The city of man, for all the width of its expansion throughout the world and for all the depth of its differences in this place and that, is a single community. The simple truth is that the bond of common nature makes

all human beings one. Nevertheless, each individual in this community is driven by his passions to pursue his private purposes. Unfortunately, the objects of these purposes are such that no one person (let alone the world community) can ever be wholly satisfied. The reason for this is that nothing but Absolute Being can satisfy human nature. The result is that the city of man remains in a chronic state of civil war.

To be prayerful is essentially to be open to God. As Augustine wrote in the quotation above, "nothing but Absolute Being can satisfy human nature." A materialistic way of life certainly cannot.

Prayer is the choice to direct ourselves toward God's friendship, to reach beyond human relationships to the love of God.

Human friendship is transformed when we do this. In the words of Antoine de Saint Exupéry: "To love does not mean simply to look at one another, but to look together in the same direction." As we join together in meeting with the personal God, whose grace moves our hearts to seek him, we are freed from self-centeredness. So community is strongest when we are all set on meeting God. Our friendships are at their deepest when we pray together. Experiencing personal relationship with God nourishes our personalities, to appreciate the vital importance of friendship, with God and with each other.

Yet the primary purpose of soul friendship is not to enhance social life. It is to promote friendship with God in the growth of our spiritual lives. Love of God and love of neighbor, what Jesus called the double commandment, do grow together. Thus Aelred of Rievaulx introduced his twelfth-century treatise on Spiritual Friendship: "Here we are two, we two; and Christ, I hope, makes the third." In other words, the human experience of friendship, itself the gift of Christ, will then lead us forward to a deeper appreciation of what friendship with God can mean. Friendship is the school of the love of God. How sad, then, that fallen human beings are so poor at it. We either isolate ourselves or we let our personalities become absorbed within the crowd. Both alternatives leave us solitary.

Dietrich Bonhoeffer put it starkly:

> Without Christ there is discord between God and man. Christ became the Mediator and made peace with God and man. Without Christ we should not know God, we could not call upon God, come to him. Without Christ we also would not know our brother, nor could we come to him. The way is blocked by our own ego. Christ opened up the way to God and to our brother. Now Christians can live together in peace; they can love and serve one another; they can become one. But they can do so only by way of Jesus Christ.

That is why the basic term used in the New Testament of community is *koinonia*. The word means sharing a common life, a common fellowship, a common source of blessings. As one body of believers, we all share Christ together. *Koinonia* is as broad as the world: When Christians experience persecution in China, or poverty in Africa, we are all called to share their experience. And it is as deep as God himself. We share in the communion of the Holy Spirit, and as fellow branches we "abide" in the same vine. It is life together in the Holy Trinity. Indeed, the Christian community is an extension of the very life of God, the three-in-one.

GOD IS A RELATIONSHIP

Christian community is not just a human ideal. It is a divine reality, rooted in the nature of God himself. This theme has been central to the structure of this book. Our new life begins when we are baptized in the name of the Father, the Son, and the Holy Spirit. Our communion is maintained as we pray to the Father, through the Son, by the Holy Spirit. And our destiny is to live forever in the presence of the three Persons in one God.

The Trinity is not just a dead church doctrine. It is the living mystery of God making himself known to us in Christ by his Spirit. And we only understand ourselves fully when we enter into communion with the Trinity. We only learn how to draw close to others when we are drawn close to the loving community of Father, Son, and Holy Spirit.

The theme of God as mutual love is developed profoundly by a twelfth-century writer, Richard of St. Victor, a Scot living in Paris. In his work, *On the Trinity,* he begins by affirming that God is love. But true love is not self-love; it is gift and exchange. So love only exists where more than one person is present:

> The perfection of one person requires fellowship with another. If God is love, then he must be at least two persons, Father and Son, loving each other.

Then Richard takes a further step by saying that love requires more than mutuality; sharing also is needed. The two must share with the third, unselfishly and without jealousy. Richard sums up his argument:

> In order for love to be true, it demands a plurality of persons. In order for love to be protected, it requires a trinity of persons ... so sharing of love cannot exist among less than three persons.

This "third" person is then the Holy Spirit, whom Richard calls "Co-Beloved." For Richard, to think of the Trinity is not to think of self-love, of God loving himself; nor of even mutual love, of Father and Son. It is divinely shared love, of Father, Son, and Holy Spirit.

Divine love is truly self-giving, as we witness the gift of God's own Son dying for us upon the cross.

In our human experience we are closed in on ourselves, opaque, with the tendency to be exclusive, all of which shut us off from others. But in the Holy Trinity there is infinite openness, transparency and receptive fellowship. Within God there is mutual interchange and indwelling, as each Person of the Godhead intertwines and "contains" the other. This is timeless dialogue, what has been called "the eternal dance" of mutual sharing in love.

The awesome consequences are that when we pray we experience the personal presence of the Trinity, not simply in being heard, but also being "prayed in" by the divine Fellowship. At the deepest level of our praying we are receiving, not just giving, prayer. Then we begin to realize that the ultimate motive for prayer is not just to express our needs, but to meet the self-revealing and self-giving character of divine fellowship, the Holy Trinity himself.

We humans were created by God in his image and likeness, to be in communion with him as well as with each other. God is love, and he would redeem us to be lovers also. That is why the human spirit has only been able to receive the revelation of divine love since Christ suffered and died, rising triumphantly to conquer everything that would alienate us from God. Therefore now the power and possibility of love is available to us in Christ, to make us people fully capable of relationship.

A deeply thoughtful theologian of the Eastern church, Vladimir Lossky, has challenged:

> If we reject the Trinity as the sole ground of all reality and of all thought, we are committed to a road that leads nowhere … in the disintegration of our being, in spiritual death. Between the Trinity and hell there lies no other choice.

The atheist Sartre observed logically that, without God, hell is other people.

I am only truly human when I am personal. And so I need you, to relate to you. Selfhood can never be individualistic; it is social or it is nothing. Authentic people cannot be egocentric, but will find their center in relationship with one another. Jesus expressed this truth in his great prayer, recorded in John 17:21–22:

> Just as you, Father, are in me, and I in you, that they also may be in us ... that they may be one even as we are one.

What an amazing longing Christ has for us that we should reflect in our families, in our friendships, in our church groups, in our congregations, and in the larger family of all God's people—this trinitarian solidarity of divine love.

Becoming God's Communities

Where does the character of the fellowship of the Trinity come most clearly into focus? Surely in our worship, when we attribute glory to God. The whole character of the Christian life becomes apparent when we praise God and express our love for him who has set us free to love.

Two beliefs give shape to the Christian life together. One is the belief that God made humanity in his image and likeness. Because he made us to be like himself, God made it possible for us to enter into relationship with him. Jesus shows this in full clarity. As God living the life of a man, he offers us the potential to be related to himself in grace—creatures capable of having union with God, appreciating and worshipping him for who he is.

The second belief is that God has called out a "church," a congregation of those chosen by God, who gather around Jesus as their center in life. So the idea of "church" means both the process of congregating in this holy and spiritual way, unlike any club or other human form of community, and the congregated community itself as those linked by the call of God. And the church is not finished and complete, but is always being called onward, to become a fit instrument to worship God. That is why we go on being worshippers; our prayers continue throughout our existence.

These two beliefs, of being made in the image of God, and of being called by God to be his church, are kept in balance. The one speaks of the potential to be God's people, the other of the reality of being that people.

In fact, God's worshipping community is often marred by two human tendencies: individualism and conformity. Individualism is the sinful tendency we all have to be isolated individuals, insensitive to the well-being of others, in quest of self-interest. Our Western society over centuries has sought to guard the individual, his or her rights and dignity. Now we are all aware that, in upholding our rights, we are in danger of forgetting our duties, the privileges we enjoy, and the responsibilities we bear. When we neglect this balance, we become alienated from others. Sometimes such alienation is caused by the pain left over from early wounds. This biography by Scott Peck shows how this can happen:

> Never once in all my years of growing up did I ever hear either of my parents say they were anxious or worried or scared or depressed or anything to indicate that they felt other than on top of things and in total control of their lives. They were good American "rugged individualists" and they very clearly wanted me to be one also. The problem was that I was not free to be me. Secure though it was, my home was not a place where it was safe to be anxious, or depressed, or dependent—to be myself. I had high blood pressure by mid-teens ... I had major difficulties being intimate ... I was left with a nameless longing.

Each one of us can insert here our own story, different, and yet not so different from the one above.

How completely opposite is the picture that comes down to us of the early Christians in Jerusalem. The Acts of the Apostles and Paul's letters describe them with such feeling: "Now the full number of those who believed were of one heart and soul, and no one said that any of the things that belonged to him was his own" (Acts 4:32 ESV). So later the apostle used the phrase "one another" very frequently, to signify how each member depended on the others. "Bear one another's burdens" (Gal. 6:2 ESV). "Encourage one another and build one another up" (1 Thess. 5:11 ESV). "We are members one of another" (Eph. 4:25 ESV). So "receive one another," "edify" and "admonish one another" (Rom. 15:7; 14:19 NKJV; Col. 3:16). "Greet one another with a holy kiss" (Rom. 16:6). "Serve one another" (Gal. 5:13). "Care for one another" (1 Cor. 12:25 ESV). "Be kind to one another" (Eph. 4:32 ESV). "Be of the same mind one toward another" (Rom. 12:16 NASB). Indeed, "love one another" (Rom. 12:10 ESV). The whole ethical fabric of such relationships in equality, mutuality, fraternity, dilutes the individualism that so hampers us today in our local churches.

But not only individualism deadens congregational worship. Conformity stifles it too. Sometimes a congregation loses sight of the primacy of worship and becomes activist and over-organized. Then a general feeling of blandness prevails, obscuring the individual needs of the fellowship. Indeed, members may feel alienated, simply because they are seen as merely "useful," "performers" in the machinery of activities and programs. Such congregations prefer to love the works of God than to love God himself, for his own sake. And this is reflected in their absence of prayer, viewed privately perhaps as rather an unproductive affair, compared with all the action necessary to get the work done. Such views of what Christians are about are actually highly secular. The question may well be asked: Is it possible we cannot convince others to join us, because we are merely asking them to exchange one form of secularism for another, religious form? No wonder such churches are unattractive.

Against all such obstacles to community, individualistic or conformist, vital prayer fellowships can begin to make changes. This is precisely because prayer encourages us not to trust in human ability but in God alone. The people I learn to trust most deeply are those who are trusting God and not themselves.

It is often said that we only see the true character of a person in the context of their own home and family. How much more true when we observe them at prayer. Often in theological debate, or in interdenominational councils, when we are naturally suspicious of each other's doctrinal positions, we do well to watch others in prayer. For it is only in the presence of Christ, and in living relationship with him, that Christians can fully express themselves and be transparent. Ananias might legitimately have hesitated from welcoming the former persecutor Saul of Tarsus into the Christian community in Damascus. But he was reassured when they told him: "Behold, he is praying!" (Acts 9:11 ESV).

DIFFERENT MODELS OF CORPORATE PRAYER

Perhaps one of the most serious problems of Christian ministry today is the great diversity of models of church leadership. This is largely the inheritance of church history, but it is exaggerated today because of the deepening tendency for everyone to define their identity in terms of function rather than relationship. "What do you do?" and not "Who are you?" is the common introductory question. Clergy are affected by this like everyone else. Having one's identity as a clergyman may be understood in four different ways: sacramental, devotional, professional, or charismatic. Each reflects a distinct approach to corporate prayer.

The *sacramental* model of ministry focuses on the need of the priest to administer the sacraments, as in the Roman Catholic tradition, or in Anglicanism, Lutheranism, and others. Worship tends to be more structured, and the use of the prayer book is significant. The use of the Anglican *Book of Common Prayer* may be recognized as having a distinct tradition of spirituality. Contrition plays a notable part. It is corporate, however, unlike the more privatized use of the confessional in the Roman Catholic tradition. Writers such as Richard Hooker, John Donne, and George Herbert give intimate treatment to the themes of aversion to sin, submission of our will to God in all our ways, the fear of God in the context of his love and offering the sacrifice of praise and thanksgiving. This reflects that we can pray and worship in all circumstances of life, so these have been revised many times according to cultural changes. Obviously too, the *Book of Common Prayer* emphasizes its corporateness. The emphasis is "we praise you ... we confess you ... we give thanks."

Yet active, shared congregational worship is not a simple matter. All take part, yet all do not take the same part. Some prayers are led by a single person; others are shared between the leader and the congregation; others are prayed unitedly. With music, words and movements, prayer and worship are passed back and forth among a variety of persons. The worshipper is welcomed into the service, as Herbert expresses so well in his sonnet, "Love Bade Me Welcome." It is a genial, joyous, open and spacious fellowship that is strongly communal, as the village parish was once accepted as a natural community. This was John Donne's conviction:

> No man is an island entire unto itself; every man is a piece of the continent, a part of the main. If a clod is washed away by the sea, Europe is the less, as well as if a promontory were, as it were, as well as if a manor of thy friend's or of thine were; any man's death diminishes me, because I am involved in mankind, and therefore never send to know for whom the bell tolls; it tolls for thee.

However, this sacramental model of ministry can take all for granted, and religious conservatism can prevail, such as Jesus condemned by the Pharisees. Each must make a personal submission to the lordship of Christ. So the *devotional* model occurs when a reformer feels called to a special vocation in ministry. Such a personal call came to John Wesley to establish what later became known as "Methodism." It so happened in 1739 that "eight to ten persons came to me in London," Wesley noted, "who appeared to be deeply convinced of sin ... they desired I would spend some time with them in prayer." Thus was born the "United Society," which Wesley defined as "a company of men having the form and seeking the power of godliness, united in order to pray together, to receive the word of exhortation, and to watch over one another in love, that they may help each other to work out their own salvation." These societies became divided into smaller groups called "classes." Ideally these were about twelve to the group with an appointed leader, and members aimed to deepen each other's desire for salvation. A strong sense of mutual accountability was established.

Today, not only Methodists, but many other denominations, such as the Baptists, may have a strong sense of calling. Group prayer and Bible study have become popular again, because the general congregational call to worship each Sunday morning needs more personal reinforcement. There can be much vitality in such groups, but much depends on the emotional strength of the ministers to be able to delegate to others, and not make their "calling" a cover-up for personal possessiveness of authority. For to organize group prayer in this context of emotional weakness can lead to much congregational uncertainty.

A model of ministry much in evidence today is the *professional*. After all, everyone has to be a "professional" in our society these days. Yet this is an inhibiting model for the church, because the world can readily undermine the church's leaders in this posture, whether it be in business management, academic skills, pastoral counseling, or in just playing politics. Indeed, this is the model where we will expect least recognition of the importance of corporate prayer, and worship will have a strong element of spectatorship. It tends to generate spiritual preacher-teacher's expertise.

Nevertheless, this appears to be the trend in many North American churches today. Declining church attendance in our society tends to direct attention toward maintenance rather than mission, and maintenance is often thought by denominational leaders to be best directed by professionals.

By the *charismatic* model of ministry we may be thinking of Pentecostal-type churches, or we may be esteeming individual leaders who have strong gifts of leadership and initiative. These are often fervent in corporate prayer, with compassionate concern for the healing of the sick, for the needs of emotional inner healing, and for fervency in witness and mission. Perhaps a danger lies in seeking to dramatize the faith too much, in extraordinary demonstrations of the presence of the Holy Spirit, or of extolling the special gifts of specialized ministry, instead of providing a more holistic nurture and discipleship for the believers.

Clearly, then, the exercise of group prayer and the fostering of communities of prayer will reflect differently in these diverse models of church life. Recognizing them may help us to understand the appropriate dynamics of prayer groups and corporate worship. The history of church communities and their denominations do carry legacies we still have to accept. Periods of renewal may emphasize the devotional fervor of the church as a worshipping sanctuary, apart from the world. Complacent congregations may reflect periods of popular preachers, when emphasis is on their personal performance. Congenial congregations may reflect more of a moral complacency, closer identification with the society around, and less evidence of personal devotion. Caring congregations may reflect the whole involvement of the congregation in caring for each other, because the leaders themselves listen deeply to the personal needs of their flock, and give of themselves.

PRAYER COMPANIONS

Whatever type of church fellowship we belong to, nothing remains more necessary than the cultivation of personal accountability in prayer. So choose a prayer companion who is committed to walk with you for a year or two in your daily exercise of prayer. To help you do this, you may want to keep a prayer journal in which you can record events, Bible verses of special help or challenge, reflections on emotions experienced, and other intimate experiences during times of prayer. Perhaps one may choose one's marriage partner as a prayer companion. If not, then it is wise to keep our partner informed of all significant events taking place in these sessions, provided of course that the wife or husband is concerned likewise in a deepening life of prayer.

In such times of soul friendship, it is of first importance to understand the threads of each other's emotional history within the family, and how it has affected our attitudes toward God. Certainly to begin with, spiritual growth will reflect personal growth. When we remove personal emotional blockages such as hidden anger, an unforgiving spirit, or inner fears, we will grow in prayer. No one has the right to extract confession of this kind too suddenly, so they will only gradually be uncovered as the friendship develops genuinely.

But if uncovering the emotional phases of our lives that require healing may prove important, strong emphasis on biblical meditation is moreso. Prayerful Bible study has been characteristic of the history of God's people. And our prayer companionships should guard against any distraction from this priority, especially in these days of so much preoccupation with feelings. We should encourage each other to read the Bible systematically, beginning perhaps with the Gospels, or the psalms, and then the New Testament letters. Daily Bible reading notes are helpful.

Soul friends will have to learn to discern the causes of peace and closeness to God, and of fear and distance from him. Feelings are deeper, often more persistent forms of consciousness, that can go in the opposite direction to the mask we put on in front of others. Noticing how our peace or fearfulness are affected by times of prayer may help us grow. So it is good for us to pay attention to our prayerful feelings, whether they are comforting or disturbing, and whether they are temporary or lasting.

Coping with temptation is a matter of importance to discuss and pray over with one's companion. Certainly do not attempt to conceal such interior struggles, for out of sight they only get worse. Help may be given to understand when and how they arise, such as, "When I am lonely I am much more susceptible to be tempted by lust." So put a label on what you are susceptible to, and then try to walk away from it, first by acknowledging to your friend what your weakness tends to be. Do not try to run away too fast from the temptation, for normally we cannot change things too fast emotionally, although some can deal remarkably quickly with some forms of addiction. Most of us have to struggle through more gradually. Remember temptations are a means of growth, and they are best overcome when we love God and do so for his own sake. Remember also that every struggle we have against temptation is a fresh opportunity to experience the grace of God, helping us to pray for divine help and guidance through it.

Finally, we need to pay attention to the phases of our lives in our spiritual journey. Each phase, from childhood through youth, mid-life, seniority, and old age, has its distinctive features and challenges. And each has its own context for living and praying before God.

The purpose of prayer friendships is not as a substitute for community prayer life, but as a personal challenge to grow and encourage others also in the life of prayer. But there may be times when the local community is insensitive or even incapable of helping us. Or we ourselves may have inner obstacles hindering us from joining with others in prayer. If so, then our own inner alienation of soul needs to be exposed and dealt with before God, with the help of our soul friend.

Prayer and personal isolation, we have been finding out, are incompatible. Yes, we must learn to be alone with God if we are ever to know true community with others. But prayer in isolation from all other Christians can never be a proper expression of fellowship with the three-in-one God who makes community possible. As the great apostle wrote to the Ephesians:

For this reason I kneel before the Father, from whom the whole family in heaven and on earth derives its name. I pray that out of his glorious riches he may strengthen you with power through his spirit in your inner being, so that Christ may dwell in your hearts through faith. And I pray that you, being rooted and established in love, may have power, together with all the saints, to grasp how wide and long and high and deep is the love of Christ, and to know this love that surpasses knowledge—that you may be filled to the measure of all the fullness of God.

Now to him who is able to do immeasurably more than all we ask or imagine, according to his power that is at work within us, to him be glory in the church and in Christ Jesus throughout all generations, forever and ever! Amen. (Eph. 3:14–21)

FOR FURTHER READING

Aelred of Rievaulx, *Jesus at the Age of Twelve, Rule for a Recluse, The Pastoral Prayer,* Cistercian Publications, Kalamazoo.

Thomas Aquinas, from *Great Souls at Prayer,* James Clarke, Cambridge.

Augustine, *City of God,* translated by Gerald G. Walsh et al., edited by Vernon J. Bourke, Image Books, Doubleday, New York.

Samuel Beckett, *Waiting for Godot,* Faber, London.

John Calvin, from *The Piety of John Calvin,* translated by Ford Lewis Battle, Baker Book House, Grand Rapids.

The Cloud of Unknowing, translated by Clifton Wolters, Penguin, Harmondsworth.

T. S. Eliot, *Four Quarters,* Faber, London.

Kenneth Grahame, *The Wind in the Willows,* Penguin, Harmondsworth.

Søren Kierkegaard, from *The Prayers of Kierkegaard,* translated by Perry D. Lefevre, University of Chicago.

C. S. Lewis, *The Great Divorce,* Macmillan, New York.

Francisco De Osuna, *The Third Spiritual Alphabet,* translated by Mary E. Giles, Paulist Press, New Jersey.

M. Scott Peck, *The Different Drum,* Simon & Shuster, New York.

Michel Quoist, *Prayers of Life,* translated by Agnes M. Forsyth and Anne Marie de Commaille, Avon, New York.

Karl Rahner, *Encounters with Silence,* Burns and Oates, Turnbridge Wells.

Symeon the New Theologian, *Hymns of Divine Love,* translated by George A. Maloney, Dimension Books, New Jersey.

Leo Tolstoy, *A Confession, The Gospel in Brief, What I Believe,* translated by Aylmer Maude, Oxford University.

Works of Richard of St. Victor, translated by Grover A. Zinn, Paulist Press, New York.